Debates in Music Teaching

Debates in Music Teaching encourages students and practising teachers to engage with contemporary issues and developments in music education. It aims to introduce a critical approach to the central concepts and practices that have influenced major interventions and initiatives in music teaching, and supports the development of new ways of looking at ideas around teaching and learning in music.

Accessible and comprehensive chapters will stimulate thinking and creativity in relation to theory and practice, and will facilitate readers in reaching their own informed judgements and rationalising their position with deep theoretical knowledge and understanding. Throughout the book, international experts in the field consider key issues including:

- the justification for music in the school curriculum
- partnerships in music education and the identity of the music teacher
- technology and conceptions of musicianship
- social justice and music education
- the place of diverse musical genres and traditions in the music curriculum
- critical thinking and music education
- autonomy and integrity for music in cross-curricular work
- the politics, sociology and philosophy of music education.

Debates in Music Teaching is for all student and practising teachers interested in furthering their understanding of the subject. Including carefully annotated further reading and reflective questions to help shape research and writing, this collection stimulates critical and creative thinking in relation to contemporary debates within music education.

Chris Philpott is Dean of the School of Education and Reader in Music Education, University of Greenwich, UK.

Gary Spruce is Senior Lecturer in Education with responsibility for Music ITT, The Open University, UK, and presently co-editor of *The British Journal of Music Education*.

Debates in Subject Teaching Series
Series edited by: Susan Capel, Jon Davison, James Arthur, John Moss

The **Debates in Subject Teaching Series** is a sequel to the popular **Issues in Subject Teaching Series**, originally published by Routledge between 1999 and 2003. Each title presents high-quality material, specially commissioned to stimulate teachers engaged in initial training, continuing professional development and Masters level study to think more deeply about their practice, and link research and evidence to what they have observed in schools. By providing up-to-date, comprehensive coverage the titles in the **Debates in Subject Teaching Series** support teachers in reaching their own informed judgements, enabling them to discuss and argue their point of view with deeper theoretical knowledge and understanding.

Titles in the series:

Debates in History Teaching
Edited by Ian Davies

Debates in English Teaching
Edited by Jon Davison, Caroline Daly and John Moss

Debates in Religious Education
Edited by L. Philip Barnes

Debates in Citizenship Education
Edited by James Arthur and Hilary Cremin

Debates in Art and Design Education
Edited by Lesley Burgess and Nicholas Addison

Debates in Music Teaching
Edited by Chris Philpott and Gary Spruce

Debates in Physical Education
Edited by Susan Capel and Margaret Whitehead

Debates in Music Teaching

Edited by Chris Philpott
and Gary Spruce

Routledge
Taylor & Francis Group

LONDON AND NEW YORK

First published 2012
by Routledge
2 Park Square, Milton Park, Abingdon, Oxon OX14 4RN

Simultaneously published in the USA and Canada
by Routledge
711 Third Avenue, New York, NY 10017

Routledge is an imprint of the Taylor & Francis Group, an informa business

British Library Cataloguing in Publication Data
A catalogue record for this book is available from the British Library

Library of Congress Cataloging in Publication Data
Debates in music teaching / edited by Chris Philpott and Gary Spruce.
p. cm. -- (Debates in subject teaching series)
Includes index.
Music--Instruction and study--Philosophy. 2. Music in education.
I. Philpott, Chris, 1956- II. Spruce, Gary.
MT1.D42 2012
780.71--dc23
2011049558

ISBN: 978-0-415-59761-6 (hbk)
ISBN: 978-0-415-59762-3 (pbk)
ISBN: 978-0-203-11744-6 (ebk)

Typeset in Galliard
by Saxon Graphics Ltd, Derby

MIX
Paper from
responsible sources
FSC® C004839
www.fsc.org

Printed and bound in Great Britain by
CPI Group (UK) Ltd, Croydon, CR0 4YY

Contents

List of figures   vii
List of tables   viii
List of contributors   ix
Series introduction   xiv
Introduction   1

PART I
Philosophical, Sociological and Psychological
Foundations   7

1   What can a reflective teacher learn from philosophies
    of music education?   9
    HEIDI WESTERLUND

2   Policy and practice in music education   20
    RUTH WRIGHT

3   Creativity, culture and the practice of music education   33
    JOHN FINNEY

4   The justification for music in the curriculum   48
    CHRIS PHILPOTT

5   What is musical development and can education
    make a difference?   64
    KEITH SWANWICK

PART II
Political Perspectives   **83**

6   Music education and social justice   85
    PAUL WOODFORD

7   The National Curriculum as manifest destiny   102
    CATHY BENEDICT AND PATRICK SCHMIDT

8   Musical ideologies, practices and pedagogies   118
    GARY SPRUCE WITH FRANCESCA MATTHEWS

PART III
The Pedagogy of Music   **135**

9   Integrity and autonomy for music in a creative and
    cross-curriculum   137
    JONATHAN BARNES

10 Assessment for self-directed learning in music education   153
    CHRIS PHILPOTT

11 Those who can, play; those who can't, use Music Tech?   169
    JONATHAN SAVAGE

12 Musical knowledge, critical consciousness and
    critical thinking   185
    GARY SPRUCE

13 Music 14–19: Choices, challenges, and opportunities   197
    KEITH EVANS

14 Partnerships in music education   209
    KATHERINE ZESERSON

PART IV
Professional Development   **221**

15 Teachers and pupils as researchers   223
    TIM CAIN AND PAMELA BURNARD

16 Professional development and music education   242
    VANESSA YOUNG

Index   259

List of figures

5.1 The Developmental Spiral (Swanwick and Tillman 1986)   69
5.2 Dimensions of development: the horizontal and the
     vertical   78
8.1 The dominant ideology of western art music   123
9.1 Hierarchical cross-curricular learning. Learning in the
     'superior' subject (Subject A) is enhanced with help
     from an 'inferior' subject (in this case music)   140
9.2 Multi-disciplinary cross-curricular learning. Discrete
     learning in two or three subjects is enhanced through
     a shared and powerful experience   142
9.3 Inter-disciplinary learning. Learning in two subjects is
     taken forward as a result of a shared learning experience
     and then brought together in a presentation or
     application to a shared problem   144
9.4 Opportunistic cross-curricular learning. Unpredictable
     and child-led learning opportunities arise from a
     powerful and shared experience   147
9.5 Double focus cross-curricular learning. Learning in
     each curriculum subject continues separately
     throughout the year but is regularly joined with one
     or two others and applied to a shared experience   149
10.1 A model for self-directed musical learning and
     assessment   164
15.1 An Action Research Spiral   227
16.1 Essential factors in the management of change
     (Knoster, T., Villa, R., and Thousand, J. (2000))   250
16.2 Teacher as enquirer process   253
16.3 Example of teacher as enquirer process from Case Study 2   253
16.4 Teaching as reinterpretation of the curriculum   256

List of tables

8.1   Aspects of praxial music and implications for the
ideology of high status knowledge   125

9.1   An example of a double focus weekly timetable
showing both separate subject studies and a
cross-curricular project   149

11.1   Martin's model of digital literacy   176

11.2   Combining Martin's and Kratus' models   177

12.1   Critical pedagogy and music education   190

14.1   Music teachers' situational roles   212

List of contributors

Jonathan Barnes is Senior Lecturer in Education at Canterbury Christ Church University. He has wide experience in all sectors of education, teaching in Africa and Asia as well as England. He finished his school career as a head teacher. He now teaches a range of disciplines in teacher education, music, art, geography and history. These broad interests have led to his interest in cross-curricular approaches to learning. His research interest is in the relationships between the curriculum, the arts and wellbeing. He writes regularly for the journal, *Improving Schools* and has presented annually at The British Education Research Association annual conference. His research into creativity is summarized in *Creative Teaching for Tomorrow*, commissioned by Creative Partnerships. He is author of *Cross-Curricular Learning 3–14*, published by Sage in 2011.

Cathy Benedict is currently the Area Coordinator of Music Education at Florida International University. She has taught classes such as Elementary Pedagogy, Orff, Curriculum Design, Critical Readings in Music Education and Music Education and Special Needs Students. Her scholarly interests lie in facilitating music education environments in which students take on the perspective of a justice-oriented citizen. To this end her research agenda focuses on the processes of education and the ways in which teachers and students interrogate taken-for-granted, normative practices. She has been published in journals including *Philosophy of Music Education Review*, *Music Education Research*, and *Research Studies in Music Education*, the Brazilian journal *ABEM*, and is currently co-editing the 2012 *National Society for the Study of Education Yearbook* (Teachers College Press).

Pamela Burnard works at the University of Cambridge, UK where she manages Higher Degree courses in Arts, Culture and Education and in Educational Research. She is Co-Editor of the *British Journal of Music Education*, Associate Editor of *Psychology of Music* and serves on many editorial boards. She is section editor of the 'Creativity Section' in the *International Handbook of Research in Arts Education* (Springer, 2007), and the 'Musical Creativity as Practice' section of the *Oxford Handbook of Music Education* (OUP, 2010). She is convenor of the British Education Research Association, Creativity SIG.

Tim Cain became a teacher–educator in music after working for 19 years as a secondary school music teacher. He is currently Professor in Education at Edge Hill University. He has research interests in mentoring, action research, music education and teacher education. He has written textbooks and other educational materials and has published a number of academic articles. He is on the editorial boards of the *British Journal of Music Education* and the *International Journal of Music Education*.

Keith Evans is Senior Lecturer in Music Education at the University of Greenwich where he teaches on both primary and secondary initial teacher training programmes. He is course leader for the secondary PGCE *Musicians in Education* programme, an innovative collaboration between the university and Trinity Laban Conservatoire of Music and Dance which aims to give teachers a more holistic view of music education through placements in alternative music education settings in addition to the formal school context. He is an experienced classroom practitioner and, prior to moving into higher education, taught music in schools in Kent for over 25 years. His publications cover teaching music musically in the 14–19 age groups and examining whether current academic and vocational qualifications are fit for purpose.

John Finney is a Senior Lecturer in Music Education in the Faculty of Education, University of Cambridge and for the last 20 years has been involved in the preparation of music graduates for teaching music in secondary schools. Prior to this, John taught in Southall, Worcestershire and Basingstoke. His recent book *Music Education in England 1950–2010: the child-centred progressive tradition* reveals not only a fascination for the ways in which public policy and classroom practice have evolved in recent times, but also, his interest in the possibility of developing an ethical approach to music education found at the heart of the relationship between pupil, teacher and what is being learnt, constructing relational knowledge and a music education with 'human interest'. In his current research John is investigating the question of music teachers as researchers as well as their professional lives as they work within a culture of 'performativity'.

Francesca Matthews studied as a singer at Trinity College of Music and works as a live and session performer in the UK. She became a secondary music teacher after several years of working as a vocal leader and singing teacher for a local authority Music Service and has worked with institutions such as the Royal Opera House and Glyndebourne Opera House as an animateur in their education departments She is now Head of Teacher Development at Trinity College London for whom she delivers professional development workshops to teachers around the world. She works for The Open University as a Music PGCE tutor, and has contributed to books and study guides about different aspects of music teaching.

Chris Philpott became a teacher–educator in music after working for 16 years as a secondary school music teacher. He is currently Dean of the School of

Education at the University of Greenwich and a Reader in Music Education. He has research interests in the pedagogy of teacher education, the body and musical learning and music as a language. He has written and edited books, online texts and resources used in initial teacher education (ITE) programmes throughout the United Kingdom. He is a member of the National Association of Music Educators (UK) for whom he has led government-funded projects for ITE in music.

Jonathan Savage is a Reader in Education at the Institute of Education, Manchester Metropolitan University. He has a number of research interests, including implementing new technologies in education, cross-curricular approaches to teaching and learning, creativity and assessment. He is Managing Director of Ucan.tv (www.ucan.tv), a not-for-profit company that produces educational software and hardware including *Sound2Picture* (www.sound2picture.net), *Sound2Game* (www.sound2game.co.uk) and *Hand2Hand* (www.hand2hand. co.uk). Free moodle courses are available at www.ucan.me.uk. He is a widely published author having written and edited for Routledge, The Open University Press, SAGE and Learning Matters. Jonathan runs an active blog at www. jsavage.org.uk and can be followed on Twitter @jpjsavage.

Patrick Schmidt is Associate Professor of Music Education at the Westminster College of the Arts of Rider University in Princeton, US. He teaches courses on the philosophy and sociology of music, research methods, secondary methods, and Hip Hop. His most recent publications can be found in the following journals: *Arts Education Policy Review; Philosophy of Music Education Review; Action, Criticism, and Theory for Music Education; ABEM Journal in Brazil;* and the *Finnish Journal of Music Education*. He is currently co-editing a 2012 NSSE book (Teachers College Press) and a special issue of the well-known education journal *Theory into Practice*.

Gary Spruce is Senior Lecturer in Education at the Open University. His primary responsibility is as subject leader for the university's flexible PGCE music course. Recently he has been heavily involved in developing a CPD course for those involved in teaching music at Key Stage 2. He has written widely on music education and presented papers at national and international conferences. He is a practising musician with a particular interest in music for the theatre.

Keith Swanwick is Emeritus Professor at the Institute of Education, University of London, where he was formerly Professor of Music Education and from 2000 to 2002, Dean of Research. His books include: *Popular Music and the Teacher* (1968); *A Basis for Music Education* (1979); *Music, Mind and Education,* (1988) (also in Spanish and Japanese); *Musical Knowledge: Intuition, Analysis and Music Education* (1994) and *Teaching Music Musically* (1999) (also in Portuguese and Japanese). From 1984 to 1998, with John Paynter, he was editor of the *British Journal of Music Education*. In 1987 he became the first Chairman of the National Association for Education in the Arts and from 1991 to 1995 was Chair of the Music Education Council (UK). During 1998 he was Visiting Professor, University of Washington and from 1999 to 2001 Advisory Professor at the Institute of Education in Hong Kong. In 2004 he held a Fellowship of the Japanese Society for the Promotion of Science.

Heidi Westerlund was educated as a music teacher and currently works as Professor at the Sibelius Academy, Finland, where she is responsible for the music education doctoral program. Her research concentrates on philosophical and theoretical research. Lately, she has dealt with issues such as higher music education, collaborative learning, multiculturalism, and democracy in music education. She is published widely in international and national journals and has served on national and international management/leadership teams, such as the International Society for Philosophy of Music Education. She has also peer reviewed for several international journals and conferences, and is editor of the *Finnish Journal of Music Education*.

Paul Woodford holds degrees from the University of Toronto, the University of Western Ontario, and Northwestern University (PhD) and is Professor and former chair of the Department of Music Education at the Don Wright Faculty of Music, the University of Western Ontario. His interests in philosophical, historical, sociological, and political issues affecting the profession have led to many publications, including four books on the history of music in Newfoundland and Labrador, a fifth, entitled *Democracy and Music Education: Liberalism, Ethics, and the Politics of Practice* (Indiana University Press 2005), contributions to *The Encyclopedia of Music in Canada* (1992), *The New Handbook of Research on Music Teaching and Learning* (2002) and *The Oxford Handbook of Music Education* (fothcoming), and many articles in professional journals. He is past chair of the executive committee of the International Society for the Philosophy of Music Education (2005–07) and is on the advisory boards of the *Bulletin of the Council for Research in Music Education*, the *British Journal of Music Education*, and the *Philosophy of Music Education Review*.

Ruth Wright has been Chair of the Department of Music Education in the Don Wright Faculty of Music, the University of Western Ontario, Canada since August 2009. Prior to this she was a Senior Lecturer at the University of Wales Institute, Cardiff for 10 years. She has more than 30 years' experience as a teacher, musician and researcher in the studio, high school and university sectors. She has written extensively on the subject of music education. She is editor of *Sociology and Music Education* published by Ashgate Press in August 2010.

Vanessa Young became a teacher–educator in music after working for 15 years in primary schools, and then for Kent LEA as a coordinator of staff development in schools. She is currently Principal Lecturer in Education at Canterbury Christ Church University where she coordinates primary music. She is passionate about the cross-phase dimension of education and for many years has led and developed the PGCE 7–14 programme. She has had a wide range of involvement in music education including CPD and ITE, consultancy and external examining. She also has extensive experience in staff development. Her writing and research interests have focused mainly on music and teacher development. She is a member of NAME and is on the editorial board for the *British Journal of Music Education*. She is currently external assessor for the ABRSM Certificate and Diploma in Teaching.

Katherine Zeserson has a national reputation as a trainer, music animateur and educator, developed over 25 years working in a wide range of community, educational and social contexts from pre-school settings to postgraduate and professional development training programmes. Since 2002 she has been a Director of The Sage Gateshead responsible for the strategic design, direction and implementation of its extensive music Learning and Participation programme. In this role she also led on the development of *Sing Up*, the national primary-age singing programme, in collaboration with Faber Music and Youth Music. She is pursuing doctoral studies exploring the relationship between quality, innovation and inclusivity in cultural organizations, and maintains an active performing career as a professional singer.

Introduction to the series

This book, *Debates in Music Teaching*, is one of a series of books entitled *Debates in Subject Teaching*. The series has been designed to engage with a wide range of debates related to subject teaching. Unquestionably, debates vary among the subjects, but may include, for example, issues that:

- impact on Initial Teacher Education in the subject;
- are addressed in the classroom through the teaching of the subject;
- are related to the content of the subject and its definition;
- are related to subject pedagogy;
- are connected with the relationship between the subject and broader educational aims and objectives in society, and the philosophy and sociology of education;
- are related to the development of the subject and its future in the twenty-first Century.

Consequently, each book presents key debates that subject teachers should understand, reflect on and engage in as part of their professional development. Chapters have been designed to highlight major questions, and to consider the evidence from research and practice in order to find possible answers. Some subject books or chapters offer at least one solution or a view of the ways forward, whereas others provide alternative views and leave readers to identify their own solution or view of the ways forward. The editors expect readers will want to pursue the issues raised, and so chapters include questions for further debate and suggestions for further reading. Debates covered in the series will provide the basis for discussion in university subject seminars or as topics for assignments or classroom research. The books have been written for all those with a professional interest in their subject, and, in particular: student teachers learning to teach the subject in secondary or primary school; newly qualified teachers; teachers undertaking study at Masters level; teachers with a subject coordination or leadership role, and those preparing for such responsibility; as well as mentors, university tutors, CPD organisers and advisers of the aforementioned groups.

Books in the series have a cross-phase dimension, because the editors believe that it is important for teachers in the primary, secondary and post-16 phases to look at subject teaching holistically, particularly in order to provide for continuity and progression, but also to increase their understanding of how children and young people learn. The balance of chapters that have a cross-phase relevance varies according to the issues relevant to different subjects. However, no matter where the emphasis is, the authors have drawn out the relevance of their topic to the whole of each book's intended audience.

Because of the range of the series, both in terms of the issues covered and its cross-phase concern, each book is an edited collection. Editors have commissioned new writing from experts on particular issues, who, collectively, represent many different perspectives on subject teaching. Readers should not expect a book in this series to cover the entire range of debates relevant to the subject, or to offer a completely unified view of subject teaching, or that every debate will be dealt with discretely, or that all aspects of a debate will be covered. Part of what each book in this series offers to readers is the opportunity to explore the inter-relationships between positions in debates and, indeed, among the debates themselves, by identifying the overlapping concerns and competing arguments that are woven through the text.

The editors are aware that many initiatives in subject teaching continue to originate from the centre, and that teachers have decreasing control of subject content, pedagogy and assessment strategies. The editors strongly believe that for teaching to remain properly a vocation and a profession, teachers must be invited to be part of a creative and critical dialogue about subject teaching, and should be encouraged to reflect, criticise, problem-solve and innovate. This series is intended to provide teachers with a stimulus for democratic involvement in the development of the discourse of subject teaching.

Susan Capel, Jon Davison, James Arthur and John Moss December 2010

Introduction

Chris Philpott and Gary Spruce

This volume is aimed at postgraduate professional development in music education. To study and develop at postgraduate level, formally or informally, involves developing a systematic understanding of the field, a critical and analytical 'gaze' and a disposition to exercise creativity and innovation. This is of particular importance given the ongoing need for music teachers to solve the educational problems that face them; for example, how to engage all pupils in meaningful musical development and achievement, an issue which has underpinned the work of music educators for many decades in the modern era.

One of the ways in which students and practitioners in the field of music education can be drawn into creating innovative solutions to educational problems is to read thought-provoking new material causing them to reflect on taken-for-granted assumptions about the nature of musical knowledge, learning and pedagogy. This volume, by international contributors leading the academic study of the subject, aims to be just such a text.

In the UK there are a range of ways to engage with postgraduate professional development from masters level credits awarded as a part of a Postgraduate Certificate in Education (PGCE, and the most common form of teacher qualification), studying for an MA, undertaking an EdD (professional taught doctorate), through to a PhD. There are also many students in the field who choose to study informally. Being a music teacher rarely leaves time for much else, and yet a commitment to continuing professional development is vital for renewal in the field. Furthermore, study and development at this level is important to the professional autonomy of music educators as they create knowledge in the field. Whatever the circumstances of those reading this volume (or others like it) we believe that the high level study of music education is vital to improving the quality of teaching and learning for young people in our schools, colleges and communities.

The international perspective offered in this book is unique for a volume which is part of a series aimed at the UK audience. The contributing authors offer a rich and creative view on music education in the UK by providing a 'lens' through which to 'gaze' at our work. In addition it is also hoped that their contribution makes the volume of genuine interest to an international audience. At international conferences it is clear that music educators the world over share similar problems and have many common aspirations that resonate across cultures. Either way, the interaction between these chapters and those emanating from the UK, has the potential to stimulate the critical and analytical thought that is a necessary precursor to creativity and innovation in music education.

Important debates in music education have been stimulated by unprecedented interventions and initiatives over the last 20 years or so in the UK, for example, the National Curriculum, the Music Manifesto, Sing Up and Musical Futures. Each of these (and others) has emerged as a result of debates involving a wide range of world views about what constitutes the musically educated state. It is important that music educators are equipped with the tools to participate in these debates at the highest possible level. What is at stake is too important to be taken for granted. Indeed, whatever one's views on the 'why and what' of music education it is crucial that the protagonists (music teachers, policymakers, academics alike) have an understanding of the issues and the capacity to both question the assumptions of others and imagine that things might be otherwise. Whether or not you agree with the views and conclusions contained in this volume, the chapters should at least pose questions and raise issues that need to be solved, offering readers valuable practice in rationalizing and adapting their own positions in the field. This is important for at the time of writing the nature and place of music in the School curriculum in the UK is once again the subject of debate. This has happened many times in the past and there is nothing to suggest that it will not happen again.

The issues confronting music educators of all types are frequently complex, as illustrated in this volume. Some of the authors have chosen to address issues of practical concern to the teaching of music while others unashamedly embrace high level theory. Having said this, the book is underpinned by an assumption that practice is symbiotically related to theory and that an interrogation of either serves to illustrate their mutual interdependence.

In each chapter the views expressed represent a personal perspective and there has been no editorial attempt to adopt anything like a common philosophy. However, there *is* a common concern with policy and national initiatives as these continue to represent significant interventions in music which deserve critique and suggestions for modification and change. Typically authors provide a critical perspective on their theme and model the synthesis of ideas or creativity which is fundamental to postgraduate professional development, wherever or however it happens.

The book is in four Parts which reflect what we believe to be the key domains of debate in music education. In the first, **Philosophical, Sociological and Psychological Foundations** we establish the foundations of music education as a subject worthy of study with five chapters interrogating its philosophical, sociological and psychological underpinnings. In Chapter 1, Heidi Westerlund establishes a firm foundation for the book by noting that 'ideological powers work in and through us all' as a consequence of our life histories as musicians and educators. She argues that an understanding of a range of philosophical positions can enable us to examine and reflect upon our musical journeys and envisage what we might want the future to be. Within this framework she examines the philosophies of a number of influential music education thinkers including Bennett Reimer, Keith Swanwick and David Elliott.

Ruth Wright (Chapter 2), also focuses on the work of an eminent educational thinker when she draws upon the work of Basil Bernstein to examine the way in which his theory of the 'pedagogic device' can be used as a 'framework for the understanding the process through which education becomes a carrier for dominant social values'. Using music education as a 'case study' she demonstrates how educational policies and the process of their enactment (filtering) can act to the benefit or disadvantage of different social groups.

Picking up once more the notion of ideologies and contested terms, John Finney in *Creativity, culture and the practice of music education* (Chapter 3) tracks the progress of the discourse of creativity in music education music from the 'child-centred creativity of John Paynter' in the 1960s to the present day. He identifies and interrogates different conceptions and definitions of creativity in music education noting, for example, that while some rhetoric reveals 'a degradation' of the concept of 'creative genius' other visions show a concern for the playful irony of the postmodern. He concludes by recommending a definition of creativity, as an essentially human characteristic.

Being able to make a convincing case for the inclusion of music in the curriculum is becoming increasingly important at a time of increasing school autonomy and where the governmental instinct is to reduce the curriculum to minimum core subjects. In Chapter 4 Chris Philpott argues that in focusing too much on the 'soft', extrinsic justifications for music we present a 'weakened case for music as a discipline in the curriculum on the basis of an incomplete account of its nature and expressive power'. By way of example he identifies a range of ways in which music operates as a symbolic mode to positive and negative effect. He proposes a reconceptualization of music as a language to underpin a stronger case for music in the curriculum and a critical pedagogy to engage with the full range of musical meanings.

A key question addressed by Keith Swanwick Chapter 5 is, *What is music development and can education make a difference?* Swanwick begins by surveying a range of developmental theories and from these identifying key characteristics which a model for musical development should exhibit in order to be serviceable and have validity. He then uses these characteristics as a means of examining his and Tillman's highly influential spiral of musical development. Swanwick concludes by considering the implications of his analysis for aspects of music education including curriculum planning and assessment.

Books on music education rarely address in a concerted way the political dimensions of the subject and the ideological forces that impact upon it. In the second Part, **Political Perspectives**, three chapters take differing positions on the interface between the political and music education and in their differing ways offer a working out of ideas presented in the first Part; particularly those relating to the way in which education can be used to sustain social structures and social inequalities. In Chapter 6 Paul Woodford identifies an inherent contradiction in many music teachers' commitment to education as a means of promoting social justice and inclusion – through, for example including in the curriculum music from a wide range of traditions and cultures- and their reluctance to 'explicitly teach students how music and music education relate to politics and other forms of social control'. Locating his chapter in the American music education context, but which nevertheless has resonance for those in the UK, he demonstrates how 'political avoidance' by teachers and the socially decontextualized paradigm of music education as aesthetic education has its roots in Cold War politics. He goes on to argue for a more socially and politically active role for music educators in order to bring about ' a more socially progressive conception of music education as empowering teachers and students to reclaim ownership of the design and direction of their musical lives …'.

From a Canadian perspective on American music education we move, in Chapter 7, to an American perspective on English music education. Cathy Benedict and Patrick Schmidt demonstrate how the English National Curriculum in Music can be viewed as a form of manifesto. Typically the government uses this as the context for appropriating the language and rhetorical devices associated with the 'revolutionary discourse of oppressed populations' for the furtherance of their own political and ideological goals. This Part concludes with Chapter 8 where Gary Spruce with Francesca Matthews argues that despite the inclusion of musics in the curriculum from a wide range of traditions and cultures, formal music education continues to promote the values and processes associated with western art music resulting in the continuing alienation of many children from the formal curriculum. They explore the potential of framing a curriculum around the concepts of musical practices rather than styles or genres as a means of beginning to address young people's alienation from music in school.

We turn now to **The Pedagogy of Music.** The chapters in this Part, whilst maintaining a high level of analysis focus on themes arising from the first two Parts and their direct impact on the pedagogy of practice and on what music teachers actually do.

In Chapter 9 Jonathan Barnes addresses the challenge of how to ensure that music does not lose its identity when it is located within a cross-curricular environment. He identifies a range of cross-curricular approaches, all with creativity at their centre, and shows how musical understanding and knowledge can be developed within each. Following on from this, in Chapter 10 Chris Philpott argues that the current orthodoxies of summative and formative assessment are incompatible for use with projects which promote self-directed and informal learning. He concludes by proposing a framework for understanding learning and assessment in projects such as *Musical Futures* based on the work of Folkestad.

In Chapter 11, Jonathan Savage argues that the use of ICT in the classroom is underpinned by an inherent conservatism which prevents music teachers from fully exploiting what it has to offer as reflected in its uses in wider society. Savage suggests that in order to gain most benefit from digital technologies teachers should recognize both what these technologies distinctively offer to music education but also use them to develop 'those specific musical skills that we know all students require as part of their music education'. Over the last few years, developing children's critical thinking skills has come to be seen as of increasing importance. However as Spruce says in Chapter 12 there is as yet no shared understanding of what is meant by critical thinking or how these might be demonstrated in music lessons. Drawing on the work of Paulo Freire (amongst others), Spruce explores the conditions for, and processes through which, critical thinking skills might be developed in music education as a means of empowering pupils to actively engage with their world.

The seemingly intractable problem of why so few young people elect to continue with formal music education once it is no longer a compulsory part of the curriculum is explored by Keith Evans in Chapter 13. Drawing on the work of – amongst others – Bourdieu and Bernstein, Evans explores the contrasting aims and philosophies of so-called 'vocational' and 'academic' qualifications on offer at post-14 particularly in relation to their perceived status. Evans argues that what is important to whether or not young people choose to continue with their music education is not the qualification but the way in which music is taught. Adopting a case study approach he demonstrates how by placing music-making and 'real' musical practices at the heart of the curriculum, one school has achieved notable success in persuading its students to continue with their formal music education.

As Katherine Zeseron points out in Chapter 14, partnership working has become increasingly important in music education over the last ten years. She suggests that fundamental to effective partnerships is for those involved in supporting music learners to have 'shared and agreed goals' and to respect and value what each brings to the partnership. Zeserson argues for a 'constellation approach' to partnership which recognizes and accommodates the 'shifting matrix' of relationships that lie at the heart of partnership working.

In the first chapter of this book Westerlund argues for the importance of teachers being enabled to envisage what kinds of futures they might want and why. The concluding Part, **Professional Development**, explores some of the ways in which teachers might be supported and support themselves in developing the conceptual and practical tools which will enable them to reflect on their practice and envisage their future. In Chapter 15, Tim Cain and Pamela Burnard explore case study and action research approaches to classroom-based research by teachers and ways in which pupils may be involved both in the research being undertaken by teachers as well as engaging in research themselves. Finally, in Chapter 16, Vanessa Young addresses key questions in relation to teacher continuing professional development such as 'What is it?'; 'Who is it for?'; 'Where should it take place?'. Drawing on Bourdean ideas of intellectual, social and organizational capital, she argues for professional development which emerges from teacher self reflection of their own needs rather than being imposed on them in pursuit of externally imposed agendas.

Whilst this book has addressed a wide range of themes there has been no attempt to achieve complete coverage. We are aware of omissions and know the commissions could have taken different paths. What we hope this book will do however is inspire debate and motivate those involved in music education to engage with some of the issues which we believe are key to its survival and enrichment.

Part I

Philosophical, Sociological and Psychological Foundations

What can a reflective teacher learn from philosophies of music education?

From personal philosophy to critical cultural readership

Heidi Westerlund

Introduction

It is widely held that as music teachers, we need to develop our own personal philosophy in order to be conscious of our own pedagogical goals, and to carry out the required educational tasks in a consistent manner. Through this personalized philosophy, we can refer to, or refer to the uniqueness of, the use of our personal practical knowledge in music education (see e.g. Clandinin 1985) or to what Polanyi (1962) calls 'personal knowledge'. Such knowledge develops over years in and through our own education and through participating in musical practices, along with teachers' own rational reflections. Personal philosophy may be related to the choice of musical styles and instruments, or possibly to a particular systematic teaching and learning approach, such as Kodaly, Suzuki or Orff. One option for the music teacher when cultivating a personal philosophy concerning teaching music is offered, in a systematic manner, by academic philosophers of music education, many of whom have during the past decades developed comprehensive theories as to how to think of music education and from what kind of basic understandings to build educational practice (e.g. Reimer 1970/1989 Swanwick 1979, 1988, 1994; Elliott 1995). A philosophy, understood in this way, provides conceptual guidelines that aim to capture the features of successful practice.

For music teachers, navigating between diverse philosophies may seem time-consuming and even frustrating as each writer tries to persuade us of the superiority of their version over others: should we educate devoted listeners through selected classics or transmit musical hands-on knowledge for amateurs to enjoy in their future lives, or should we simply feed the existing musical institutions, symphony orchestras and the ilk, with new practitioners? However, rather than taking philosophies of music education as professional 'bibles' encompassing absolute truths, we could view these as *cultural prophecies*, each creating a critical *vision for the educational culture* (Bruner 1996). This view of philosophy, held by the pragmatist philosopher John Dewey, views philosophers as defining 'the larger patterns of continuity which are woven in effecting the enduring junctions of a stubborn past and an insistent future' (Dewey LW 3: 6).

Reading philosophy as thoroughly thought-out cultural critique, and as justified prophecy, allows teachers to further estimate the arguments against the cultural starting points; against their own specific educational culture, historical background and futures. It makes us teachers more conscious of how traditions and practices have nurtured our history and our own growth and path in musical learning; of how they implicitly or explicitly feed our present life and of what kind of future they suggest. Indeed, it is those very habits and beliefs that we grew up with and values that we learned to cherish that will have to be reflected upon when alternative paths and landscapes for music education are opened through philosophical cultural critique.

In this chapter, philosophies of music education will thus be understood as the ordering of ideas in critical and inspiring ways, not for the good, but rather, against certain kinds of practices in a given time and context, some of which will be examined in what follows as they have been presented during the past decades. Their practical power, in this proposed pragmatist approach, will be tested in relation to the meanings they enhance in teachers' conscious work when developing cultural readership, and within individual and collective attempts to improve educational practices. Thus, philosophical critique provides heuristic points of reference, not necessarily answers, for teachers' critical reflection.

Appreciation through subjective musical experiences

The call for a philosophy of music education has, by and large, arisen from the need to justify the existence of music in general education. When previous rationales[1] were no longer relevant, it became increasingly evident that a new rationale was needed for why one should be musically educated. At the time when in many countries the school subject was renamed 'Music' rather than 'Singing' it also became necessary to find a philosophical justification that would point out the specifically musical, rather than the non-musical, outcomes of the profession (e.g., Mark 2002). New technology, such as record players and tape recorders, allowed previously unheard of practices to come into schools, such as listening to professional performances.

One of the most influential post-Second World War philosophical ideas was the recognition of the subjective meaning that music has for human beings and recognition of the value of *individual musical experiences*. In his *A Philosophy of Music Education*, Bennett Reimer (1970/1989) suggested that making space for musical experiences within the best works of musical cultures could form the basic rationale that teachers would need to justify their work in schools and to decide on which aspects of music and music education should be emphasized. Students should be educated through the classics of the world's music cultures in order to learn to *appreciate* the art of music. Something deeper and more personal that could be carried throughout the students' life span would be needed in schools where previously most energy had been put into choirs or bands with a limited repertoire, and in which one perhaps would learn a single instrument, later to be abandoned. According to Reimer:

> ... we have largely neglected the musical needs of the majority of people in our culture – as serving the few who choose to perform – and only secondarily serving the people who will become (and already are) musical partakers of the music produced by specialists. We have so emphasized the few over the many that most people regard us as special education for the interested and talented.
>
> (Reimer 1997: 34.)

Deep musical experiences, that can be called *aesthetic experiences*, should therefore be the focus of teaching. This emphasis has certain practical implications. Reimer writes:

> In the general music curriculum, the point is to experience the great diversity of musics in the only way possible for all people when music is required – through listening as the fundamental behavior. Performing, in the general music program, is an essential but contributory mode of interaction with music. It is a powerful means, among others, for enhancing musical understanding and experience. But the balance between listening and performing will *favor listening*.
>
> (Reimer 1989: 185, italics added).

Hence this approach remains critical of such lessons that approach musical learning merely from the perspective of advancing skills and music making. Music education as *aesthetic education* does not expend valuable school hours simply on breathing techniques or fingering, but rather is highly concerned with the musical experiences that one can gain by cultivating an aesthetic mode of knowing, by teaching the 'distinctive cognitive domain' through attentive and active listening (Reimer 1992: 25).

Reimer's philosophical position views students primarily as potential audiences for the musical practices of professionals. Consequently, there are also opposing views. As this approach in its own way starts with the problematic division between potential professionals and those who only appreciate art, studies increasingly point out the consequences of education in which students are selected according to their potential for a professional career, and of silencing those with an assumed lack of talent in order to secure musical products of as high a quality as possible: indeed, one can learn to be unmusical in a school that is in principle based on the idea of equity and democracy (see e.g., Trehub 2003; Numminen 2005; West 2009). Furthermore, as Numminen's (2005) study on adult poor pitch singers shows, learning how to make music, for instance, learning how to sing, can be made possible for everyone since *anyone* can advance in it. It has been argued that the enjoyment one gets from performing music ought to be one of the main goals of music education since school may be, and often is, the only place where such enjoyment is made possible (see e.g., Elliott 1995). Furthermore, worldwide emerging online music communities exemplify how the hard boundaries between professional and amateur musicians are becoming more obscure today and how amateur musicians increasingly want to make music just for the sake of the meaning and value that *music making* and *being a musician* brings into their life (Partti 2009; Partti and Karlsen 2010). X-Factor type competitions, new television programmes in which anyone can participate in choir competitions or learn alongside professionals, manifest an emerging wider tendency towards a 'participatory culture' (see, e.g., Jenkins *et al.*, 2006).

Understanding musical meanings and values through multiple activities

Another approach, within one that could be called 'music education as aesthetic education' (Regelski 1996), is to categorize the practice of music education into a set of activities that each, in their own valuable way, contributes to the overall goal: *musical understanding*. Schools may not be seen as extensions of a professional division of labour in which a few produce music, just as equally we do not teach mathematics only to those who have the potential to become mathematicians. This approach, taken, for instance, by Keith Swanwick, aims to open multiple doors for all students.

In his *A Basis for Music Education* (1979), Swanwick develops a 'comprehensive model of musical experience' (p. 55) for organizing music studies, arguing that they should involve composition (C), literature studies (L), audition (A ; meaning 'the act of attentive and responsive listening, with aesthetic understanding as part of the experience' (p. 51)), skill acquisition (S), and performance (P) – ('CLASP'). Swanwick emphasizes the significance of knowledge *of* music, the direct cognitive and affective experience and personal knowledge that easily gives way to knowledge *about* music, or 'to measurable skills, such as playing scales and writing in manuscript from dictation' (p. 54). He warns teachers not to take 'short cuts that actually manage to avoid the beauty spots which are the ultimate destination of our journeys' (p. 54; see also, Swanwick 1994: 16). Music, as such, involves multiple 'layers of meaning', some of which are intuitive and some more explicable, and by carefully unwrapping those layers it is possible to learn from others (Swanwick 1994: 2; see also, Swanwick 1999: 36). Our personal interpretations arise from within this meeting point of intuition and explicit analysis in musical events (Swanwick 1994: 176).

Perhaps Swanwick's most important contribution to the *international* discussion in music education has been the recognition of composing as a way of understanding music. As music education in many countries still deals first and foremost with a pre-existing musical repertoire that is there for the teachers to teach and students to learn (e.g., Georgii-Hemming and Westvall 2010), composing as a working method and educational activity gives room in a unique way for students' imagination, creativity and innovation, at the same time as it deals with cognitive tasks, structures, concrete material and tradition (Swanwick 1979: 56).

Both Swanwick and Reimer examine music in schools as subject content in which musical meanings and values transcend particular socio-cultural contexts: 'Music has a life of its own' and in education one ought to get rid of its 'strong idiomatic boundaries' (Swanwick 1988: 112) that may prevent students from understanding the musical in music. For both thinkers, what is specifically musical in the subject ought to be cultivated in teaching so that it is possible to justify the subject matter in an educational system. Reimer questions any other values that may be considered as the rationale for music education: 'Why teach social skills through music, if one can do the same with sports?' (Reimer 2009: 11). In other words, for example, choosing repertoire should be done with musical criteria, not social issues in mind; or, one should avoid 'strongly culturally loaded idioms until their context has eroded' (Swanwick 1988: 111).

This kind of ranking of values and the separating of musical values from any other 'minority values' (Reimer 2009: 11) is a logical solution considering that the point is to find a rationale that is specifically musical. However, from the school teacher's point of view, this search may have major consequences. If considering the social values of music is 'a moral crime', as it is for Reimer (*Ibid.*), teachers may even end up setting their own philosophies against national guidelines for music and schooling in general that in many contexts emphasize social values. A more holistic approach may therefore resonate with the ideas of a teacher who is also obliged to design musical learning environments that aim to socially reward musical experiences. This receives support from Dewey: he argued that there is a stubborn idea of 'educating specific faculties' and that this idea is repeated in the thought that different subjects represent specific values in the curriculum. According to Dewey, this idea represents 'the obverse side of the conception of experience or life as a patchwork of independent interests' (Dewey MW 9: 254). Against this starting point, one can then also wonder if the question of a rationale for music education can be answered by setting values against each other: musical values against any other values; individual against social; global against contextual and situational.

Contextual musicianship as musical understanding

If in Reimer's and Swanwick's philosophies the meanings and value of music education arise from the meanings and values of musical works or discourses that exist 'out there' as something anyone can learn to value in a global sense, another possibility would be to consider music as something people in various cultures *do* and the value of the subject matter as arising from students' actions and activities. From this kind of starting point, music is seen as involving musicianship and culture-specific craftsmanship through which people express their cultural beliefs and values.

Much influenced by the ethno-musicological research that began to flourish in the 1980s, David Elliott's (1995) music education philosophy starts from the premise that each musical culture has its own set of values and goals and it is musical knowing-in-action that students need in order to be able to navigate in our present multicultural world and to value the epistemological, i.e. knowledge-related, differences of diverse musical practices. A culture-specific musical praxis should therefore be at the centre of education. By praxis, Elliott means 'action committed to achieving goals (*telos*) in relation to standards, traditions, images, and purposes (*eidos*) viewed as Ideals that are themselves open to renewal, reformulation, and improvement' (Elliott 1995: 69). By challenging Reimer's philosophy, Elliott argues: 'in real life, people do not learn how to make music just to improve their ability to listen to music' but rather they find it worth doing 'for the sake of musicing itself' (Elliott 1995: 76). Elliott envisions a school in which students gain experiences of 'musicing' in the widest sense of the concept: it involves musical performing, improvising, composing, arranging, and conducting that also all include musical listening (p. 173). This approach has similarities to that of Swanwick, yet, as Elliott points out, music listening is involved in all forms of musicing. The value of musicianship is in the enjoyment one gets from the subjective optimal experiences, i.e., flow experiences, when deeply involved in one's doing and when meeting the musical challenges (p. 122). Understood in this way, music-making in education affects students' self-growth and self-knowledge so that these wider educational goals are also gained through musicing (p. 121).

Much in the same vein as Reimer and Swanwick, however, Elliott sees musical cultures and practices as carrying *positive* values that are then reproduced in education as authentically as possible (Elliott 1995: 72). Despite valuable considerations, this stance protects education from any wider critical perspective emerging: in this light any human practice seems ethically good as long as it has traditions, cultural meanings and values that are cherished. Moreover, it ignores the fact that music may change its socio-cultural and situational meanings when 'travelling' and that this can take place also in education; it is worth noting that people have been tortured using music, even with their own music (see, e.g., Alanne 2010), an observation that forces us to see the situational aspects of musical values and to reflect on how our students actually experience music and music education (Westerlund 2008). Furthermore, we may not even adopt a single approach to cherished musical traditions, since different musical practices have differing attitudes towards what is considered authentic. As Schippers (2010) notes, '[w]hile early music practice aimed at faithful reproduction of historical originals, rock musicians emphatically do not want to copy an original but aim to be original', both paradoxically having the same goal of creating 'the most 'truthful' musical experience possible' (p. 53). Our basic understanding of what is valuable in music-making may thus differ radically depending upon the tradition and musical genre one favours and the context in which it finds itself.

Music teachers as critical cultural workers

It may be symptomatic of the philosophy of music education that as it is making efforts to justify the subject in schools, at the same time it presents music, musical works or practices as idealized without dealing critically with their faults: for instance, how music may be used to ridicule ethnic minorities, to present sexual power, or depict violence, to mention but a few. Students are expected to learn to appreciate or actively make music, but it is not common for theorists to encourage teachers to point out the ideological and possibly prejudicial sides of music: rather that is to be avoided (see, Swanwick 1988: 104–15). In this respect, Lucy Green's (2008) experiment in the UK, in which students copied music as music makers, took a stronger critical approach. Students, according to Green, develop 'critical musicality' through their 'informal, aural learning involving their own choice of music' (p. 84). While musical appreciation carries 'connotations of a struggle to impose a superior, complex, autonomous classical musical taste upon the "masses" ' (p. 83), 'the concept of 'critical musicality' includes the idea that all music can be listened to more or less analytically, with more or less under-standing' (p. 84), and that all musical meanings include musical and non-musical delineated meanings.

An even stronger critical practice could be deduced from the standpoint of critical pedagogy in which teachers are seen as *critical cultural workers* (Freire 1998) whose task is to lead students into critically perceiving their cultural condi-tions and to change them. Besides receiving, analysing and celebrating music's artistic features, the teacher ought to be able to identify possible inequalities and undemocratic practices and work towards better conditions (McLaren 1998). With the purpose of separating conscious and unconscious political agendas in education, Henry Giroux, one of the leading North American critical peda-gogues, makes a distinction between *politicizing education* and *political education*. The former refers to such educational practices in which the political aims of the practice are hidden behind the expert, or scientific discourse on objectivity, whereas the latter refers to an understanding that education has connections to economic, social and cultural issues which are seen as a use of power – even in classrooms (Giroux 1999: 198–199).

Music educators as critical cultural workers do not treat aesthetic education in isolation from the other critical goals of schooling but rather see any subject, including music, as offering possibilities for becoming increasingly conscious of the world's ideological constraints. They see that as any state of affairs is ideo-logically loaded in some ways, even music education is structured by values that have been institutionalized and taken for granted. It is, for instance, not difficult to find white, middle-class, Christian values in music curricula in countries whose school system explicitly defends multiculturalism, democracy and reli-gious neutrality. For a critical music educator, the task is to be constantly conscious of how the ideological power works in and through all of us: what kind of assumptions lay the groundwork for our educational practices and how these assumptions are seen in our teaching. Recognition of this ethical task of schooling is a necessity even in music education in order to avoid hegemonic, unequal practices in schools and in future societies.

As the critical music teacher's work is not simply about delivering the subject content, musical idioms or structures, or even about their delineated non-musical meanings, designing and *re-designing* educational environments and using imagination in creating new social spaces becomes important. Understanding music in schools as a social endeavour means that the music teacher constantly searches for meanings in dialogue with the students: the school culture becomes a co-constructed culture. Consequently, in the curricula even music history and past have a connection to today's society and the students' lives. The teacher gives space for students' own ideas even when working with a pre-existing musical repertoire, and she trusts her students in choosing working methods yet, at the same time, acts as the responsible coach and facilitator. The teacher constantly asks: How does music education best support all students' identity, work and agency?

Experimenting with materials and working methods is a way of resisting the kind of teacher-proof curriculum and 'banking approach' (Freire 1970) that tends to ignore students' innovative moments, prevent open-ended creative processes and students' own criticism. Openness to change, surprise and critical views means that the musical meanings and traditions that we have inherited from previous generations are understood as *re-contextualized* in education (see Westerlund 2002; Schippers 2010) in the sense that investing effort and overcoming struggle when studying is felt to be worthwhile for students. The critical mindset is not simply set on how authentic students' music making is, by comparing it to music outside school, but on reflecting on the meaningfulness of the learning; on how the students' 'learnings' are put to use in their own lives and how the activities empower each one of them.

It is obvious that this kind of pedagogy is perpetually in the making: it regularly faces tension and, therefore requires the teacher's constant use of creative intelligence. The teacher's philosophy should be to accept a continuous search for better and more meaningful practices, to engage ourselves not only with reflection-in-action but also with reflection-on-action, in which the latter refers to the reflective work the teacher does before or after having made practical decisions (Schön 1987). Such reflective thinking is 'thinking through options before prematurely foreclosing them', as Estelle Jorgensen suggests (2003, 18) – however, always keeping an educator's larger critical societal and cultural tasks as the backdrop of any single practical act.

Discussion

To start planning one's teaching with existing repertoires and commonly used textbooks is an easy road to begin with. Repertoire, even when well tested through other teachers' use, says little, however, about potential activities and about how music may function socially within the school itself and in its surrounding contexts: It says nothing about who the students are. Reflection on educational practices means looking beyond textbooks and established practices. It demands envisioning the meanings of activities, the purposes of educational processes and the attitudes that school creates in students, independent of whether one is thinking of concentrating critical minds, the efforts put into learning instruments or of students negotiating when composing together. Studying the society and culture of our schools and envisioning how their futures may look is, however, a lifelong professional learning process for a teacher. It is in this ongoing reflective work that theoretical work and the philosophy of music education may help us to look beyond the most obvious and what seems 'natural'.

As suggested here, the starting point of the teacher's reflective pathway lies in being able to break the boundaries of one's own educational background: learning to read the culture of music education may best start from reading our own education. 'What has been meaningful musical learning for me and why, and how does it inform me as a teacher of others?' And 'how is my students' musical life different from mine?'. Yet, even this reflection may be a lifelong process in which no perfect final stage can be achieved. We may even say that the better one becomes in questioning, the less sure and unreflective one allows oneself to be, since imagination and creativity are also involved when considering options.

Dewey realized the challenges of this intellectual and practical task when encouraging teachers to study not just their societies now but also what future will unfold within them. He described the challenge of change when writing:

> [t]ransformation, readjustment, reconstruction all imply prior existences: existences which have characters and behaviors of their own which must be accepted, consulted, humored, manipulated or made light of, in all kinds of differing ways in the different context of different problems. Making a difference in reality does not mean making any more difference than we find by experimentation can be made under the given conditions – even though we may still hope for different fortune another time under other circumstances.
>
> (Dewey MW 4: 141)

Thus, a reflective teacher's professional life is neither cynical nor hopeless, and it does not even necessarily demand great revolutions. However, it will involve an ethical dedication to alertness, to the renewing of oneself as a professional and one's pedagogy, as they will inevitably become part of other people's lives and our future society. At best, this ethical dedication is sustained and critical cultural readership developed in professional communities in which theory and practice constructively meet and feed each other.

Reflective questions

1   What kind of personal philosophy did your own music teacher exhibit during your general education? Give some practical examples of this philosophy in their teaching.
2   How is musical culture in your society changing and how would you take this change into account in transforming music education?
3   What are the particular taken-for-granted assumptions of your country's music education that may influence the music teacher's freedom to choose

music and working methods and how do these ideological features implicitly impact the teacher's personal philosophy?

4   In what ways do the above discussed philosophical approaches challenge your prior understanding of music education?

5   How has your philosophical position changed now as a teacher, comparing your position as a student?

Note

1   e.g. Music and the Arts in general as an entry point to Christianity; or patriotism-fuelled singing.

References

Alanne, S. (2010) 'Music Psychotherapy with Refugee Survivors of Torture. Interpretations of Three Clinical Case Studies', *Studia Musica*, 44. Helsinki: Sibelius Academy.

Bruner, J. (1996) *The Culture of Education*, Cambridge: Harvard University Press.

Clandinin, J. (1985) 'Personal Practical Knowledge: A Study of Teachers' Classroom Images', *Curriculum Inquiry* 15: 361–85.

Dewey, J. (1996) Middle Works, in L. Hickman, (ed.) *The Collected Works of John Dewey, 1882–1953*, The Electronic Edition.

Dewey. J. (1996) Later Works, in L. Hickman, (ed.) *The Collected Works of John Dewey, 1882–1953*, The Electronic Edition.

Elliott, D.J. (1995) *Music Matters. A New Philosophy of Music Education*, Oxford: Oxford University Press.

Freire, P. (1970) *Pedagogy of the Oppressed*, New York: Continuum.

Freire, P. (1998) *Teachers as Cultural Workers: Letters to Those Who Dare Teach*, Boulder: Westview.

Georgii-Hemming, E. and Westvall, M. (2010) 'Music Education – A Personal Matter? Examining the Current Discourses of Music Education in Sweden', *British Journal of Music Education* 27(1): 21–33.

Giroux, H. (1999) 'Performing Cultural Studies as a pedagogical practice', in D. Slayden and R. K. Whillock (eds) *Soundbite Culture: The Death of Discourse in a Wired World*, Thousand Oaks: Sage.

Green, L. (2008) *Music, Informal Learning and the School: A New Classroom Pedagogy*, Aldershot: Ashgate.

Jenkins, H., Clinton, K., Purushotma, R., Robinson, A.J. and Weigel, M. (2006) *Confronting the Challenges of Participatory Culture: Media Education for the 21st Century*. Online. Available : <http://www.digitallearning.macfound.org/> (accessed 14 January 2008).

Jorgensen, E. (2003) *Transforming Music Education*, Bloomington and Indianapolis: Indiana University Press.

Mark, M. (2002) 'Historical Precedents of Aesthetic Education Philosophy', in M. Mark (ed.) *Music Education Source Readings from Ancient Greece to Today*, New York and London: Routledge.

McLaren, P. (1998) *Life in Schools. An Introduction to Critical Pedagogy in the Foundation of Education*, Reading, MA: Allison Wesley Longman.

Numminen, A. (2005) *Laulutaidottomasta Kehittyväksi Laulajaksi: Tutkimus Aikuisen Laulutaidon Lukoista ja Niiden Aukaisemisesta.* (Helping adult poor pitch singers learn to sing in tune. A study of the stumbling blocks confronting developing singers and the means of surmounting them). Helsinki: Sibelius Academy.

Partti, H. (2009) *Musiikin Verkkoyhteisöissä Opitaan Tekemällä. Kokemisen, Jakamisen, Yhteisön ja Oman Musiikinteon Merkitykset Osallistumisen Kulttuurissa.* (Learning by doing in an online music community. The meaning of experience, sharing, music making and community in participatory culture.) *Finnish Journal of Music Education,* 12(2): 39–47.

Partti, H. and Karlsen, S. (2010) 'Reconceptualising Musical Learning: New Media, Identity and Community in Music Education', *British Journal of Music Education.*

Polanyi, M. (1962) *Personal knowledge: Towards a Post-critical Philosophy,* London: Routledge.

Reimer, B. (1989) *A Philosophy of Music Education,* 2nd edn, Englewood Cliffs, New Jersey: Prentice Hall.

Reimer, B. (1992) 'What Knowledge Is of Most Worth in the Arts', in B. Reimer and R. A. Smith (eds) *The Arts, Education, and Aesthetic Knowing 91. Yearbook of the National Society for the Study of Education,* Part II, Chicago: The University of Chicago Press.

Reimer, B. (1997) 'Music Education in the 21st Century', *Music Educators Journal* 84 (3): 33–8.

Reimer, B. (2009) *Seeking the Significance of Music Education – Essays and Reflections,* Lanham, New York, Toronto and Plymouth, UK: MENC and Rowman and Littlefield Education.

Regelski, T.A. (1996) 'Prolegomenon to a Praxial Philosophy of Music and Music Education', *Finnish Journal of Music Education* 1(1): 23–38.

Schippers, H. (2010) *Facing the Music. Shaping Music Education from a Global Perspective,* Oxford and New York: Oxford University Press.

Schön, D. (1987) *Educating the Reflective Practitioner: Toward a New Design for Teaching and Learning in the Professions,* San Francisco: Jossey-Bass.

Swanwick, K. (1979) *A Basis for Music Education,* London: Routledge.

Swanwick, K. (1988) *Music, Mind, and Education,* London and New York: Routledge.

Swanwick, K. (1994) *Musical Knowledge. Intuition, Analysis and Music Education,* London and New York: Routledge.

Swanwick, K. (1999) *Teaching Music Musically,* New York and London: Routledge.

Trehub, S.E. (2003) 'Musical Predispositions in Infancy: An Update', in I. Peretz and R. Zatorre (eds), *The Cognitive Neuroscience of Music,* Oxford: Oxford University Press.

West, S. (2009) 'Selective Mutism for Singing (SMS) and its Treatment: Conceptualising Musical Disengagement as Mass Social Dysfunction', in W. Baker (ed.) *Musical Understanding: Proceedings of the XVII National Conference,* Launceston: Australian Society for Music Education.

Westerlund, H. (2002) *Bridging Experience, Action, and Culture in Music Education, Studia Musica* 16. Helsinki: Sibelius Academy.

Westerlund, H. (2008) 'Justifying Music Education. A View from the Here-and-Now Value experience', *Philosophy of Music Education Review,* 16(1): 79–95.

Chapter 2

Policy and practice in music education

A sociological perspective

Ruth Wright

> The first wisdom of sociology is this: things are not what they seem ... Social reality turns out to have many layers of meaning. The discovery of each new layer changes the perception of the whole.
>
> (Peter Berger 1963: 23)

Introduction

In this chapter we explore some of the ways in which policy impacts upon practice in music education. A sociological perspective will be applied to show how educational policy is used as one of the ways in which dominant social groups may be seen to act to perpetuate their values in society. Policy is a framework that links ideologies, political affiliations, social groups and social institutions to agendas for change. Along with policy comes allocation of material resources to enable policy to change society in the desired ways. This has a substantial impact upon the lives of teachers and their students. Some key questions are presented around which this chapter revolves:

- Who are the actors in each policy arena?
- What resources are distributed? To whom are they distributed and on what scale?
- Who benefits from a policy and who is left out? (Fitz, Davies and Evans 2006).

We then explore how Basil Bernstein's (1996; 2000) theory of the pedagogic device can provide a framework for understanding the process through which education becomes a carrier for dominant social values. This theory will be presented and applied to examples drawn from music education.

Sociology and the sociological perspective

One of the main services that sociology renders to us as music educators is that it helps us make the familiar strange. As the sociologist Peter Berger so simply but acutely observed 'things are not what they seem.' Sociology urges us to become aware of this fact in our everyday lives. It helps us to be like the fish that becomes aware of the water in which it swims. By seeing our classrooms, studios, rehearsal halls – the familiar – through a new set of lenses, those of sociological theory, we can 'make them strange'–observe them as an outsider might. This can be a salutary experience and may present to us new ways to think and act in our roles as music educators. In this chapter we try to move perceptions of policy, and its impact on music education from the familiar, taken-for-granted facts of life for educators – to the strange, subject to critique and reflection. In so doing we hope to open up areas of debate about the effects of policy on knowledge, on practice and on equality of access to music in education.

Sociology may be described as the systematic study of human societies, particu- larly those that have developed since the industrial era. This discipline examines among other things how those societies came to be, how they have developed and become organized and how they reproduce themselves and function. Sociology also embraces the study of social relationships and social institutions. It offers a viewpoint drawn from outside the field of music and education that we can adopt to examine the issues facing our subject, bringing new perspectives to bear on persistent problems. Furthermore, it is a theory-rich perspective, theory being something that has arguably been lacking in many of our previous efforts to research music education. Sociological theory brings with it languages of description and frameworks of analysis that may assist us in depicting and under- standing the worlds of classrooms, studios, concert halls, schools, ministries of education and many other contexts that touch our lives. Moreover, the breadth of sociological theory provides powerful frameworks for consideration of the world in which we live from the macro – the very largest scale of humanity as it is organized in societies; to the micro – the close-up inspection of the interactions between individuals in their real life contexts, such as musical learning and teaching. As the pioneers in this field in relation to music education such as Christopher Small, Hildegard Froehlich and Lucy Green have shown, socio- logical thinking can be illuminating both as a means to deeper understanding of the issues themselves and as a means of raising consciousness of the large-scale (macro) issues of power and control by which music education is often constrained.

Perhaps the necessity for music educators to become aware of the sociological water within which we swim may be perceived as particularly pressing within an era of increased manipulation of societal institutions, such as education, by governments with ever more potent and practically articulated policies towards education. As education policies become increasingly focused on what the soci- ologist Basil Bernstein (2001: 31) termed 'trainability', the purpose of schools and schooling becomes increasingly oriented towards preparing young people for constant, flexible re-training to suit the requirements of the economy. Bernstein saw this as a 'socially empty' process, still acting effectively to disadvantage those not privileged by home and family to preferentially acquire the resulting skills and qualifications. Alternative vistas of the future, alternative rationales for education and for the lives of young people may be offered through subjects such as Music but to do so effectively music educators need to understand the context within which we are living and working from a sociological perspective.

This context is commonly underpinned by policy. Moreover 'Policy by definition arises out of ideas and struggles of the past and seeks to shape social developments in the future' (Fitz *et al.*, 2006: 17). In other words, a policy is a means by which ideology, often derived from political philosophy, in turn connected to certain social groups is made manifest in and through society's institutions.

Sociologist Anthony Giddens (1984: 24) tells us that: 'Institutions by definition are the more enduring features of social life.' Typically, contemporary sociologists use the term to refer to complex social forms that reproduce themselves: such as governments, the family, human languages, universities, schools, hospitals, business corporations and legal systems. For those of us engaged in music education, our lives are closely entwined with any number of social institutions and the effects of policy initiatives upon these institutions will have a direct bearing upon our lives and on those of the students we teach.

Policy to practice

As Fitz *et al.* (2006: 17) assert, policies 'can be thought of as outcomes of contested preferences expressed within the state and civil society, some of which go forward as practical programmes involving the allocation or reallocation of resources.' In other words, a policy is the end result of an ideological battle, carrying with it resources to make the ideology real. Let's take an example from music education – the formation of the English National Curriculum for Music. The idea of a national curriculum was characteristic of a government ideology of the 1980s that sought to extend and tighten central control over education, specifically curriculum content, pedagogy and assessment. This ideology was subject to debate and parliamentary process and enshrined in policy and law in the Education Act 1988, with the creation of the National Curriculum and attendant assessment apparatus. Subsequent to the 1988 Act, financial and human resources were deployed to put the National Curriculum into action in schools with the production of documentation and in-service training for teachers.

As Fitz *et al.* (2006) suggest, some researchable questions arise from this process, such as 'who are the actors in a particular policy arena?'; 'What resources are distributed?'; 'To whom are they distributed and on what scale?'; 'Who benefits from this policy?', 'Who is left out?'. These questions could be usefully applied to many educational policies affecting music educators at all levels of the educational context from local, school or council policies to regional or national ones. The resulting answers might shed interesting light on those whom policy serves and those whom it disadvantages or excludes.

As government education policies seeking to produce officially sanctioned knowledge (e.g. national curricula, national standards or their global equivalents) mushroom around the world, the question of who has control of the knowledge content of the curriculum and the values for which it is a vehicle become key issues. Official curricula in turn become entwined with practice in such a way that the two may become indistinguishable. An example of this is the National Strategy Key Stage 3 Music Programme (England) to all intents and purposes a pedagogic manual for delivering the National Curriculum. In such circumstances, the questions discussed above become far from academic as the embedding of policy in practice like this makes it invisible.

The knowledge that finds its way into schools as the music curriculum is never neutral. It is the result of ideologically impregnated policy through which it becomes filtered to enhance and preserve the cultural and economic interests of the dominant social group. As such, it is a relay for certain social and cultural values. For Antonio Gramsci, the Italian Marxist, the control of knowledge is critical to preserving the ideological dominance of certain classes, a process he terms *hegemony*. Gramsci identifies schools as playing a central role in this process by distributing to students the form of knowledge required to preserve and produce that society's institutions (Apple: 2004). In other words, as Brian Davies (Wright and Davies: 2010) so acutely observed 'schools exist to do it over' that is, schools function to reproduce society through reproducing the knowledge and culture valued by the dominant social group.

A case study of the process of ideology into policy can be found in the formation of England's National Curriculum for Music. Gammon recounted events related to the 1991 report by the National Curriculum Music Working Group:

> ... which reflected the best practice of music teachers as it had developed since the 1970s [...] they made a number of references to different musical styles including Bhangra beat, pop-flamenco, penillion singing, Gamelan, and Scottish Gaelic psalm singing (DES, Welsh Office 1991a: 26, 51, 40, 41). In mentioning these musical styles they were reflecting an increased diversity in practice in schools, with steel bands and samba bands being equipped and organized and some LEAs even providing lessons on such instruments as the tabla, the Indian harmonium and the Northumbrian bagpipes. A significant list of publications dealing with the teaching of 'ethnic' music in school emerged since the 1970s.
>
> (Gammon 1999: 1)

The recommendations of the Working Group however required explicit official endorsement before they could pass into policy and the cultural inclusivity of the proposed music curriculum suggested by the list of activities above did not meet with universal approval. David Pascall (in Gammon 1993), chairman of the National Curriculum Council seconded from British Petroleum, and who scrutinized all pre-legislative subject group reports, declared that: '(A)ny domination of popular and temporary cultural movements in our approach to the curriculum will only serve to separate our children from their inheritance which has shaped society today.' The idea of a curriculum that did not foreground the seminal importance of western art music provoked a storm of controversy, not least from the conservative media, fuelled by neo-conservative philosophers, such as Roger Scruton and Anthony O'Hear (1991), the latter contending that:

> On this curriculum, pupils will be able to study music for 10 years without gaining a sound knowledge of either the history or the techniques of Western classical music, which is surely one of the greatest achievements of our civilization.
>
> (O'Hear 1991)

These statements are witness to a worldview so deeply entrenched that they imply both a complete confidence in the form of culture embodied within it as superior (represented by the ingrained belief by O'Hear that the conception of 'our civilization' or, in the case of Pascall, 'our society', was commonly held), and an inability to comprehend that other races or classes might see these things completely differently.

After a celebrated media battle, with exchanges of letters in the Press from the great and the good of the classical music world defending the more liberal curriculum proposed by the Music Working Group, Kenneth Clarke, then Secretary of State for Education, capitulated to reactionary pressure and eventually published a much more prescriptive draft English National Curriculum for Music, detailing historical periods and genres of western art music, with suggested composers and works with which pupils must become familiar. This was greeted with despondency by many (e.g. Sir Simon Rattle) as being a retrogressive step for music education. What it exemplified perfectly, however, was Gramsci's concept of hegemony in action: the control of knowledge, in this case musical knowledge, to preserve the ideological values of the dominant social group, in this case through the reproduction of the form of culture valued by the dominant group.

A critical understanding of the basis of education policy in government economic ideology may help to provide some reflective distance for educators, before we embrace unthinkingly the latest edicts from 'on high'. As Apple (2004) proceeds to argue, the underlying economic rationale for much current education policy around the world, with its roots in the global economic crisis and subsequent relationship problems between social authority and the populace has been 'exported *onto* the schools'. It has been made our problem and in many cases portrayed as our responsibility:

> If teachers and curricula were more tightly controlled, more closely linked to the needs of business and industry, more technically oriented, with more stress on traditional values and workplace norms and dispositions, then the problems of achievement, of unemployment, of international economic competitiveness, of the disintegration of the inner city, and so on would largely disappear, or so goes the accepted litany.
>
> (Apple 2004: xix)

It becomes very clear from this analysis and from reflection upon government education policies in many countries around the world over the last 25 years at least (see, e.g. Woodford 2011) that the effects of government education policies to achieve just this 'tight control', this close link to the needs of business and industry, have had significant impact upon the lives of teacher–musicians working in education. For example, music has become increasingly marginalized in many curricula, particularly at the earlier stages of education where the focus is increasingly upon literacy, numeracy and scientific/technological knowhow – the cogs that are perceived to keep the economic machine turning. The purpose of a music education has become reconceptualized in terms of what it can do for other more work-related skills: the generic enterprise of student engagement in education, creativity, problem-solving, team work and leadership, not for the intrinsic value of music education itself. Not that many of these generic issues are not worthy and deserving of our time and attention as music educators. They have in many instances, however, changed what we do and how we do it and we may benefit from observing and reflecting upon how this has happened and to what ends.

It is for these reasons amongst others that a sociological consideration of the effects of policy and its effects on practice in music education may be particularly helpful to those reflecting upon our field. We now turn to the work of Bernstein to provide us with a conceptual framework for analysing the process of policy formation and implementation in music education.

Enter Basil Bernstein

Basil Bernstein was a British sociologist and linguist, holding the Karl Mannheim Chair of the Sociology of Education at the Institute of Education, University of London, England. Born into a Jewish immigrant family, in the East End of London, his career was centered around his desire to understand and eliminate the barriers to upward social mobility. He came late to an academic career, gaining a doctorate at the age of 40. Prior to this he had served as an under-age soldier in the Second World War, worked in a London boys' club for underprivi-leged Jewish children, put himself through university at the London School of Economics by working at various menial jobs, and completed teacher education. He subsequently taught various subjects, including mathematics, physical education, driver education and motor repair, despite the fact that he could not drive; a fact that he successfully concealed from his students.

Bernstein's contribution to the fields of sociology, sociology of education and sociolinguistics have made him one of the most significant academic figures of the twentieth century. His work has made particularly strong contributions to theory in the sociology of education. He is not 'easy' to read but worth persevering with, as the brilliance of his work in helping us describe, analyze and understand how education still acts to differentiate between children of various social classes is unparalleled. He has formulated a well-articulated and complex theorization of the ways in which society and education interact in his theory of the 'pedagogic device'. Through this theory he explains *how* education works as a vehicle for social reproduction. This allows us to follow the journey of knowledge from the point of its origination, through the process of selection and filtration to becoming curriculum, through the interactions of school and teacher with pupils, to the point at which the pupil reproduces their understanding of what has been taught. His work therefore enables us to answer Fitz *et al.* (2006) questions about how educational policy produces our curriculum for music. Let us remind ourselves that these questions involve *actors* (who are the actors in any policy arena?), *resources* (what resources are distributed? to whom are they distributed?) and *outcomes* (who benefits from a policy? who is left out?).

Bernstein: policy and the pedagogic device

Who are the actors in a particular policy arena?

Bernstein saw the actors involved in policy as acting in two interrelated contexts – the primary and the secondary.

At the primary context (the macro context) Bernstein saw two fields existing within which recontextualising agents (change agents) transformed discourses (knowledges) into pedagogic discourses (pedagogic forms of that knowledge or school/university subjects). He observed struggles occurring within and between these fields to determine which knowledge was to become sanctioned to be taught to others. The first field was called by Bernstein the *official recontextualizing field* (ORF; or *official field of change*). The ORF is a creation of the state. It is governed by state selected ministries and approved agents (e.g., state agencies for curriculum, assessment, inspection). The second field Bernstein named the *pedagogic recontextualizing field* (PRF; or *specialist educational field of change*). This field is dominated by educational bodies such as education departments in universities, subject journals and associations such as NAME (the National Association of Music Educators), private research bodies (e.g. Paul Hamlyn Foundation), textbook publishers and others who transform subjects into school subjects (e.g., music into school Music). Bernstein argued that:

> If the PRF can have an effect on pedagogic discourse independently of the ORF, then there is both some autonomy *and* struggle over pedagogic discourse and its practices. But if there is only the ORF, then there is no autonomy.
>
> (Bernstein 2000: 33)

He identified a steadily increasing threat to the autonomy of the PRF through enhancement of ORF activity and intervention. Examples of this might be state-formulated curricula and schemes of work. The struggles for domination and shaping of the National Curriculum for Music as briefly exemplified above (see also Wright and Davies 2010) exemplify the tensions inherent in battles for control of pedagogic discourse between the PRF and the ORF.

All of this previously described activity then occurs at what Bernstein termed the primary context. Bernstein referred to this primary context as the level where 'new ideas are selectively created, modified and changed and where specialized discourses are developed, modified or changed' (Bernstein 1999: 59). For us the 'specialized discourse' is the school subject of Music. The first actor in this policy arena then is the State and its agents, or the ORF; and the second the pedagogic bodies or the PRF. Within these two fields, knowledge is selected which will be legitimized for transmission to others through the distribution of social power and control so that the dominant principles of society are expressed. Bernstein differentiates between two types of knowledge which he terms the 'thinkable' and the 'unthinkable'. The thinkable consists of approved knowledge and usual practices whereas the unthinkable consists of taboo or new knowledge. What might this mean in terms of music education? What is thinkable musical knowledge and what unthinkable? It tends to be that knowledge moves from unthinkable to thinkable over time, for example jazz, 'world' musics and popular music were once unthinkable official knowledge to be taught in schools. Now they have entered the curriculum. Bernstein pointed out that what is unthinkable to some may be thinkable to others, depending on social class and other social category membership and previous experiences. Pedagogic discourses have traditionally emphasized academic knowledge as most useful to the needs of society's dominant class in its ability to generate new knowledge and technological advancement. New knowledge, that yet to be discovered or yet to be thought, is termed a 'potential discursive gap'.

The secondary context (the micro context) is where the policy is acted out as it is put into practice in the micro context, i.e. most typically those who work in schools. Various agents within schools, however, not only reproduce but, in some degree, may further recontextualize the official pedagogic discourse.

The National Curriculum for example does not cease to be filtered and altered once it arrives within individual schools. School administrations, department heads and individual teachers also impose their stamp upon the subjects that are taught. Power and control have already been exercised upon knowledge in the primary context but they may act further within this secondary context (the school) so as to ideologically transform that subject. Think for example of whole school policies that act upon your subject or the school ethos and how that shapes what you are permitted to do within your music program. Bernstein (1990) described how knowledge was decontextualized and then recontextualized (taken apart and put back together again) at this level so that it might be transformed for reproduction. This involved processes of condensing, refocusing, simplifying, modifying or elaboration so that, at their end, 'the text is no longer the same text'. One might argue that there have been numerous examples of this process occurring within music, as originally spontaneous and relatively unregulated genres such as jazz and rock have become codified and regimented to produce pedagogic forms of themselves, probably unrecognizable to their original proponents. The notion that teachers not only reproduce discourse but may also play a significant part in its recontextualization before introducing the material to students is therefore of central importance.

What resources are distributed? To whom are resources distributed and on what scale?

For our purposes, distribution of resources concerns who transmits what musical knowledge to whom and under what circumstances.

This has a great deal to do both with the pedagogic discourse – the subject – that has been produced at the primary context and with what occurs inside the teaching situation – the secondary context or the school. Bernstein identified that within any teaching situation, two things are occurring. First, something is being taught – the interchanges occurring here he termed 'instructional discourse' (ID). Instructional discourse is concerned with the teaching content delivered, received and evaluated. Second, social order is being maintained, students are being shown how to behave, identities are being created, affirmed, challenged, a teacher persona and value system is being projected. Bernstein called this 'regulative discourse' (RD). Regulative discourse is always dominant, telling learners what they can do and where they can do it. It provides values, beliefs and rules. It defines the thinkable and unthinkable within the curriculum for pupils and teachers, as well as creating and maintaining classroom order. Instructional discourse is necessarily embedded within regulative discourse. What Bernstein named 'pedagogic discourse' is, therefore, a principle by which the 'what' of teaching or pedagogic practice is assimilated by the 'how'. In simple terms, the 'what' is always wrapped up in the 'how' – we never just pass on knowledge, we always consciously or unconsciously transmit values at the same time. Pedagogic discourse is, therefore, defined by Bernstein (1990) as the rule whereby one discourse is embedded within the other to create one subject or one discourse. There is no distinction between transmission of skills and what he reports educators as calling 'the transmission of values'. He refers to this as the 'secret voice' of pedagogic discourse, disguising the fact that there is, in fact, no separation between these two elements of teaching. The two become one. As teachers teach 'music' within pedagogic strategies, school policies (on behaviour, classroom conduct etc.), their own lived experiences and conscious or unconscious value systems and myriad other 'filters'– the teaching that emerges is an amalgam of the musical pedagogy and the framing or filtering regulative pedagogy. In this way it is thus possible for teachers to transmit to pupils, consciously or unconsciously; that they value this music more than that, this response over that; that this type of creativity is allowed but not that. This is where it is perhaps possible to perceive dangers in national pedagogic strategies as they insert a particular regulative discourse around the instructional discourse. They direct teachers' attention towards the particular types of knowledge that are to be valued, the regulative messages that are to surround instructional discourse. The National Strategy Key Stage 3 Music Programme (England), for example, suggests intrusion of the Official Recontextualizing Field into one of the last remaining areas of autonomy left to the Pedagogic Recontextualizing Field. A new layer of official control is now inserted into the very heart of the learning and teaching process, into the very classroom. This brings regulative discourse firmly under official control, effectively ensuring that the text resulting at the end of the recontextualization process is that desired by the policy. At the end of this process, the 'text is no longer the same text' (Bernstein 1990). Music has become a series of knowledge bites to be internalized and reproduced by pupils to evidence their attainment of 'musical understanding' (whatever that may be?). The creative and experiential aspects of the subject become subservient to the attainment of this goal. Given our earlier statement that pedagogic discourses have traditionally emphasized academic knowledge as most useful to the needs of society's dominant class in its ability to generate new knowledge and technological advancement, one might wonder whose interests are best served by such a reshaping of the focus of music education?

Who benefits from policy? Who is left out?

In terms of who benefits from the education occurring and who is left out, this can present answers to crucial questions that have been puzzling analysts of education for a long time. Why is it that despite comprehensive education, little change in patterns of social mobility has been detected in most industrial countries around the world? Why does education still appear to work selectively for some students and not others? Why despite compulsory school music education in the UK for the past two decades and more, a national curriculum and the expenditure of much time, money and effort in training teachers and others to teach music effectively, does there still appear to be a substantial disparity between social classes in their ability to access and benefit from school music? Why do the same strata of society's young people still by-and-large go on to become music teachers?

The answer perhaps is that large-scale systemic change, however well intentioned, may not address the problematic effects of social stratification upon music education. Hiding behind what Arnot and Reay (2007) describe as 'the mask of neutrality', a curriculum (here perhaps we may read also pedagogic strategy) carrying with it the knowledge, values and habitus of one dominant social group may merely disguise the effects of social stratification upon music education. The particular emphasis upon academic knowledge (think here the theory necessary to access A-level music, e.g.) may serve to undermine the best efforts of teachers working for the inclusion of all their students in the music class. The skills, knowledge and understanding they are required to develop in their students as they progress through the stages of schooling may move progressively more towards the academic end of the spectrum. The covert message therefore being sent is that music can be inclusive until you want to be taken seriously in it and then you need to develop academic skill in the discipline in order to proceed. As the ability to 'pay to play' in terms of access to additional instrumental and theory tuition outside school has long affected the nature of the student group able to elect for GCSE and BTEC/A level and other 16+ examinations in music, the subject becomes increasingly socially stratified as we move through the stages of schooling. Those from more affluent families have preferential access to music as a curriculum subject once additional tuition becomes necessary.

We suspect that little progress will be made in addressing issues of socially based exclusion from music education until educators become critical consumers of education policy. We need to ask of music education policy the type of Fitz *et al.* questions about actors, resources and inclusion that we are addressing here. Teacher awareness of the power of regulative discourses ('the how' in all its complexity), to colour and alter pupil perception of instructional discourse ('the what') might prompt consideration of the covert messages being sent to pupils of varying social backgrounds as to who and what is recognized as valued and worthy within the school and the music classroom. Is emphasis upon 'musical understanding', academic knowledge *about* music the goal of music education? Or is such emphasis an assault upon the potential inclusive and socially transformative power of music education? Do we need to teach and learn all subjects in the same way? Do we need pedagogic strategies to help us deliver the pre-packaged learning goods required by our governments, or is some pedagogic autonomy more beneficial to the healthy musical growth of our students? One thing is certain, the more we delve into the 'layers of meaning' embedded in our lives as music educators, the more we become aware that 'things are not what they seem' (Berger 1963).

Conclusion

This chapter has attempted to explore some of the ways in which dominant social groups may be seen to act to impose their values upon education through policies such as national curricula and pedagogic strategies. Policy can be seen as a framework that links ideologies, political affiliations, social groups and social institutions to agendas for change. With policy goes allocation of resources to enable the policy to change society in the desired ways. As Fitz *et al.* (2006) suggest, some crucial questions arising from this process relate to the actors, resources and outcomes in a particular policy arena. Policy concerning knowledge takes many forms. In this chapter the focus has been on knowledge policies in the forms of national curricula and national pedagogic strategies. A critical understanding of the basis of education policy in government economic ideology may help to provide some reflective distance for educators, before they embrace new policy uncritically. Here Antonio Gramsci's view that the control of knowledge is critical to preserving the ideological dominance of certain classes, a process he terms *hegemony,* provides an important perspective. Basil Bernstein has also provided, in his theory of the pedagogic device, a conceptual framework for exploring how education becomes a vehicle for social reproduction. The pedagogic device is a series of processes of filtration through which knowledge passes until at the end 'the text is no longer the same text': e.g., carpentry becomes Woodwork, music becomes school Music. We have suggested that this may be happening to unfortunate effect in music education. Of crucial importance to the continued autonomy and healthy development of music education is that music educators continually reflect on these ways in which the process of policy formation and implementation impinges on their day-to-day practice. Such understanding is essential if they are to become influential in the development of future policy and part of a more inclusive music education.

Reflective questions

1   Identify a current policy that you see affecting music teachers.
    Use Fitz *et al.*'s (2006) questions to examine this policy:

    a   Who are the actors in this policy arena?
    b   What resources are distributed?
    c   To whom are they distributed and on what scale?
    d   Who benefits from this policy?
    e   Who is left out?

2   a   What constraints can you see the field of music education presenting to students of differing:
        • social classes
        • ethnicities
        • sex/sexuality
        • cultural groups?
    b   How might these constraints be overcome?

3   How do the 'what' and the 'how' of your teaching or that of a teacher you have observed become entangled? What ideological messages does this send?

References

Apple, M.W. (2004) *Ideology and Curriculum*, New York: RoutledgeFalmer.

Arnot, M. and Reay, D. (2007) 'A Sociology of Pedagogic Voice: Power, Inequality and Pupil Consultation', in *Discourse: Studies in the Cultural Politics of Education*, 28(14).

Bernstein, B. (1996) *Pedagogy, Symbolic Control and Identity: Theory, Research, Critique*, London: Taylor and Francis Ltd.

Bernstein, B. (2000) *Pedagogy, Symbolic Control and Identity: Theory, Research, Critique* (rev.edn) London: Rowman and Littlefield.

Bernstein, B. (2001) 'Symbolic Control: Issues of Empirical Description and Agents', *International Journal of Social Research Methodology*, 4(1): 21–33.

Darder, A., Baltadano, M. and Torres, R.D. (2003) *The Critical Pedagogy Reader*, New York, RoutledgeFalmer.

Fitz, J., Davies, B. and Evans, J. (2006) *Educational Policy and Social Reproduction Class Inscription and Symbolic Control*, London: Routledge.

Gammon, V. (1993) 'Dominance or Diversity? David Pascall, The National Curriculum Council and Culture', *Arts Education,* April.

Gammon, V. (1999) 'The Cultural Politics of the National Curriculum for Music 1991–1992', *Journal of Educational Administration and History,* 31(2): 130–45.

Giddens, A. (1984) *The Constitution of Society: Outline of the Theory of Structuration,* Cambridge: Polity Press.

Macionis, J.J. and Gerber, L.M. (2008) *Sociology,* Upper Saddle River, NJ: Pearson.

Meyer, J.W. (1977) 'The Effects of Education as an Institution', *American Journal for Sociology,* LXXXIII, 51–77.

Morais, A.M. (2002) 'Basil Bernstein at the Micro Level of the Classroom', *British Journal of Sociology of Education,* 23(10).

Morais, A.M., Peneda, D. and Madeiros, A. 'The Recontextualizing of Pedagogic Discourse: Influence of Differential Pedagogic Practices on Students' Achievements as Mediated by Class, Gender and Race', paper presented at The International Sociology of Education Conference, University of Birmingham, 1991.

O'Hear, A. (1991) 'Out of Sync with Bach', *The Times Educational Supplement,* 22 February.

Philpott, C. (2010) 'The Sociological Critique of Curriculum Music in England. Is Radical Change Really Possible?', in R. M. Wright (ed.) *Sociology and Music Education,* Farnham: Ashgate Press.

Whitty, G. (1974) 'Sociology and the Problem of Radical Educational Change', in M. Flude, and J. Ahier (eds) *Educability, Schools and Ideology,* London: Halstead Press.

Williams, R. (1961) *The Long Revolution,* London: Chatto and Windus.

Willis, P. (1981) *Learning to Labor: How Working Class Kids Get Working Class Jobs,* New York: Columbia University Press.

Woodford, P.G. (ed.) (2011) *Re-Thinking Standards for the Twenty-First Century: New Realities, New Challenges, New Propositions; Studies in Music from the University of Western Ontario.*

Wright, R. and Davies, B. (2010) Class, Power, Culture and the Music Curriculum, in: R. Wright, (ed.) *Sociology and Music Education,* Farnham: Ashgate Press Limited.

Chapter 3

Creativity, culture and the practice of music education

John Finney

> I think creativity is an irritating term. It sets up walls and ramps – we have to be on one side or the other or somewhere on them. Is this creativity? Am I being creative? Is she more creative? What do I have to do to be more creative?
>
> (Secondary school music teacher)

Introduction

Emerging conceptually in the first half of the twentieth century (Pope 2006), it was in the 1950s that creativity fully gained purchase on problems associated with the prospect of technological change and the need to adapt to uncertain futures. Adaptability, imagination, breakers of stereotypes and solvers of problems were needed. In *Towards a Theory of Creativity* published in 1954, and then again as part of a collection of papers establishing wider debate (Vernon 1970), Carl Rogers made a case for creativity as a social good. He noted tendencies towards conformity, passive use of leisure time, work seen as the execution of technical tasks and the dreariness of well-ordered family life as impelling a need to understand the nature of the creative process and the realization of undiscovered human potentialities. This new interest in creativity was drawing together what were mostly psychological perspectives making links to personality, intelligence and a variety of conscious and unconscious thought processes. For Rogers the creative process was viewed as 'the emergence in action of a novel relational product, growing out of the uniqueness of the individual on the one hand, and the materials, events, people, or circumstances on the other' (p. 139). While such definitions are attractive, they do, as Estelle Jorgensen points out, frequently rely upon circular arguments.

> ... certain products are recognized by others to be creative in the sense that they diverge from the norm while also meeting and possibly exceeding particular criteria; products are regarded as creative because they are produced by people who are known to be creative.
>
> (Jorgensen 2008: 234)

Notwithstanding such criticism, the drive to promote particular ways of construing creativity and of extending its rhetoric has a contemporary virility that is not easily ignored. In what follows I examine the idea of creativity as voiced and musically practiced over the last 50 years, a period characterized by the final flourishes of high modernism yielding to a new cultural phase artistically and culturally understood as postmodernism. My purpose is to create a reasonable historical narrative presented through a series of cases showing ways in which creativity has been constructed in relation to the social, cultural and political conditions of this period.

I begin by reviewing the idea of 'creative music' coming into prominence in the 1960s and as led by composer–educator John Paynter, bringing together the notion of child as artist and a commitment to artistic modernism. From here the idea of the creative child, *sui generis*, is displaced by seeing the child, the individual, as socially located where communities, standards and gatekeepers exist to mediate and validate creative activity and its products. This in turn is disrupted by creativity thought of as common, shaping and being shaped by material culture of the everyday made legitimate by a grounded form of aesthetics. This is a creativity that is both ordinary and profane and which yields finally to a postmodern creativity of the present with an invitation to act playfully, ironically and make irreverent pastiche.

While the case of a child-centred creativity is exemplified in the work of John Paynter, no such synergy with the thinking of key music educators of the period has been attempted in the cases that follow, although the reader may well conjecture in this direction should they choose. Together the cases selected reveal a degradation of the rhetoric of 'creative genius' linked as it is to the personality traits and achievements of 'great' artists. Furthermore, the cases show little interest in the more recent idea of creativity as 'economic imperative', of creativity as utility and in which music and the arts might be expected to play a central role. However, both the creativity of the 'creative genius' and creativity as 'economic imperative' may well be found playing in the shadows of what follows and the latter will be raised again in the concluding paragraph.

Creative music

> … in a healthy society all men should be artists to some extent and in some
> way, in proportion to their capacity to live creatively.
>
> (Mellers 1946/2008: 18)

Such was the need to express a major turning point in music educational thought and practice in 1960s England, that there emerged talk of 'creative experiment', 'creative process', 'creative work', 'creative music making' and 'creative music'. There was talk too of 'experimental music', itself a direct reference to the experimentalism of the avant-garde of late modernism.

Exceptionally, a facet of contemporary culture interrupted the practice of music education. The break with traditional music education was dramatic, verging on the iconoclastic, and for many disorientating. Arnold Bentley, speaking for an ordered past, could only conceive of creativity as uncommon and exceptional and noted that, '... in practice, these "creative" activities in schools are by their nature, so time-consuming that 'traditional reading and playing techniques tend to be neglected' (Bentley 1975: 60). With the dumb-founding and silencing of tradition, the creative movement's Diaspora proved to be rapid as Paynter and Aston's creative primer *Sound and Silence* moved through translation into many parts of the world. By seeking out the practices of the contemporary artist new directions were opened up. Writing about creativity in the music curriculum and promoting music as a creative art, Paynter maintained that '*all* musical activity – listening, composing and performing – is essentially creative'. The characteristic of creativity is the process of:

> ... making inward imaginative models from which we can extrapolate. The models are based on aspects of our experience but are, of course applied beyond the boundaries of that experience to determine new possibilities.
>
> (Paynter 1982: 94)

Quite unlike the convergent and potentially deterministic nature of musical training, here was a breaking out, a reaching out and a finding out. The child, like the contemporary artist discovers, innovates. The child's newly made 'prepared piano music' lives alongside the prepared piano music of John Cage. The sovereignty of childhood is celebrated.

For Paynter 'creative music' was not to be seen as an alternative method but a principle of music education capable of embracing all. It could sharpen and direct music educational purpose. Music was an art, and artistic behaviour fundamentally involved a process of making, where decisions were taken, judgements made, responding to what was coincidental and working towards a fresh model of musical reality. While the composition of music took a central position in this, engaging with music in whatever way called for its making and re-making in the imagination. Paynter reports how this was for a class of ten-year-old children imagining and creating in response to observing birds flying in the wind above the Yorkshire countryside in the 1960s. After writing about their experience they talk about making some music.

> Someone suggested that we would have tambourines to be the beating of the rook's wings. We agreed. We thought what we would have for gliding. Someone tried top 'c' and 'g' (on recorders). It goes 'c' then the tambourines, then 'g' and so on. The leaves were falling all the time. The leaves were falling all the time. The leaves were the xylophone. We had to think of something for the banking of the seagull. Pamela thought of four notes on the piano. I thought it was an excellent idea. As well we had recorders and a

drum for the wind. I played a part in the finch music. I played the swooping of the finch. Guy played the flapping of the finch by tapping the drum. I had the piano. Then we replayed the first line.

(Paynter 1995: 130–31)

Throughout, the children's ideas were continually evaluated in practice, empirically tested – a process which artistically intuitive judgments worked towards what was felt and 'known' to be right. In this case a piece in ternary form with codetta had been created containing far more than could be known by the makers in the process of making. Skills had been developed, techniques mastered and musical conventions revealed. The model of learning is inductive and in this way there could be a 'coming to know', a process of making and revealing. In this model of creativity the child is first endowed with the capacity to make. The artist lies within. The instinct to make is spontaneous and autonomous.

Facilitating environments and creativity

This commitment to the instinctual spontaneity of childhood was of interest to Martin Buber speaking at the Third International Conference of Education in 1925. Buber had pointed out that this becoming, free from the will to power, implied a particular kind of relational knowledge. The child's creative utterances needed to be received in reality or imagination by another (Buber 1925/2004). Paynter's children needed a teacher and each other. There needed to be in Donald Winnicott's term a 'facilitating environment' in which the symbolic gestures of the child are consummated through reception and reciprocation. In this way creativity becomes an inter-human matter through which is achieved 'psychic integration' (Winnicott 1987), or in Paynter's terms, satisfaction and a sense of wholeness (Paynter 1997), achieved through a 'symbolic search for order and integration' (Paynter 1982: 92). In this the quality of the teacher–pupil, pupil–pupil relationship is a significant determining factor. The *process* of relating is creative as well as the products of the relationship. Crucially, the child as artist needed the teacher as artist, the child as composer needed the teacher as composer, a demanding requirement that was not always easy to satisfy. For the creative movement of the 1960s and 70s the child's creative music making thrived on its own terms. Mellers' sentiment that 'all men should be artists to some extent' had been boldly enacted (with the implication that fields of judgments existing beyond childhood were of little or no relevance). However, it is precisely these that are central to a systems approach to creativity. In this the work of Csikszentmihalyi is taken as guide.

Domain creativity and its flow

Now the child as artist floating free yields to authority; for music is viewed as an established cultural domain within which exist conventions, traditions and models to be incorporated and emulated. The place to start is through examining extra-ordinary human achievement and those minds that change the domain, and in this Gardner's study of creative genius plays a part (see Gardener 1993). Accepted as a significant form of human activity with symbolic rules and procedures, music qualifies as a domain free to spawn and elaborate its sub-domains, its own styles, genres and traditions. Within domain and sub-domains there exists a 'field' made up of individuals who through consensual recognition become qualified to act as gatekeepers maintaining its integrity (Csikszentmihalyi 1990). It is the field that selects, promotes and secures bodies of knowledge that establish authority and seats of judgment. In the case of music it is the creators, composers, performers and interpreters who command positions of authority within the field. It is the individual who innovates, who sets new standards, who opens up new pathways, whose work is recognized as a shaper of the domain and who is deferred to. Might Miles Davies, Jay-Z, Simon Rattle be recognized as gatekeepers of what are the sub-domains of Cool Jazz, Hip Hop and the interpretation of Brahms' symphonic works? In this model, creativity is conditional upon learning the rules of the domain through surveying and assimilating all that is already known. Mastery is a pre-condition. Only then can boundaries be pushed and a new consensus found. Together, domain, field and individual form an interrelationship that is a system (Csikszentmihalyi 1996).

Little 'c' and big 'C' and the flow of creativity

This approach proceeds to examine creative individuals who have successfully internalized their domains and who it is discovered demonstrate common traits, one of which is intrinsic motivation. They love what they do. They enjoy their work and this is because of the way they engage with it. Their enjoyment begets a continual search for challenge and discovery. In their acts of creativity they discover 'flow'. Across domains such creative individuals identify 'flow' as a common experience understood through the delineation of nine dimensions. There are: clear goals every step of the way; immediate feedback to one's actions; balance between challenge and skills; merging of action and awareness; excluding distractions from consciousness; no fear of failure; self-consciousness disappears; sense of time becomes distorted; the activity becomes autotelic (Csikszentmihalyi 1996). In this way a bridge is built between what is the 'big C' creativity of the master and the 'little c' creativity potential of all.

Custodero examining the case of music makes possible the recognition of 'flow' through observation of behaviour indicative of 'flow' (Custodero 2005). These are generalized into three types: 'Challenge Seeking Indicators'; 'Challenge Monitoring Indicators'; 'Social Context Indicators'.

Challenge Seeking Indicators come from independent behaviour and include:

- *Self-assignment*: self-initiated purposeful activity, suggesting a concern for skill acquisition and mastery.

- *Self-correction*: error adjustment in response to immediate feedback and clear goals.
- *Gesture*: deliberate control and focus of movement as a result of intense concentration.

Challenge Monitoring Indicators relate to responses to information or material presented by another, usually an adult. These include:

- *Anticipation*: attempts to guess or demonstrate that which is to follow as a result of immersion in the activity and of the merging of action and awareness.
- *Expansion*: transforming the material to become more challenging.
- *Extension*: continuing to engage with the material beyond the end of the activity as a result of it having become autotelic.

Finally, Social Context Indicators relate to an awareness of others present. These include interactions with others such as a prolonged gaze, head-turning, directed movement or verbal communication. The first two of these types of 'flow' indicator relate well to Csikszentmihalyi's nine dimensions of flow. Social Context Indicators seem to relate rather less to 'flow' explicitly, since 'flow' is often experienced alone. A music teacher with the assistance of an observer records how all this works in the classroom working as a Samba Band (see Box 3.1).

The teacher here is asking whether the Samba Band and her leading of it can induce 'flow', and if so, how can flow be maintained? In this example there is evidence of 'flow'. The music teacher is encouraged, and I observe that she becomes more playful in her interactions. The social context is enhanced and the classroom can become a place where creativity can flourish. But what kind of creativity is this? While we may be able to observe 'flow', what is it that we can say about creativity in this situation? Is all this small 'c' creativity? Isn't the classroom some considerable distance from big 'C' Samba, where field leaders are generating new grooves, fusing disparate elements and extending Samba's reach and cultural significance, and might this be in the Carnival processions of Sao Paulo or somewhere quite unknown? Whatever and wherever, this is the creativity not of the child but of their immediate classroom community and the communities and institutions, virtual and real, to which they defer and into which they may choose to grow. The creativity of classroom Samba exists within a particular cultural setting helpfully discussed by Burnard and Younker in the light of activity theory. These creative group music making contexts need to be seen as:

> … situated activity of people acting in a place. The combination of time, place and experience is conditioned by the rules or norms that govern activity, the communities of social settings in which activity takes place and the ways in which activity and responsibility are shared or divided amongst participants.
>
> (Burnard and Younker 2010: 167)

BOX 3.1: FLOW AND WORKING WITH SAMBA

Examples of 'Flow' indicators

Challenge Seeking Indicators
Self-assignment: When given an instrument, or when rotating seats students practice the appropriate rhythm without instruction. Students mime other rhythmic parts while watching them being played by others. Students on surdos mouth counting from one to four in order to play on the correct beats. In a short agogo sectional lead by the teacher, the other students correctly judge when the rhythm has been mastered and join in with the three other instrumental parts.

Self-correction: A boy on a tambourim struggles with the rhythm; he stops, watches the other tambourim players, nods his head in time, then re-enters playing the rhythm correctly. Pupils keep their eyes on the maestro.

Gesture: Pupils move in time with the groove: swaying, tapping feet, moving heads. Students sit up straight when given an instrument. The movement of surdo and ganze players in particular appears to be deliberate and automatic. Agogo and tambourim players hold their instruments up when playing.

Challenge Monitoring Indicators
Anticipation: Students sit up straight when given an instrument. Students mime parts before they play.

Expansion: Once playing has finished some students test how quickly they can play their rhythm pattern.

Extension: Pupils play during packing-away.

Social Context Indicators
Awareness of adults and peers: Pupils smile at one another and at the teacher. Pupils carefully watch each other and the teacher. Pupils congratulate and encourage each other. Pupils smile in response to praise from the teacher.

(Ambrose 2010: 24)

This leads to consideration of the complexities of authority relationships within the Samba class where, while there may be distributed leadership, it is the teacher, nominally at least, who acts as gatekeeper. The extent to which the rules and conventions of Samba are socialized, the extent to which space is made for the re-generation of and divergence from the material given, the extent to which the incoming personal vernacular musical knowledge of the students becomes incorporated and hybridity celebrated or not becomes of great interest. The idea of a domain/sub-domain as fluid or fixed, with weak boundaries or strong, unwilling or ready and available to travel, intersects with what will be viewed as acts of creativity.

These are the kinds of questions raised by a systems approach to creativity where 'big C' is in dialogue with 'little c'. Central to this construction of domain, sub-domain and field as part of a system, there is the assumption of a consensual forming dynamic at work bringing about unity, integration and progress. However, in a field of creators, composers, producers, performers and interpreters who are masters of their particular genres and traditions there is interaction with concert promoters, government agencies, arts foundations, benefactors and patrons, radio presenters, school curriculum authorities, media moguls, examination boards, commentators and critics and more. Taken together the players in the field are unlikely to be seeking consensus or acting benevolently in moving the field forward. With a less naïve view of the field it would be as valid to see the workers of the field bringing about its continual fragmentation, the proliferation of difference in the cause of gaining in cultural, social, symbolic and economic capital (Bourdieu 1993; Jenkins 2003). Set alongside the seeking of consensus within the systems approach to creativity, the quest for recognition through maintaining difference can be in itself construed as a strategic form of creativity. Thus, creativity is viewed as opposing and resisting systems, domains and the institutional norms that they project. To better understand this it is the material creativities of everyday life that move against the hegemony of the artist, the arts and music thought of as a domain or discipline.

Creativity as necessary symbolic work

While music as an art and the child as artist were foundational to creativity as conceived by the creative movement and in a 'systems approach' to under-standing creativity through the authority of domains and sub-domains, we now explore another way by working with the idea of creativity as symbolic of lived experience and grounded in material culture, where lives do necessary work to manage and make, for the time being at least, the essence of identity. This is a theory of social action concerned with the formation of individual and collective identities. There is no interest in domains of practice or with the making of art works deferential to domain masters; for symbolic creativity lies in the production of new meaning in the lives of young people (Willis *et al.*, 1990). This is crea-tivity beyond the reaches of the institution and freed from the standard concep-tions of the arts. Willis maintains that the traditional arts play very little part in young people's lives. It is not the arts that beget culture but culture that yields activity spread across the whole of life as a grounded form of aesthetics. The approach is anthropological. The arts as institutionalized are redundant to mean-ingful existence. In this view the love of work, of school life is rarely possible. Thus common daily activity draws upon creativity and is to be found in the place where 'vital capacities, the powers of the self and how they might be applied to the cultural world' can be 'developed and affirmed' (Willis *et al.*, 1990:12). This is a process rejecting any kind of regulated formalities and allows for the blurring of distinctions between consumption and production. Through the process of cultural consumption '... the received world is made human and, to however small a degree, controllable' (p. 14–15). In the case of music – and remember Willis is writing in 1990 – the acts of listening and buying, home taping, interpreting sounds, dance and the interpretation of songs and symbols all represent the creativity of symbolic work. Sound systems are used and in the case of Afro-Caribbean young people there is spontaneous oral poetry; and finally there is the formality of music making and performance. All this represents symbolic creativity and is possible only in the spaces created by individuals and groups in their 'free time'.

Willis takes popular music to be the central cultural interest of the young. By copying sounds from records and cassettes, applying knowledge of genre and taste and making value judgments, music and meanings are produced. When this creativity moves into the worked-up condition of musical performance in the form of collective public expression through bands, profound significance is achieved and marked potentially by large shifts in understanding and the creation of new meanings 'intrinsically attached to feeling, energy, to excitement and psychic movement' (p. 18). This is a creativity of appropriation and the everyday.

The creativity of material sonic culture

Willis is writing on the cusp of globalized cultural formations where the local is also the global. Hall (1997) creates the idea of the 'global postmodern', in which visual representations dominate and cross national and socio-cultural borders. The global postmodern is able to adjust itself to contemporary migration, transnational movements, and mass media and is characterized by a 'proliferation of difference'. Grounded aesthetics is now on global ground aided by the advancement of technologies. Eglinton (2008) captures this 'glocalized' condition in her ethnography of the youth of the New York Bronx. Here the ubiquitous rap/hip-hop is freely appropriated across class, race, place and gender. Working with a group of young people aged eight to fourteen years, Eglinton shows how young peoples' Visual Material Culture is infused with musical/sonic significance as they create identities of place, race and gender. These young people forming socio-musical identities draw from a host of local, national and global discourses through the most basic of electronic devices. Here symbolic creativity is globally networked, yet intensely localized, where identities shift fast while being vigorously protected. For Eglinton's on-the-edge Latino and Black youth, musical creativity is about 'representing' as Jeremy insists:

> [In rap] 'you'll always represent where you was from. You gotta represent. If you was from Bronx you be like 'oh the Bronx is hot'. You know you be like that unless you move to Manhattan then you be like 'oh Bronx is where I'm from' all the time.'

Jeremy goes on to tell how hand gestures are a part of rap aesthetics and crucially signify place. In registering this lies an authenticity sustained through a personal lexicon of signs and significations. Jeremy is gatekeeper and authenticator of his uniquely-made urban forms. This is a creativity of appropriation, agency, allegiance and identity protection claiming difference in a postmodern world of moving cultures. If Jeremy's material visual-sonic culture represents one facet of the postmodern then composer Mark Anthony Turnage presents another in his new work 'Hammered Out' performed at the BBC Promenade Concert of August 2010.

Creativity 'hammered out'

> Its opening sounds are fabulous – vast, radiant, angry chords, alternating with silly little rapid flurries; this is the Turnage one knows and loves… But then something beyond weird happens; bless my soul, can Turnage really be drawing on *Beyoncé Knowles* in the work's first episode?!
>
> (Blog 28.8.10 5:4 11.11.10)

Composer Turnage has made a 'mash up', a term equally significant in the fashion world of clothing and body decoration as in music – 'an explosion of contrasting things, all stuck together', a youthful friend tells me. Turnage might be thought of as a domain leader, a master of contemporary musical composition as conceived of within a Western European 'art' tradition and thus entitled to innovate. And now a 'mash up', the willful juxtaposition, or if you prefer, a postmodern blend of difference and with some of the characteristics of Eagleton's postmodern artifact described as:

> … playful, self-ironizing and even schizoid; and that it reacts to the austere economy of high modernism by impudently embracing the language of commerce and the commodity. Its stance towards cultural tradition is one of irreverent pastiche, and its contrived depthlessness undermines all metaphysical solemnities, sometimes by a brutal aesthetics of squalor and shock.
>
> (Eagleton 1987: 14)

Frederick Jameson's analysis of the shift in the cultural order from modernism to postmodernism is insightful. For Jameson as for others (e.g. Harvey 1990) the growth of post-Second World War consumer capitalism created a landscape that witnessed the exhaustion of artistic modernisms. Modernism's construction of artistic creativity as belonging to the artist expressing a unique, private world in a style of their own was over. Stylistic innovation was no longer possible. Where the modernist had parody and the occasional cross genre reference at their disposal there is now pastiche, and in music, fusion and reuse of the past with the possibility of originality diminished. The big 'C' – little 'c' dialectic finds synthesis and the modernist distinction between mass popular culture and high culture dissolved as seen in the work of Riley and Glass, for example (Jameson 1998). In this view the postmodern creative musician makes new musics by playfully deconstructing the past and working with the material culture of the present. If this is the case, what questions are asked of a contemporary creative music education? How might a contemporary creative music education embrace the postmodern, hold up a mirror to society and in doing this would the 'mash up' act as an ideal form of mediation representing the past as present, a perfect concentration of time and space that resonates with the logic of consumer capitalism as Jameson maintains?

Creative pedagogy in music education

In a secondary school concert recently attended there was performance of the music of Pergolesi, Lennon and McCartney, Britten, the Carpenters, music composed by the music teacher and a student songwriter's performance of her latest work. The event began with a Samba procession and ended with a sophisticated multi-part choral performance of *Fly Me to the Moon*. Thus we see a considerable gap between notions of the creative postmodern and music in school presented through its traditional end-of-term concert. However, in the same school there is an after school 'Rock School' open to all students. Here students work with whatever material they choose, and students in their weekly classroom music lessons have the opportunity to work digitally. It is here that their musical creations appropriate material given by their teacher and may come to be 'well mashed' through collisions with the students' invasive material sonic culture. In this context Field (in Finney and Burnard 2010) proposes a series of creative strategies that the teacher might introduce to students. Field thinks of these as new forms of composition in which there is not only scope to play with time and space in new ways afforded by the technology, but opportunity to comment on life and other music. Irreverent pastiche, fusions and mash-ups; refreshed arrangements of *Fly Me to the Moon*, kitsch celebrated through popular song renditions and Sambas with new grooves may reveal something of the creativity of a contemporary music education, a creativity of difference. A secondary school music teacher explains further through description of 'inbetween times' music making of school life (see Box 3.2).

The image is of the school as a place where continually emerging, as well as more stable, communities of musical practice collide, co-exist and co-extend. It is a place where a facilitating environment is made by music teachers and students together imagining and curiously exploring what Paynter called 'new possibilities', sometimes protecting, sometimes breaking out and finding new ways of representing music within the cultural politics of the school. Creativity and music education is being 'hammered out'.

BOX 3.2: MUSIC MAKING AND SCHOOL LIFE

Schools are full of collisions and communities – different people with different affiliations and the same person with different affiliations – Glen rehearses his Beethoven in a room in which Max and Joe explore funk and in which Karl sometimes comes and teaches younger students the guitar and in which I sometimes teach Grade 5 theory (and sometimes it gets mixed up), which is adjacent to the room with the Emo guitarists and the room with the 'Glee club' inspired by Ambition singing/piano group and adjacent to the computer room where Manny is the keeper of the hip-hop gate, Ryan the keeper of the (very playful) dance/electronica gate – they are making meanings, new meanings, forming – at times individual identities and at times collective ones (Manny has a crew – they make raps about themselves, their faith, their love lives or some generalized vision – they are making meanings but they are not breaking stylistic musical or lyrical ground. It's all there in the Streets, Dizzie Rascall etc., etc. Manny's Sixth Form workshops gave voice to a group very cross about a new Sixth Form uniform – protest was made) (Ryan has fallen for the logic sequencing package. He writes electronic/dance tracks – some are 'straight', others are for people and times – a version of Happy Birthday caused much delight – and it spreads – people turn up at lunchtime and plug in). Emma, Beth and Justin (leaving behind their chamber choir and school orchestral identities) are also there – doing their advanced level compositions – or just mucking about. It's noisy and messy but it regulates itself (with occasional small interventions).

All this is the informality of lunchtimes and after school and I suppose it is less easy within the formal curriculum and in lessons when there is a small pool of people and a limited age range but each class can be a colliding community. We are experimenting with year 9 areas of expertise and different pathways through the same projects – we rely on people to find routes through.

We imagine that if we provide instruments, space and things rich with possibilities that people might be provoked to take a look inside and that they might get carried away in one direction or another. It doesn't always work but it seems worth the risk.

Concluding thoughts

The Third International Educational Conference held in Heidelberg in 1925 had as its theme 'The Development of the Creative Powers of the Child'. These were modern times and the idea that childhood was no longer simply thought of as a preparation for life, to be passed through as quickly as possible, could once again be considered. Childhood could be 'a time in itself' as the meandering tradition of child-centered education would have it. In the almost 100 years since, we have passed to a cultural condition in which post-traditional societies experience fragmentation and heterogeneity in place of organic solidarity, inherited identities and stable tradition. Culture is glocal and the postmodern turn, with its pastiche and musical mashing (that glued together explosion of contrasting musics), is offered now as the source of new musical energy awaiting a response from the music educator.

While definitions of creativity abound I recommend just one. I think it helpful. It recognizes that creativity can be thought about as a capacity, a potentiality and this is in terms of making, doing and becoming. And because creativity can be realized through an object including 'another', an action or an ongoing process, there is the possibility of making new and novel things; and this may involve refreshing things and revealing these in a new light. All this is valuable because what is made, done or experienced is worth sharing with others, worth knowing about more widely. Thus we might agree that central to the practice of music is '... the capacity to make, do or become something fresh and valuable with respect to others as well as ourselves' (Pope 2005: xvi).

However, music education must choose, or at least debate, whether to turn towards the dominating rhetoric of a creativity bound to entrepreneurship and productive economic futures, whether and how to embrace music as a dynamic cultural element of consumer capitalism. Might Pope's definition slip too easily inside and be swallowed up by a contemporary rhetoric that announces the arrival of *The Creative Age* (Seltzer and Bentley 1999), where knowledge and its creative application is seen as the source of economic growth driven by the energies of a flexible workforce? Indeed, Pope's generous way of thinking is easily accommodated to governmental policy statements across the world uniformly emphasizing notions of innovation, entrepreneurship and industrial creativity bound to an image of cultural energy and dynamism. At the same time those advocates of music education wishing to demonstrate utility are quick to point to a relationship between musical creativity and the so called 'creative industries' giving to music education attractive and steadfast wealth creating credentials. Is Pope's definition in need of protection? It would seem now that the idea of creativity, like the idea of culture, is condemned to extend its reach and endlessly expand its designations and meanings. Creativity can be an irritating word!

Reflective questions

1   Creativity in music is most usually thought of in terms of musical improvisation and composition. To what extent is Paynter's creativity of performance and listening equally significant?
2   'Big C – little c creativity' has some 50 million entries on the internet. The idea is persistent in providing a way of thinking about what might be considered novel and innovative. Is this helpful?
3   Who is best qualified to be the gatekeepers of musical creativity?
4   To what extent might music education work imaginatively with postmodern culture as a response to a culture of consumerism?

References

Ambrose, K. (2009) *Year 8 Samba as a Model of Engagement in the Cause of Developing Positive Musical Identity in the School*, In-depth Assignment, University of Cambridge.

Bourdieu, P. (1992) *The Field of Cultural Production. Essays on art and literature*, Cambridge: Polity.

Bentley, A. (1975) *Music in Education: A Point of View*, Windsor: NFER Publishing Company.

Buber, M. (2004) *Between Man and Man*, London: Routledge.

Burnard, P. and Younker, B. (2010) 'Towards a Broader Conception of Musical Creativity in the Classroom: A Case for using Engestrom's Activity Theory as a basis for researching and characterizing group musicmaking practices', in R. Wright (Ed.) *Sociology and Music Education*, Farnham: Ashgate.

Cohen, A. (1979) 'Martin Buber and Changes in Modern Education', *Oxford Review of Education*, 5(3): 81–103.

Csikszentmihalyi, M. (1990) *Flow: The Psychology of Optimal Experience*, New York: HarperPerennial.

Csikszentmihalyi, M. (1996) *Creativity: Flow and the Psychology of Discovery and Invention*, New York: HarperPerennial.

Custodero, L. (2005) Observable Indicators of Flow Experience: a Developmental Perspective on Musical Engagement in Young Children from Infancy to School Age, *Music Education Research*, 7(2): 185209.

Eagleton, T. (1987) 'Awakening from Modernity', *Times Literary Supplement*, 20 February 1987.

Eglinton, K. (2008) 'Making Selves, Making Worlds: A Ethnographic account of Young People's Use of Visual Material Culture', unpublished PhD thesis, University of Cambridge.

Finney, J. and Burnard, P. (2010) *Music Education with Digital Technology*, London: Continuum.

Gardener, H. (1993) 'Seven Creators of the Modern Era', in J. Brockman (ed.) *Creativity*, New York: Simon & Schuster.

Hall, S. (1997) *Representations: Cultural Representations and Signifying Practices*. London; Thousand Oaks: Sage.

Harvey, D. (2008) *The Condition of Postmodernity: An Enquiry into the Origins of Cultural Change*, Oxford: Blackwell.

Jameson, F. (1998) *The Cultural Turn: Selected Writings of the Postmodern*, London: Verso.

Jenkins, R. (2003) *Pierre Bourdieu*, London: Routledge.

Jorgensen, E. (2008) *The Art of Teaching Music*, Bloomington and Indianapolis: Indiana University Press.

Mellers, W. (1946/2008) *Music and Society. England and the European Tradition*, London: Travers and Emery.

Paynter, J. (1970) *Sound and Silence: Classroom Projects in Creative Music*, Cambridge: Cambridge University Press.

Paynter, J. (1982) *Music in the Secondary School Curriculum. Trends and Developments in Classroom Teaching*, Cambridge: Cambridge University Press.

Paynter, J. (1995) 'Working on One's Inner World', in E. Webb (ed.) *Powers of Being: David Holbrook and His Work*, London: Associated University Press.

Paynter, J. (1997) 'The Form of Finality: a Context for Music Education', *British Journal of Music Education*, 14(1):5–21.

Pope, R. (2005) *Creativity, History, Practice*, London: Routledge.

Seltzer, K. and Bentley, T. (1999) *The Creative Age: Knowledge and Skills in the New Economy*, DEMOS.

Vernon, P. (1970) *Creativity*, New York: Penguin.

Willis, P., Jones, S., Canann, J. and Hurd, G. (1990) *Common Culture: Symbolic work at play in the everyday cultures of the young*, Milton Keynes: Open University Press.

Willis, P. (1990) *Moving Culture: an Enquiry into the Cultural Activities of Young People*, London: Calouste Gulbenkian Foundation.

Winnicott, D. (1987) *The Maturational Process and the Facilitating Environment*, London: Hogarth Press.

Chapter 4

The justification for music in the curriculum

Music can be bad for you

Chris Philpott

Bad is an adjective used to indicate something as evil, naughty, rotten, ill, distressing, offensive, unpleasant. In slang Bad is used when something is relatively good, excellent or positive. This linguistic device is called an antagonym.

Introduction

It is the ongoing fate of music to be perpetually justifying its place in the school curriculum. This chapter argues that an over reliance on the 'soft' justifications for educational music have ultimately undermined it being taken seriously by pupils, teachers and policymakers alike. These 'soft' justifications are predicated on the popular assumption that 'music is good for you'. Furthermore, the notion that 'music is good for you' derives from a particular narrative surrounding western classical music that *good* music is good for you and that the impact is universal. These justifications typically construct music as being a 'special case', often based on dubious evidence, instigating an unseemly protectionism in relation to other 'subjects' *and* perpetuating an arts–science dualism constructed as a 'soft', subjective counterbalance to a 'hard'-nosed objectivity.

The upshot is a weakened case for educational music as a discipline in the curriculum on the basis of an incomplete account of its nature and expressive power. This chapter will explore how these 'soft' justifications have permeated past and present policy for music and will argue that this partial account of musical meaning, understanding and knowledge is inadequate. In order to 'complete' our account we need to consider that the 'language' of music might be *bad* for us (even if this appears counter intuitive) and that the relationship between music, individuals and society is complex and problematic. The implications for music in the classroom is a critical pedagogy where such issues are explicitly part of the learning and not hidden within it.

Soft and hard justifications

What are the 'soft' justifications for music in the curriculum and how do they manifest themselves in policy and pedagogy? These usually hang around the notion that music is 'good' for us and come in the following forms:

- *Instrumental justifications*: in which the experience and understanding of music uniquely reaches other dimensions of human cognition, e.g. developing mathematical skills, spatial skills, language ('the Heineken effect'). It is also suggested that contact with 'great' music can develop intelligence ('the Mozart effect');
- *Therapeutic justifications*: in which an engagement with music can have cathartic and healing powers; it can promote health, develop self-esteem and cure damaged lives;
- *Civilizing justifications*: in which learning in music makes for a better and more rounded human being;
- *Emotional justifications*: in which music making is a means of developing our emotional intelligence.

These justifications are predicated on the assumption that, at worst, music is seen as servicing other areas of human understanding, and at best as a necessary counterpart to a 'harder' and more rational world. Even some of the more 'academic' justifications are touched with 'softness' and dualism. For example:

- *Rational justifications*: in which music is seen as a unique form of human rationality serving different human needs to the sciences (see Witkin 1974);
- *Symbolic justifications*: in which music is a type of 'language' for our 'felt world' (see Langer 1978);
- *Liberal justifications*: in which music is seen as an important differentiated component in a well-educated person (see Abbs 1987).

In short, these justifications have undermined the case for music and the arts. This is not to deny their importance but to suggest that they present an over-sanitized and romantic vision of music. While they derive from the best of motives they are based on a partial exposition of the nature of musical expression, meaning and understanding. In emphasizing the essential difference of music and its 'special' qualities such justifications have also ignored the process of meaning making which music shares with other symbolic modes.

What might it mean for us to view music as a 'hard' discipline? First, it is not clear that some of the justifications noted above are based on anything but a generalized reality. For example, musicians are not always so very psychologically 'rounded'. Furthermore, certain types of 'delineated' musical meanings can induce hatred; ask the loyalist in the presence of a rebel song. For music to be taken seriously as a 'hard' discipline we should not deny the complex nature of meaning and understanding. Music can be 'soft' and civilizing but can also be 'hard'; it can offend, harm, present unsavoury ideas. It might be the case that music 'heals' or enables us to become more socially adept, but we should also entertain the idea that music might actually cause us to be psychologically ill or excluded.

However, there are no absolutes here – one person's healing is another person's pain. Justifications for music in the curriculum need this 'completion' of expression, meaning and understanding. Such completion has the potential to offer important perspectives on musical understanding in the classroom. For example, it can help to explain how musical meaning contributes to 'tribalism' and why there are so few well-known women composers in western 'art' music. It can help us to understand how to manage misogyny and homophobia when these appear in the delineated meanings of music arising out of children's 'interests'. These are not necessarily problems – just the way things are! Music may well be different and special and yet it also shares a great deal with other symbolic modes in terms of how meaning is constructed.

Music educators have been quick to promote uniqueness at the expense of unity, and this has been to the detriment of the discipline, preventing it from being taken seriously as a 'hard' subject. Furthermore, given that the so-called 'hard' subjects (popularly conceived of as maths and science) have been busy adding 'values and feelings' to their rationales, it is even more important that music begins to construct itself as it really is, and not like a soak in a warm soapy bath.

It is not the purpose of this chapter to fully deconstruct such claims but to problematize their foreground prominence. In what ways have the 'soft' justifications manifested themselves in policy and writing in music education?

The current context

The contention is then that the 'soft' justifications have made it easier to take music (and the arts) less seriously and that they are derived from a partial analysis of musical meaning. Given that any symbolic mode is subject to wide and powerful political, social and cultural forces, this construction of educational music has not helped the cause.

One of the most pervasive notions of the 'soft' lobby is that music has powers of transfer to other aspects of education and wellbeing. This theme can be traced over millennia but the words of John Harvey Kellogg (of Cornflakes fame) make the point:

> I have been particularly impressed with the value of singing. It is not only a diversion and wholesome mental occupation, and on this account health-promoting. But also excellent lung gymnastics and promotes not alone breathing but the circulation as well. It especially aids circulation through the liver, stomach and other digestive organs, and so promotes digestion.
>
> (quoted in Clift and Hancox 2001)

In the same paper Clift and Hancox (2001) go on to say that:

> Of all the arts, music may justly claim to have the greatest significance in relation to health and healing. The idea that music can have significant health benefits has deep historical roots in Western culture ....
>
> (Clift and Hancox 2001: 249)

By invoking the uniqueness of music such justifications not only perpetuate the soft/hard dualism, they also raise notions of 'specialness' for music which, as Plummeridge points out, are dubious:

> It is one thing to say that the study of music has transfer effects but quite another to claim that this makes music unique which in turn provides its justification as a curriculum subject. The point is that transfer of skills from one discipline to another occurs all the time in everyday life and is, of course a vital part of the educational process.
>
> (Plummeridge 2001: 24)

Box 4.1 shows a selection of writings from the current discourse on the justification for music in education taken from policy, national initiatives and influential twenty-first century sources. The 'soft' themes are in the foreground, i.e. that music has a special impact for the better on our lives.

BOX 4.1: JUSTIFICATIONS FOR MUSIC IN THE CURRICULUM

Secretary of State's guidelines to instigate the Henley Review
www.education.gov.uk/inthenews/inthenews/a0064925/
education-secretary-michael-gove-announces-review-of-music-education
'Government priorities recognize music as an enriching and valuable academic subject with important areas of knowledge that need be learnt, including how to play an instrument and sing. Secondary benefits of a quality music education are those of increased self-esteem and aspirations; improved behaviour and social skills; and improved academic attainment in areas such as numeracy, literacy and language. There is evidence that music and cultural activity can further not only the education and cultural agendas but also the aspirations for the Big Society.'

The aims of Sing Up www.singup.org
'Every child deserves the chance to sing every day. Singing improves learning, confidence, health and social development. It has the power to change lives and help to build stronger communities.'

Howard Goodall's introduction to a Teachers' TV series, Take 10 Weeks – Singing School filmed in early 2007: www.howardgoodall.co.uk/singing/singing%20 ambassador.htm
'Singing in schools, after suffering a period of relative decline, is finally back on the agenda, with a vengeance. There's no doubt that all children, whatever their background, get enormous benefit from singing as a group. It enhances their self-esteem, it boosts their ability to learn and it is also great fun. Schools where singing thrives are happy schools. Scientific studies from all over the world show that singing accelerates learning by improving a child's memory skills, it is a fun way of teaching languages and numeracy, it builds a sense of teamwork and is a great opportunity to bring together children from very different backgrounds into one sociable and enjoyable activity. What's more, you don't have to teach

singing like you do a language or a sport or a mathematical skill – all infants automatically know how to sing. Nature's already done the job!'

Music Education Council's aims www.mec.org.uk
'Music must remain integral to the national educational strategy and remain part of the national curriculum. Music supports attainment in numeracy and literacy and MEC will ensure that Head Teachers and community leaders understand its importance in living a well-balanced and enriching life.'

National Curriculum for Music http://curriculum.qcda.gov.uk/key-stages-3-and-4/subjects/key-stage-3/music/index.aspx
'Music is a unique form of communication that can change the way pupils feel, think and act. Music forms part of an individual's identity and positive inter-action with music can develop pupils' competence as learners and increase their self-esteem. Music brings together intellect and feeling and enables personal expression, reflection and emotional development. As an integral part of culture, past and present, music helps pupils understand themselves, relate to others and develop their cultural understanding, forging important links between home, school and the wider world.'

Hallam, S. And Creech, A. (2010) Music Education in the 21st Century in the United Kingdom
'Chapter 1: The power of music: its impact on the intellectual, personal and social development of children and young people.'

'Notwithstanding the wide-ranging benefits of music that have been outlined in this book, it is perhaps most fitting to conclude by celebrating the rich musical diversity that is evident across the UK. The wider benefits of music making are indeed impressive and should not be ignored. However, the value of music in its own right must not be forgotten (p. 345)'.

Voices Foundation www.voices.org.uk
'Transforming children through singing'

Part of the problem here would appear to be the absence of a strong epistemological discourse for educational music beyond the notion of 'transfer'. The construction of music as life-affirming is indeed laudable and yet this 'popular' discourse is more fully developed than that which surrounds the wider nature of musical meaning. Questions such as: 'What is music?'; 'How is meaning constructed in music?'; 'What does it mean to understand music?', are relatively underdeveloped in much current discourse about the 'why?' of music education. It is not as if this deeper analysis is even 'hidden away' in these documents (although it is conceded that the national curriculum text does a better job here).The fact is that the 'complete' discourse is either absent or relatively immature with celebrated issues of transfer as the default discourse.

This is not to say that authors have shied away from this project (see Swanwick 1988 and Elliott, 1995) but such writing has failed to make an impression on much populist writing and policy documents surrounding why music should be in the curriculum. The benevolent interpretation is that the 'hard' discourse is inevitably complex and challenging, although such a partial account of the nature of music continues to allow it to be constructed as an adjunct (and an amelioration) to a harder and more rational world. The more cynical political interpretation is that in a culture of outcomes and accountability ministers are more likely to look favourably on music if it can be shown that it has an impact on child development and wellbeing. The attraction for politicians, and indeed for those who wish to promote various initiatives, is that there is the possibility of 'measuring' such impact. However, a cosy relationship with these assumptions merely serves to adopt the very dualism that has subjugated music (and indeed the arts) in the curriculum and wider culture at the expense of other 'harder' subjects.

In short, there is a discourse that continues to perpetuate a view of educational music that does little for the integrity of the discipline. What might constitute a more complete account of music that is truer to its essential nature and thus part of a more convincing argument for its inclusion in the curriculum? The sense of 'hard' being postulated here is not derived from any populist notion of music needing to be 'academic' or 'rigorous' but from the idea that music deserves to be justified in the curriculum as a language(s) capable of the full expressive range found in all symbolic modes.

The wider meaning of music: completing the picture

Green (1988) has provided a useful theoretical framework for the construction of musical meaning that helps to explain what is going on here. She proposes two types of musical meaning that are ultimately inextricably linked: inherent meaning and delineated meaning. Inherent meaning is constructed directly through the 'temporal musical experience' (1988:25) of musical materials as they sound and pass us by. However, music 'must mean something apart from itself' (p. 26) for:

> No sooner do the first sounds of any music reach our ears, than we begin to assimilate them within a web of meanings in the social world: our past, our future, our friends, family, taste.
>
> (Green 1988: 27)

This for Green is delineated meaning, as music not only points to self but out from itself to social meanings and social relations, and as such are subject to wider ideological and cultural processes.

Brown and Theorell (2006) suggest that the delineation of 'music is good for you' is derived from the western classical tradition.

> Western people have a need to believe that the music of the European classical tradition is something noble and good, the kind of thing that works positively for humankind.
>
> (Brown and Theorell 2006: 151)

These assumptions are also underpinned by a notion that 'classical' music is the best of music, that it emanates from the very best of societies and that it appears both autonomous and universal (see Spruce 1999); what Tagg calls a 'suprasocial phenomenon' (2006: 179). In this way the ideology of western classical music permeates and controls the narrative surrounding much popular discourse in music education.

> Good–music–brighter–children has become the clarion call of those trying to oppose budget cuts for music education in schools. But this laudable goal should not obscure people's judgment of reality. One could easily dismiss the Mozart effect as a blatant tactic to promote the musical tastes of the dominant class on rationalist grounds. If hard rock music were empirically shown to enhance spatial-temporal reasoning more than does Mozart, would classical music enthusiasts petition to promote hard rock music education in school? The answer seems quite obvious to us.
>
> (Brown and Theorell 2006: 152)

It is clear that the 'music is good for you' discourse is both partial and ideological and as such not in the best interests of children or their teachers. Brown and Theorell go on to point out that:

> The notion that music is some kind of universal elixir that smartens and cures remains one of the most contentious issues in the sociology of music even though it is rarely recognized as such … Music is a mixed bag. It can be both good and bad for people.
>
> (Brown and Theorell 2006: 153)

The relationship between music, the individual and society is a complex one. The next section aims to exemplify some of the components of this complexity that enable us to arrive at a more complete account of the nature of musical meaning, understanding and knowledge. If anything the argument is that music is *more* important than is suggested by the 'music is good for you' strapline.

Music is tribal, exclusive and can enshrine prejudice

An English footballer playing for a Scottish team once famously stirred sectarian tensions by imitating the playing of a flute in front of the opposition supporters. This was at once recognized by them as him miming *The Sash* (also known as *The Sash My Father Wore*) a ballad from Ireland commemorating the victory of King William III in the Williamite war in Ireland in 1690–1691. It is a popular tune amongst Protestant loyalists in Northern Ireland and is taken as being offensive and provocative by Catholic republicans. Quite apart from the media indignation, this example serves to illustrate that music is rarely neutral and autonomous. It is always born of a particular set of social, political and historical circumstances that renders its meaning rich and complex not least when reinterpreted between generations. More benign forms of tribalism (but no less strongly contested) can be found in, for example, opera lovers and the subgroups of 'metal' music e.g. death, black etc.

Music is dangerous

Plato understood the danger of music to the extent that he was in favour of the censorship of certain 'modes'. In more recent times Richard Taruskin has questioned the notion of autonomous art for art's sake, what he calls utopian music. The 'danger' of this view, he maintains, is that it ignores the potency of music to be intolerably insensitive.

> What is called for is self control .... There is no need to shove Wagner in the faces of Holocaust survivors ... Censorship is always deplorable, but the exercise of forbearance can be noble ... Art is not blameless. Art can inflict harm.
>
> (Taruskin 2009: 173)

Whether or not one agrees with his controversial views on the censorship of John Adams *The Death of Klinghoffer* post the 9/11 tragedy (the opera re-enacts and comments on the murder of an American Jew by Palestinian terrorists), his writing serves to illustrate that music provokes competing definitions of value in relation to its nature and purpose.

Music is manipulative of behaviour

It has been known for some time that music can be used to influence purchasing (see North and Hargreaves 2006), and that it can influence behaviour in busy times at railway stations. Indeed, the argument that 'music is good for you' is based on an assumption that our behaviour and psychology can be manipulated through a positive engagement with music e.g. better teamwork, higher self-esteem. However, it is clear that music has far wider powers of persuasion, enculturation and socialization (see Brown 2006).

Manipulation in this sense is not necessarily a negative process but it could be if, for example, the powers of 'persuasion' in music led to inequities that were not transparent.

Music is gendered

A further example of how music in education and society can underpin social control is in relation to gender. Green (1995), in analysing the construction of gender stereotypes in music, notes that the most abundantly successful job for a female in all styles of music in the western world is that of singer. Females, she maintains, predominantly perform on an instrument which is their body as an affirmation of their femininity. For centuries the singing woman has been associated with the sexual temptress and also the idealized mother singing to her child and these have constructed our perceptions of the role of females in society and as participants in music. She also asks us to consider the way in which women composers have been written about often in terms of the idealized vision of the male composer.

> A great deal of music by women composers has been denigrated for its effeminacy; other music has been more favourably received as displaying positive feminine attributes such as delicacy or sensitivity; a tiny amount of music by women has been incredulously hailed as equal to music by men.
>
> (Green 1995: 127)

While over-generalized for this snapshot, this analysis serves to show how music plays a role in perpetuating gender stereotypes in music and society.

Music enshrines ideology

Ideology comes sharply into focus when we make value judgements about life and about music. These values are the basis for us thinking and acting and their pervasiveness, while giving the impression of free will, are derived from wider social structures. An example of this can be seen in how the values of western classical music permeate assessment criteria in the secondary music curriculum in the UK (Philpott 2010). Despite huge changes to the national curriculum for music post-1992 which embraced a wide range of 'musics' from around the world, Green notes that:

> ... when teachers, curricula, syllabi, or books *theoretically supported* the value of popular music, they tended to do so by appealing to the very same qualities of universality, complexity, originality, or autonomy upon which the values of classical music rested.
>
> (Green 2003: 266)

The point about complexity and originality is important. The assessment criteria used in many post-1992 syllabi in the UK have been written on the assumption that the more complex the music 'produced' by the pupils the higher the marks it is likely to gain and to the detriment of music which does not aspire to these values. The upshot is the perpetuation of the 'classical' ideology in what seemingly *appears* to be a more inclusive and diverse curriculum.

Music is propaganda

It is well known that both the Nazi and Soviet regimes of the last century criticized art for art's sake. In both cases any music composed was expected to be close to the spirit of the people and in particular the aims of the regime. In the case of the latter the philosophy of 'Socialist Realism' required artists and musicians to glorify the 'struggle' through positive affirmation. Indeed, there was an explicit expectation that music should be good for you (but not for its own sake). However, the propagandist dimension to music is common in all cultures, for example, nationalism and patriotism, both of which can be seen as tribalism depending on which side of the anthem you are listening to or singing.

Music reflects social structures

Authors such as Shepherd and Small have suggested ways in which music is related to social structures. Shepherd (1977) for example, has theorized the links between functional tonality and the values and structure of western society. Martin has summarized his position as follows:

> In its hierarchical and centralized nature, then, in its expression of time as linear (rather than cyclical) and above all in its representation of the notion of progress, functional tonality is seen by Shepherd as 'encoding' the 'industrial world sense'.
>
> (Martin 1991: 122)

Shepherd also postulates that different visions of society are encoded in other types of tonality, for example, pentatonicism where the lack of a definitive tonal centre smacks of a more decentralized and localized society. For Adorno, music plays a role in sustaining social structures especially through the narrative of music as the expression of emotion (as it happens another feature of the 'music is good for you' discourse).

> Emotional music has become the image of the mother who says, 'Come weep, my child' .... music that permits its listeners the confession of their unhappiness (*or happiness*) reconciles them, by means of this 'release', to their social dependence.
>
> (Adorno 1991: 313–14)

The examples above serve to illustrate that music is a complex symbolic system and the limited discourse of the 'soft' justification will not do. If the examples err on the side of the negative it is to provide an antidote to the 'music is good for you' narrative. The aim is to 'complete' the account of music as a powerful symbolic mode.

There are two important implications of the analysis thus far which we now need to consider. First, that music should be considered as a language system that is vital to the ways in which we construct meaning, culture and ideology. Second, that in light of this music educators at all levels need to engage with a critical pedagogy which aims to facilitate pupils, students and teachers to engage with the complex webs of meaning which arise as part of making music.

Music is a language

Music has had a problematical relationship with language and knowledge which rests on its non-discursive nature. The assumption is that music is not really a language at all (see Sloboda 1985), except in a very special sense, and thus cannot be regarded as a way of knowing. Music fails the test of being a language, the argument goes, as it is impossible to find any causal link between sounds and meaning (in the same way that there is between words and meaning), despite several attempts to do so (see Cooke 1959). This 'logical' view of language is synonymous with an 'objective', mind-independent view of knowledge. If music cannot show that its meanings are somehow objective and testable through logic or observation then it cannot be taken seriously as a language in which knowledge can be held. The consequence for music has been an epistemological barrier to being regarded as a language and consequently not being fit to 'hold' objective knowledge. In any case, it is argued, music speaks of the subjective realm of feelings and emotions which are the essential counterbalance to the objectivity of the sciences. It is easy to see how these assumptions about language and music have helped to promote the 'soft' accounts noted earlier in this chapter. Music cannot be 'hard' as it does not live up to the criteria which would make it so, and many who have chosen to justify music in the curriculum have condoned this duality.

However, a careful analysis of these assumptions behind the music–language comparison, calls into question the 'logical' view as an adequate account of any language system. An examination of certain strands in literary theory and semiotics have shown that the relationship between the word/sound (signifier) and the object of meaning (the signified) is (a) open to a multitude of cultural, ideological delineated influences, and (b) is an ever-shifting and unstable horizon where any 'signified' is open to many interpretations of its meaning. Such a vision of a language has the potential to provide a more fruitful account of language and knowledge, a more rational basis for a music–language comparison i.e. multiple and complex relationships between signifiers and the signified, and thus a sound epistemological basis for music as a language.

Drawing on the work of semiotics and continental literary theory, Philpott (2001) has highlighted the consequences of this 'shift'. Using the semiotics of Nattiez (1987) he suggests that the meanings of both language and music (as a language) are always complex and constructed out of 'webs' of meaning.

> Indeed, his [Nattiez] notion of musical meaning is grounded in the 'infinite and dynamic interpretant' of C. S. Pierce. He argues that the sign (interpretation) sparks off many other signs (interpretations) and each interpretation adds to a web of musical meaning ... (while) these interpretations are not utterly random .... but neither are they fixed to a precise sound – meaning basis. The web is part of a complex interpretative process ... .
>
> (Philpott 2001: 39)

A conception of music as a language, which like other types of language, is characterized by complex webs of meaning is required if we wish to develop a 'hard' discourse when justifying music in the curriculum. The concept of webs of meaning is more amenable to accounting for the role of, for example, gender, culture and ideology in musical meaning and both its danger and therapeutic powers. While there is much work to do on these ideas, the notion that music is a language and shares a process of meaning making with all languages, is a strong basis for proposing the notion that music is capable of 'hard' and complex meaning including and beyond those meanings assigned to music in the 'soft' discourse. A 'harder' discourse can underpin a justification for music in the curriculum that celebrates the full breadth of its power of expression. A discourse for educational music that moves beyond 'music is good for you' and embraces both the strength and subtlety of musical meaning, is required if a justifiable justification is to be mounted.

In the final section of this chapter we argue that given the complexity surrounding the construction of musical meaning (as a basis for justifying the discipline) then these meanings logically become the remit of the curriculum, facilitated through a critical pedagogy. This implies that teachers could, for example, engage their pupils in the political and ideological issues that are embedded in complex webs of musical meaning. In the sense used here critical pedagogy also implies that teachers accept hermeneutical (interpretative) relationship with music is that this becomes a valid part of our classroom transactions. To do otherwise betrays music as a significant and 'hard' language and compromises its status as a curriculum subject.

A critical pedagogy for music education

The act of understanding music is one of interpreting complex webs of meaning. The theme of interpretation is central to the work of Gadamer (1975) whose treatise on hermeneutics argues that understanding is always an interpretative act. Each piece of music (whether we are performing or creating it) comes with an 'attitude' of its own and along with our own values and beliefs (which Gadamer calls 'prejudices') engages in a playful dialogue in order to construct meaning. Both sides of this dialogue will be shot through with tacit assumptions in relation to, for example, culture and ideology. Gadamer developed the concept of 'fusions of horizons' to describe this process of interpretation. It is here at the 'fusions of horizons' that the 'hard' discourse of music education can be found and offers a legitimate dimension to the music curriculum.

Having said this, Swanwick (1988) has warned us against engaging pupils too closely with such interpretative acts that might uncover, for example some of the 'tribal' dimensions to musical meaning.

> When music has become emotionally embroiled in local cultural practices or fads we would do well to avoid it in the curriculum, the song being for the

while lost in 'noise' either literally or metaphorically ... Most music, though, is not so tied down to cultural practice and is accessible to us if we give it a chance to speak.

(Swanwick 1988: 101)

He argues that music as a language has much by way of meaning that operates at the level of cultural universals, a position that involved him in a celebrated dialogue with the sociologist John Shepherd who conversely felt that music can only be fully understood by the culture that creates it (see Shepherd and Vulliamy 1984). Swanwick warns that the music curriculum is no place to expose and make explicit what might turn out to be unsavoury and possibly tribal.

While this is a legitimate concern for music educators, at a time when pupils/students 'interests' are at the centre of significant curriculum developments (see *Musical Futures* projects at www.musicalfutures.org) it could be that music education needs the maturity to embrace curriculum content that deals with the mysoginism, sexism, ideology and tribalism that *might* arise during the process of musical learning. The arguments of this chapter would suggest the need for a critical pedagogy as part of a mature justification for music as a language in the curriculum.

Elsewhere in this volume both Westerlund and Woodford have suggested that music teachers should explicitly engage pupils/students in the political and ideological dimensions of the music. But what does this actually mean in practice? How can music teachers engage with the controversial issues highlighted by Lucy Green when she writes about the representation of women in music in western cultures?

But the woman singer not only appears sexually available, for in her private capacity she conjures up an inversion of this public image that of the idealized mother singing to her baby. Pivoted upon the binary division between whore and Madonna, harlot and virgin – is one of the reasons why – women have been more abundant and successful in singing than any other single musical role.

(Green 1995: 124)

We should countenance that such issues can form the basis of valid interventions in music education in the form of discussions and musical responses from teachers and students alike, e.g. playing music which is a challenge to musical stereotypes. It is clear that there is much scope for research and development here, since the subtleties of a critical pedagogy have received little attention compared with the 'neutral' activities of composing, performing and listening.

Bennett Reimer (1989) wrote that the nature of music education should reflect the very nature of music itself. His wisdom was a clear mandate for music educators to put what musicians do at the heart of the curriculum i.e. performing, creating and consuming musical products. A critical pedagogy for music education suggests that we go further than this and regard the complex meanings

of music as valid and significant curriculum content during the pedagogical transactions of teachers, pupils and students. This involves raising the tacit and implicit
meanings of music to the level of the explicit and is a logical consequence of
viewing music as a language characterized by complex webs of meaning. There is
much work to be done here for subtle and sensitive issues inevitably arise and yet
if we accept music as a language then music education remains incomplete if
these are silenced.

Conclusion

This chapter is not meant to present a negative picture of musical meaning and
the incidence of 'bad' examples are in the name of balance. These arguments do
not displace the uniqueness of music as a mode of expression and understanding
which may or may not be responsible for the celebrated 'effects'. Indeed, it could
be that music is more important than any of us think it to be. The proposed
project is one of completion through resurrecting in the discourse of educational
music, the notion of music as a language, which is capable of many diverse and
intricate webs of meaning. To settle for less is to consign the language to limited
powers of expression and a 'soft' romanticized discourse. Furthermore, it is
suggested that a 'hard' discourse is the legitimate remit of learning and teaching
in music through a critical pedagogy that explicitly engages with the hermeneutics
of musical meaning.

 And so we need to understand, along with John Harvey Kellog, that music
'aids circulation through the liver, stomach and other digestive organs, and so
promotes digestion'. But also to bear in mind Adorno when he sensitively adds:

> Emotional music ... is catharsis for the masses, but catharsis which keeps
> them all the more in line .... One who weeps does not resist any more than
> one who marches.
>
> (Adorno 1991: 313–14)

Music can be Bad – *Bad*; music can be Wicked – *Wicked*. How many antagonyms
do you know?

Reflective questions

1 What does music mean to you? Why do you engage with music and what
   types of musical meanings are important to you? How does this analysis
   relate to your own justification for music in the curriculum?
2 Do you agree with Swanwick that aspects of musical meaning which are
   'embroiled in local cultural practices' should be left well alone in the music
   curriculum?
3 What strategies can be employed in a critical pedagogy that enable music
   teachers to embrace the full expressive power of music in the classroom?

References

Abbs, P. (1987) *Living Powers: The Arts in Education,* London: The Falmer Press.

Adorno, T. (1991) *The Culture Industry,* London: Routledge.

Brown, S. (2006) '"How Does Music Work?" Toward a Pragmatics of Musical Communication', in S. Brown, and U. Volgsten (eds) *Music and Manipulation: On the Social Uses and Social Control of Music,* New York: Berghahn Books.

Brown, S. and Theorell, T. (2006) 'The Social Uses of Background Music for Personal Enhancement', in S. Brown, and U. Volgsten (eds) *Music and Manipulation: On the Social Uses and Social Control of Music,* New York: Berghahn Books.

Clift, S. and Hancox, G. (2001) 'The Perceived benefits of Singing: Findings from Preliminary Surveys with a University College Choral Society', *Journal of the Royal Society for the Promotion of Health,* 121(4): 248–56.

Cooke, D. (1959) *The Language of Music,* Oxford: Oxford University Press.

Elliott, D.J. (1995) *Music Matters: A New Philosophy of Music Education,* Oxford: Oxford University Press.

Gadamer, H.G. (1975) *Truth and Method,* New York: Seabury Press.

Green, L. (1995) 'Gender, Musical Meaning and Education' in G. Spruce, (ed) *Teaching Music,* London: Routledge.

Green, L. (1996) 'The Emergence of Gender as an Issue in Music Education', in C. Plummeridge (ed.) *Music Education: Trends and Issues,* London: Institute of Education, University of London.

Green, L. (2003) 'Music Education, Cultural Capital and Social Group Identity' in M. Clayton, T. Herbert, and R. Middleton (eds) *The Cultural Study of Music,* London: Routledge.

Hallam, S. and Creech, A. (eds) (2010) *Music Education in the 21st Century in the United Kingdom: Achievements, Analysis and Aspirations,* London: Institute of Education, University of London.

Langer, S.K. (1978) *Philosophy in a New Key,* Cambridge, Mass: Harvard University Press.

Martin, P.J. (1995) *Sounds and Society: Themes in the Sociology of Music,* Manchester: Manchester University Press.

Nattiez, J.J. (1987) *Music and Discourse: Towards a Semiology of Music,* Princetown, NJ: Princetown University Press.

North, A.C. and Hargreaves, D.J. (2006) 'Music in Business Environments', in S. Brown, and U. Volgsten (eds) *Music and Manipulation: On the Social Uses and Social Control of Music,* New York: Berghahn Books.

Philpott, C. (2001) 'Is Music a Language', in C. Philpott, and C. Plummeridge (eds) *Issues in Music Teaching,* London: Routledge Falmer.

Philpott, C. (2010) 'The Sociological Critique of Curriculum Music in England: Is Radical Change Really Possible?', in R. Wright (ed.) *Sociology and Music Education,* Farnham: Ashgate.

Plummeridge, C. (2001) 'The Justification for Music Education', in C. Philpott, and C. Plummeridge (eds) *Issues in Music Teaching,* London: Routledge Falmer.

Reimer, B. (1989) *A Philosophy of Music Education,* Englewood Cliffs, NJ: Prentice-Hall.

Shepherd, J. (1977) *Whose Music? A Sociology of Musical Languages,* London: Latimer.

Shepherd, J. and Vulliamy, G. (1984) 'Sociology and Music Education: a Response to Swanwick', *British Journal of Sociology of Education* 5: 49–56.

Sloboda, J.A. (1985) *The Musical Mind: The Cognitive Psychology of Music*, Oxford: Oxford University Press.

Small, C. (1977) *Music – Society – Education*, London: John Calder.

Spruce, G. (1999) 'Music, Music Education and the Bourgeois Aesthetic: Developing a Music Curriculum for the New Millennium', in R. McCormick, and C. Paechter (eds) *Learning and Knowledge*, London: Oxford University Press.

Swanwick, K. (1988) *Music, Mind and Education*, London: Routledge.

Tagg, P. (2006) 'Music, Moving Images, Semiotics, and the Democratic Right to Know', in S. Brown, and Volgsten U. (eds) *Music and Manipulation: On the Social Uses and Social Control of Music*, New York: Berghahn Books.

Taruskin, R. (2009) *The Danger of Music and Other Anti-Utopian Essays*, Berkeley: University of California Press.

Witkin, R. (1974) *The Intelligence of Feeling*, London: Heinemann.

Websites

www.education.gov.uk/inthenews/inthenews/a0064925/education-secretary-michael-gove-announces-review-of-music-education (accessed 27 September 2011)

www.singup.org (accessed 27 September 2011)

www.howardgoodall.co.uk/singing/singing%20ambassador.htm (accessed 27 September 2011)

www.mec.org.uk (accessed 27 September 2011)

http://curriculum.qcda.gov.uk/key-stages-3-and-4/subjects/key-stage-3/music/index.aspx (accessed 27 September 2011)

www.voices.org.uk (accessed 27 September 2011)

www.musicalfutures.org (accessed 27 September 2011)

Chapter 5

What is musical development and can education make a difference?

Keith Swanwick

Introduction

Theories of development and musical development

The question 'what is musical development?' is surely central to music education. Yet it seems rarely considered at the present time. Instead, ideas of 'musicality' or 'progression' may be implicitly assumed but usually remain explicitly unexamined. In this chapter this question will be foremost, as we consider theories of music and musical development which may illuminate music education transactions.

We expect to find developmental patterns in maturing children, for example in linguistic or sensory-motor development, and there are things we can learn from the broader field of studies in child development, especially from a consideration of the concept of 'stages'. According to Crain, developmental theorists, such as Piaget, Erikson and Kohlberg, took the view that any theory of cognitive stages should meet five quite stringent criteria (Crain 1992). These criteria are quite challenging to musicians and music educators, indeed they may be resisted by some.

- Stages imply qualitatively differentiated patterns of behaviour.
- Stage descriptions deal with general issues rather than specific achievements.
- Stages unfold in an invariant sequence.
- Stages are cultural universals.
- Stages are hierarchic, in that early structures are integrated into later ones.

The first of these seems particularly important. Although some development can be seen as *quantitative*, in the sense that children become more skilled in doing something, for instance, throwing a ball, major aspects of developmental change are usually *qualitative*, with the emergence of new characteristics, rather than 'more of the same'. So, for example, the transition from a child able to stand supported to walking unaided, or the emergence of meaningful speech from infant babbling, can be seen as qualitative shifts. It seems reasonable to look for similar qualitative changes in musical development.

'Cultural universals' may be thought problematic. However, we might expect a good theory to be capable of application beyond a single cultural group (though 'widespread' might be a better and less contested term than 'universal'). Developmental expectations need not ignore individual or cultural differences and the concept of a stage need not be so fixed as to leave no possibility for unique interpretation, cultural difference, or maturational variation. The notion of hierarchy is also important, especially in the sense of the integration of early developments into later ones, an issue we shall revisit later.

Hargreaves and Zimmerman (1992) identified four criteria for specifically evaluating developmental theories for music. These, taken with the more general formulations given above, seem to be a good basis for evaluating any contribution to a discussion of musical development.

- Any theories and associated evidence should comprehensively reflect the nature of musical behaviour.
- Theories and underlying assumptions should be valid across a range of musical activities or 'modalities': composing (including improvisation), performing and audience-listening.
- Evidence should be systematically and reliably produced to support or challenge theoretical assertions.
- Developmental theories should take into account both the natural developmental inclinations of individuals and the cultural environment in which their development is realized.

The first of these criteria is fundamental: musical behaviour, or perhaps better, musical understanding, should be comprehensively addressed. The essential nature of musical activity in all its potential richness should be the focus of any investigation into musical development.

In brief then: a serviceable music development model is likely to involve a hierarchy of evolving qualities, it ought also to be capable of mapping development across a range of musical and cultural settings. And most important, a valid developmental theory should encompass the essential nature of musical activity and not some limited aspect in isolation, such as tonal or rhythmic discrimination, or vocal production.

There have been many attempts to isolate and measure the development of specific musical functions. From Seashore through to Bentley and more recently, there have been claims that particular musical abilities develop before or after others. For example, Hargreaves (1986) has asserted that the development of rhythmic skills are among the first to emerge, echoing Bentley (1966), who argued that the ability to discriminate rhythm develops earlier than an ability to discriminate pitch or to perceive chords. We notice though, that evidence for this is derived from separate test scores for each 'ability'. There is an obvious problem with such claims. We cannot compare, say, a measure of rhythm pattern discrimination with chord discrimination, any more than we can compare the tyre pressures on a car with the oil level, unless we can identify some connective element, perhaps the number of miles travelled. There can be no baseline for comparing melodic with rhythmic development using separate tests without an overarching theory of music and musical development.

Mary Louise Serafine is unimpressed by what she sees as a reductionist organization of research into the measurement of separate parameters, such as time, timbre, pitch and loudness (Serafine 1980). She categorizes entities such as tones and chords *per se* as sound 'materials' rather than musical elements. This is a helpful distinction, one made some time ago by Suzanne Langer and expanded by others, including Swanwick (Swanwick 1979: 8–10). A fundamental question for Serafine is 'what is the nature and source of musical thought?' (Serafine 2980: 1). For her, the main characteristic is awareness of movement in time (p. 69). Tones are not heard in isolation nor as pairs of stimuli to be identified or discriminated, but are sensory experiences from which the listener constructs musical properties, perhaps phrases. This constructive temporal process takes place in two ways, first as 'succession', where basic coherent units are conceived and transformed into longer configurations through processes of motivic chaining, by patterning through repetition and alternation and by the boundaries between phrase groupings. Second is the dimension of 'simultaneity', when two or more meaningful sound events or units are heard together. Serafine did not deal systematically with age-related changes but she does begin to set out a theory of music which can inform ideas on musical development.

This is an important issue. To understand children's linguistic development requires us to have a theory of the functions and purposes of language. Similarly to understand musical development requires some view of how music functions. This is hard to find. For example, Sloboda and Deliège bring together a number of reviews on developmental issues, including pre-natal auditory experience, infants' auditory sensitivity towards acoustic parameters of speech and music, parenting and musical stimulation in infancy, the development of artistic and musical competence and the young performing musician (Sloboda and Deliège 1996). However, these contributions by various authors do not really contribute to an emerging developmental theory. Nor can one be found in *The Child as Musician* (Mcpherson 2006). In spite of the subtitle, *A handbook of musical development*, this collection of essays rarely addresses the issue of development in the usual sense. One exception is Bamberger's contribution, *What develops in musical development?* She writes:

> Thus, I argue that rather than being a unidirectional process, musical development is a spiralling, endlessly recursive process in which multiple organizing constraints are concurrently present, creating an essential, generative tension as they play a transformational dance with one another.
>
> (Bamberger 2006: 71)

This is beautifully put and her initial question 'what develops in musical development?' is very important and is related to the first of the Hargreaves criteria.

There have of course been many studies of various aspects of development, often with younger children. Early attempts to observe and record musical development in early childhood include the pioneering work of Moog (1976). Fairly recently we have those by Davies (1992), Barrett (1999) and Tarfuri (2009). It is not my intention to review these, except to note that most writers tend not to offer any generic theory or model of musical development. Indeed, they seek to avoid this, concentrating instead on ethnographic details and participant observation, often with individual children. Valuable as these insights may be, the lack of a theoretical perspective limits the possibility of generalizing from the findings to developmental expectations over a period of time, for example during the years of schooling, or to developing classroom strategies.

Many music development researchers have placed significant weight on the analysis of childrens' notations, for example Davidson and Scripp, Christensen, Upitis, Gromko and Barrett (Davidson and Scripp 1988; Christensen 1992; Upitis 1992; Gromko 1994; Barrett 1997). This approach is justified by Barrett, who claims that invented notations of musical experience may be viewed '... as indicators of musical thinking' (Barrett 1999: 71), that the notations children use represent their thinking about the world.

However, music itself is an activity that is in some way representative of our experience of the world, a multi-layered primary symbolic system. Notations, verbal descriptions or graphic representations are *secondary* systems, offering a visual translation from the aural domain. In this process some loss of information is inevitable, and in any case, notating music is by no means culturally widespread. Evidence based only on notations is therefore likely to be unreliable, culturally limited and of doubtful validity. Researchers who rely on secondary forms of representation may overlook important features of musical development. Observing actual musical production is likely to be more informative.

The Swanwick/Tillman developmental spiral

Swanwick and Tillman's work on musical development is based on multiple observations of actual music making under varied conditions (Swanwick and Tillman 1986). The work has been widely cited, extensively reviewed and appears to meet most if not all of the Hargreaves/ Zimmerman criteria. Questions have of course been raised about its validity and reliability and, since the present author has a long association with this theory and its critics, it seems appropriate to focus on it here and on some theoretical antecedents.

During the 1970s, Swanwick developed a series of objectives for music teaching (Swanwick 1979: 67). These included skill acquisition, later to become 'materials', recognizing and producing expressive gesture, later to be designated 'expression' or 'expressive character', identifying and displaying the operation of norms and deviations, subsequently taken into the concept of 'form' and aesthetic response or 'meaning for', eventually to be called 'value'. Swanwick further developed this paradigm in a public lecture given in 1982, linking it to Piagetian concepts of assimilation and accommodation (Swanwick 1983). This was an attempt to synthesize several strands of debate in music aesthetics. Technique, expression, form and value are not seen as competing but as complementary aspects of music experience and controversial issues of 'formalism' and 'referentialism' are bypassed. Music is seen as a multi-layered experience, where layers not only interact vertically but also laterally, as minds assimilate and accommodate to musical processes. This epistemological perspective and its subsequent incorporation into a developmental model are first made explicit in the 1986 article.

Un-notated compositions were produced by children, mostly aged three to 14, from several ethnic and cultural groups in London schools. The compositions were part of normal classroom activities and were tape-recorded over four years, nine times each year, yielding 745 compositions from 48 children. There was a cross-section of music from children of different ages and, in some cases, a longitudinal spectrum of compositions from individual children. This rich data, systematically collected and carefully interpreted by June Tillman (Tillman 1987), was crucial for evolving the initial theory of music into a developmental theory. The compositions ranged from brief spontaneous utterances to more sustained and rehearsed musical inventions. Studying a large number of musical inventions in this way was thought to be both ecologically sensitive, with greater validity than setting specific tests, conducting interviews or theorizing (generalizing) from small samples. During repeated hearings the compositions were subsequently grouped into clusters perceived as sharing similar properties. These clusters were consonant with Swanwick's original conception of four levels or layers of musical experience and became 'materials', 'expression', 'form' and 'value' (Swanwick and Tillman 1986).

Further evaluation of the compositions led to seeing that in each of four levels there is a transformation from assimilatory, personal response to music (the left side) to accommodatory 'social sharing' (the right side). Social contexts are implicit in the right-hand dimension, in the concept of manipulative control which makes it possible for people to make music together, in the idea of the vernacular – common shared music processes and in the idiomatic with its implications of social conventions of style and genre. Even the 'systematic', with its connotations of creating new musical processes and forms, can be seen as socially situated, in that existing conventions may be challenged. For these reasons the original spiral diagram (and this one here, Fig. 5.1) had an arrow running from left to right captioned 'towards social sharing.'

Although the word 'spiral' was used from the start of this project, in reality the concept is of a *helix*, a three dimensional continuous curve. It is unnecessary to alter the terminology here but it is important to recognize the intention to depict a process where there may be vertical change but also a continuous return to each side of the horizontal plane.

The developmental helix or spiral thus eventually consisted of eight layers. Some of the terminology for these drew on observations by Robert Bunting (Bunting 1977) of children composing in a secondary school. He does not place

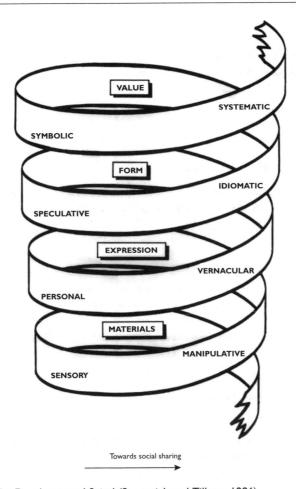

Figure 5.1 The Developmental Spiral (Swanwick and Tillman 1986).

his observations into a developmental sequence but he does identify some qualitative differences in the way children compose. Swanwick and Tillman also report
such differences emerging over time as children mature. An initial phase of
exploring sounds transforms into manipulative control. With this technical ability,
musical expression becomes possible, at first spontaneous but later more conventional with vernacular commonplaces of phrase and sequence. These conventional processes are transformed into coherent musical forms, initially in a
speculative way and then in identifiable styles or idioms. Beyond this lies the
possibility of symbolic value for the individual and systematic musical commitment.
The concept of 'value' involves much more than immediate enjoyment and
denotes the phenomenon of people becoming consciously aware of the importance of music for them, a meta-cognitive process that involves considerable

personal autonomy. The essence of these developmental layers has been captured in the following short descriptions. Layer eight is a theoretical extrapolation, since it is difficult to find evidence for this among school age children. Confidence in the seventh layer was initially limited by the small number of older children involved in the initial study but is confirmed in the Cyprus replication to be discussed later.

MATERIALS

Layer one – Sensory

Children take pleasure in sound itself, particularly in experimenting with timbre and extremes of loud and soft. They enjoy exploring instruments in a spontaneous, loosely-organized way.

Layer two – Manipulative

Control is shown by repetitions and regular pulse. Ideas may be suggested by the physical structure and layout of available instruments, such as glissandi, scalic and intervallic patterns, trills and tremolo. Compositions tend to be extended with repetitions as the composer enjoys the feeling of managing the instrument.

EXPRESSION

Layer three – Personal Expressiveness

Expressiveness is apparent in changes of speed and loudness levels. There is an impression of spontaneity with phrases – musical gestures – which cannot always be exactly repeated. There may be drama, mood or atmosphere, perhaps with reference to an external 'programmatic' idea.

Layer four – Vernacular

Melodic and rhythmic figures are repeated. Pieces may be based on established general musical conventions, often falling into two, four or eight-bar units, metrically organized, with devices such as syncopation, melodic and rhythmic ostinati and sequences. Compositions tend to be fairly predictable and show influences of the repertoire from other musical experiences; singing, playing and listening.

FORM

Layer five – Speculative

Deviations and surprises occur as expressive characterization is subject to experimentation, exploring structural possibilities, contrasting or varying musical ideas. After establishing repeated patterns, a frequent device is to introduce a novel ending.

Layer six – Idiomatic

Structural surprises are integrated into a recognizable musical style. Contrast and variation take place on the basis of emulated models and clear idiomatic practices, frequently, though not always drawn from popular musical traditions. Harmonic and instrumental authenticity seems important. Answering phrases, call and response, variation by elaboration and contrasting sections are common. Structural control is revealed in longer compositions.

VALUE

Layer seven – Symbolic

Technical mastery serves musical communication. Formal relationships and expressive character are fused together in an impressive, coherent and original musical statement. Particular groups of timbres, turns of phrase and harmonic progressions may be developed and given sustained concern. There is a strong sense of personal commitment.

Layer eight – Systematic

Further to the qualities of the previous layer, musical compositions may be based on sets of newly generated musical materials, such as a scales and note rows, novel systems of harmonic generation, electronically created sounds or computer technology. The possibilities of musical discourse are systematically expanded.

Several formulations of these layers have been used to evaluate the musical work of students in a variety of settings. The following and shortest version may help to make it clear that they are cumulative. These criteria are also wholly positive and can be applied to composing, performing and audience-listening settings. The later statements take in all preceding ones. It is therefore possible to read down through the layers to where the evolving description best matches the music.

Eight cumulative developmental layers

Layer one	We enjoy/explore sounds
	(*and*)
Layer two	we classify/control sounds
	(*and*)
Layer three	we identify/produce expressive shapes, mood/ atmosphere
	(*and*)
Layer four	we identify/produce expressive shapes within common musical conventions

	(and)
Layer five	we perceive/produce expressive shapes in transformed or contrasting or surprising relationships
	(and)
Layer six	we locate structural relationships within specific idioms or styles
	(and)
Layer seven	musical perception/production shows strong personal identification and commitment
	(and)
Layer eight	we relate to music with sustained, original and involved independence.

It is important to stress that it has never been an intention to use criteria of this kind to assess students *per se*, but rather to evaluate the *music* they make and their conversations about music at a particular time. Only when a portfolio of such observations becomes available might it be possible to say something about the usual mode of a student's musical understanding.

Questions of validity

A major issue of validity concerns the extent to which the theory can 'comprehensively reflect the nature of musical behaviour' (Hargreaves and Zimmerman 1992). The integration of expressive, formal and value dimensions seems musically more comprehensive than many previous attempts to model musical development in terms of limited functions, for example measuring discrimination between sound materials (higher and lower, or longer and shorter) or attempting to study conservation of melodic or rhythmic elements. Nor is development assessed through secondary media, such as ability to handle graphic or notational representation, or by verbal description. The four levels with their eight layers between them capture something of the richness of musical understanding. There is also evidence that, although the original work focussed on composing, the theory may also contribute to our understanding of other musical activities. For example, the development of audience-listening may follow the same developmental sequence as composing (Hentschke 1993). The criterion statements have also been examined. França (Silva 1998) conducted a study using a version of the audience-listening criteria in Portuguese and found significant accordance between judges unfamiliar with the spiral in sorting the randomized sets of statements into a hierarchy which matches the predicted order (Swanwick and França 1999).

A second validity issue concerns the relationship between the developmental layers. Here there have been misunderstandings. For example, both Davies (1992) and Marsh (1995), observe that a child might work in several layers at the same time. This is of course true once the layers are present but it is necessary to distinguish between the sequence of their initial developmental emergence and subsequent interaction between them. A related point of criticism seems misplaced and is based on an incorrect view that Piaget thought each stage somehow separate from the others. For example, Gardner claimed that for Piaget 'the child does not even have access to his earlier forms of understanding. Once he is out of a stage, it is as though the prior stage had never happened' (Gardner 1973). Hargreaves also refers to 'Piagetian-style developmental discontinuities in thinking' (Hargreaves, Marshall *et al.* 2003: 153). This is a fairly widespread misreading. When writing about the development of children and what he calls the successive structures (sensory-motor, symbolic, preconceptual, intuitive and rational), Piaget (1951) tells us plainly:

> ... it is essential to understand how each of these behaviours is continued in the one that follows, the direction being from a lower to a higher equilibrium. It is for this reason that in our view a static analysis of discontinuous, stratified levels is unacceptable.
>
> (Piaget 1951: 291).

The same fundamental misunderstanding can sometimes be found among reviewers of the Swanwick/Tillman theory. For example, Barrett (2007: 612) claims that children are thought to 'move progressively through stages' and Burnard assumes that the theory asserts that children 'move from' one stage to another (Burnard 2007). Yet the original 1986 article took a quite different view when writing about the layers.

> We would emphasize that each one of these is swept up into the next developmental thrust and is repeatedly revisited. We regard these developments as cumulative and cyclical.
>
> (p. 316)

This point was stressed again in a subsequent publication.

> We do not merely pass through one of these modes but carry them forward with us to the next.
>
> (Swanwick 1988: 63–4)

The process of musical development is not a once-in-a-lifetime, linear affair. The broken ends of the helix indicate that the layers are recursive: for example, when people encounter new music or a performer begins to work on a new piece, or when a composer engages with a new computer music program, or an improviser starts up in a new acoustic or with a new group. In these situations of challenge they are likely to find themselves once again at the start of the process, exploring and controlling sound.

  There is of course individual difference at any age. In general though, very young children do not usually aspire to idiomatic authenticity but enter the world of music with some excitement over sound materials and enjoy control of them before engaging with vernacular conventions. By the age of 14 years or so, making music in idiomatic ways becomes a strong imperative for so many young people.

The spiral is not 'dualistic'. There is no separation of affective responses from cognition: they are integrated. Response to 'form' is a cognitive/affective construing of relationships between expressive gestures and has its own affective charge (Meyer 1956). In any case, we must not assume that responses to expressive, affective elements are developmentally inferior to those relating to structure and form (Barrett, 2007: 612). Simply because certain responses tend to be developmentally 'prior' does not denigrate them. Are the first infant words inferior to the speech of a five-year-old or, in developmental terms, a staggering achievement? At the age of one, a child might be able to stand, at the age of two she may walk and at three will probably stand, walk or hop, though she may also choose just to stand. The hierarchical initial emergence of these developmental processes is not usually a cause for concern and, in music, sound materials, expression, form and value become integrated and interactive.

There is also a dialectic relationship between the processes of assimilation (the left) and accommodation (the right). Once the layers have initially emerged, they become dynamic, interactive and recursive, playing what Bamberger calls 'a transformational dance with one another' (Bamberger, 2006: 71). Although they appear initially and developmentally in a fairly predictable sequence, sound materials are perceived as linked into expressive shapes and these expressive gestures may be combined into organic forms of feeling which have the power to reach into and relate to our personal and cultural histories. This is 'affective cognition' that characterizes musical encounters, permeates musical environments and lies at the heart of musical development.

Reliability

Questions have been raised as to whether the initial assessment of the compositions was sufficiently objective (Hargreaves and Zimmerman 1992). In addition, there are issues concerning the sample of children: for instance, could these findings be repeated in another cultural setting? Partly to meet such legitimate concerns, a replication of the original study was conducted in a different cultural setting, that of the Greek part of Cyprus (Swanwick 1991). Over 600 recordings of children's compositions were collected and from these, 28 were selected at random with a single sorting rule, that there should be seven items from each of four age groups: four–five; seven–eight; ten–eleven; 14–15. Seven primary and secondary music teachers were asked to independently assign each of the compositions to one of the criterion statements on a 'best fit' basis. The relationship between the actual ages of the children and the placing of compositions by the spiral criteria was statistically significant. There was a clear ascending relationship between age and the order of the criteria and high levels of inter-judge agreement (Swanwick 1994). The 'observers' in this study also attributed more developmental layers to the compositions of children when their composing was integrated with listening to music as part of a project called '*Contrasts*' (Stavrides 1995).

The developmental spiral has also been used comparatively in both England and Brazil to examine children's perception of music as 'audience-listeners' (Hentschke 1993; Hentschke and Ben 1999). Younger children tended to comment on sound materials and expressive character while recognition and enjoyment of the inter-relationships of musical form appears around the age of ten.

França argued that the theoretical basis of the spiral offers a valid general theory of musical understanding. Over several months she studied the musical activities of 20 Brazilian children between 11 and 13 years of age. Each child made tape recordings of three memorized piano performances, recorded three of their own compositions and discussed and/or made written notes on three recorded pieces of music, all of which were heard three times. These 'products' in the three modalities of performing, composing and audience-listening were assessed by judges – experienced teacher–musicians – using criterion statements based on the eight spiral modes. There were high levels of inter-judge reliability. An interesting finding is that, while most of the children's work displayed matching levels of musical understanding for composing and audience-listening, their performances of memorized music were usually less developed.

The education relevance of this kind of study may be significant, particularly in terms of the range of activities suggested in or mandated by curriculum guidelines or expected in schools. Musical development may not be symmetrical across performing, composing and audience-listening for different individuals and this suggests the value of access to engagement in all three modalities. It is also clear that activities in one modality, for example performing, can influence and enhance another, such as composing and audience-listening. Other researchers have drawn on this developmental paradigm while investigating various aspects of teaching and learning and to assist in curriculum evaluation and development and music therapy (Hentschke and Oliveira 1999; Markea 2003; Uricoechea 2003). In the current UK music national curriculum, the eight 'Attainment Target' levels contain oblique similarities to the developmental spiral, from exploration and control of sounds, to idiomatic performances and independent musical judgement. Though little is said about musical expression or structural relationships, there seems to be a recognition of the broad sweep of musical development, though no references are given.

Bearing in mind the criteria discussed earlier, this theory still seems valid, in that it is founded on a broad and comprehensive view of the nature of musical experience observed across a range of activities. The various empirical replications and extensions of the initial project strengthen claims of reliability. The model is premised on qualitatively differentiated elements and early structures are integrated into later ones. There is no evidence to contradict the claim that the musical layers initially unfold in an invariant developmental sequence and there is some evidence that this developmental sequence is culturally widespread.

Implications for the curriculum

The first main implication is in terms of broad curriculum planning and provision. Curriculum activities may be focused toward specific aspects of musical development at different broadly identified stages, working with the grain of development. In the very early years of schooling and at pre-school level, sensory exploration and the encouragement of manipulative control would be the main aim. In the first years of schooling this could be taken further forward and expressive elements of music would come more sharply into focus. This may involve movement, dance, drama and visual images, all of which might help promote, stimulate and intensify awareness of expressiveness. By the age of ten or so we would also be looking to further the production and recognition of musical speculation, an awareness of the uniquely contextual nature of the contrasts, transformations and repetitions essential to musical form. Older students in high schools will be seeking to enter a 'grown-up', idiomatic world of music. The resources of formal education are not always organized to match their musical development. Lucy Green has shown how rock musicians teach themselves, perhaps with a little help from their peers. They tend to choose the music they want to work with and towards, learning informally, by aural copying from admired models, usually on CD or some other recorded format. During this process they move easily between the roles of audience-listening, composing and performing. They often work in haphazard ways, beginning by approximating whole pieces and are strongly influenced by peer groups (Green 2001). This reminds us of Vygotsky's 'zone of proximal development', the space between any level of independent learning and additional levels of possible achievement, perhaps with adult guidance but also in interaction with more advanced peers (Vygotsky 1978).

Idiomatic requirements include appropriate instrumental and performance settings and equipment, along with the expertise of a range of teachers or music leaders, so that there can be some basis of choice for the student who is becoming idiomatically aware or who has a strong commitment to music. Drawing on the resources of musical agencies and musicians outside of the school setting is one powerful strategy in providing elements of idiomatic authenticity which makes more likely the emergence of musical autonomy and valuing.

Individual development

The second way in which an understanding of musical development might inform music education is in individual development. Although schools are organized into classes, people develop as individuals. It is surely helpful for a teacher to be able to relate to developmental change for individuals, with awareness of subsequent possibilities. This may enable the teachers to ask a stimulating question, make a suggestion or choose material that may have more meaning and developmental consequences for the individual. Teachers can become alert to the next layer, for example helping students to move from the repetitions of the vernacular to more interesting and engaging deviations, speculating with musical form. It may be necessary from time-to-time to move to a prior layer in order to move to other layers more securely musical. For instance, it may be of benefit to take a facile instrumentalist back to the enjoyment of the exploratory sensory mode. This may help counteract habits of inattention to sound quality that may have been acquired by learning a performance repertoire by rote, imitation and decoding of notation.

Evaluating the work of students

Furthermore, if teachers have access to a musically comprehensive theory of development, they may be better able to make sensitive evaluations of students' music making and perception. This is particularly true of projects, such as those sponsored by *Youth Music*, and of such schemes as *Sing Up* and the widening range of activities in which students may be involved. In the UK, *Musical Futures*, an emphasis on non-formal teaching and informal learning is encouraging 'a shift in the role the teacher takes in facilitating and supporting music activities'. This is bound to produce diverse and often unpredictable outcomes and it seems important for those involved to have some general understanding of underlying musical development, whatever the specific context. In situations where specific, limited outcomes are not predicted and activities are open-ended, it is crucial to have generic ways of evaluating what students are doing, if only to be able to make appropriate formative responses.

Progression

The recursive nature of musical development is particularly suggestive for organizing teaching sequences or musical projects. In one sense progression in music may be thought of as linear, quantitative or horizontal. We may see education in music as proceeding from relatively simple to more complex and technically advanced material. But progression may also be seen as layered, as qualitative or vertical. For example, a curriculum sequence may be viewed as recurring spirals along the horizontal where the level of musical material changes over time, perhaps from high-low or loud-soft distinctions, through pentatonic melodies to other tonal series or harmonic progressions. The 'vertical' dimension informs the critical judgment of teachers and students in the 'here-and-now' and raises the question of how many layers are involved in musical production or in-audience response. The vertical is to do with the *quality* of music education encounters whenever and in whatever setting. It is also an attempt to answer Bamberger's question *What develops in musical development?* We might hope that the leaders of music education projects and those who develop National Curricula in various countries are aware of the implications.

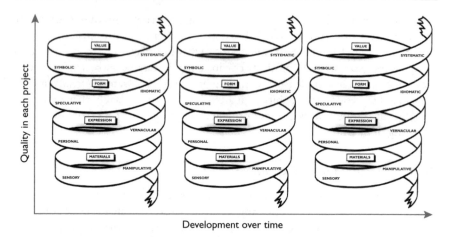

Development over time

Figure 5.2 Dimensions of development: the horizontal and the vertical.

Conclusion

In summary we have seen that:

- Musical development may be construed as consisting of cumulative layers, each bringing in an additional quality.
- Once students have developed beyond early childhood, they may move freely between all or any of the qualitative layers, provided that the activity is rich enough in musical possibilities.
- Developmental sequences are recursive and will be reactivated in new musical contexts.
- Understanding musical development is suggestive for curriculum design, for organizing educational activities and for interpreting the music making and musical responses of students.
- Integration of different musical modalities may provide richer opportunities for musical development.
- As well as providing musical models and structures in cultural settings, it is important to leave room for assimilatory activity, where the student absorbs and decides for him or herself.

The potential richness of activities is important. Using spiral-related criteria, Jane Cheung-Yung found in Hong Kong secondary schools that some computer programs limit what is musically possible (Cheung-Yung 2001). Similarly, it appears that Bamberger's 'natural experiment', which gave students opportunities to work at their own pace with sound feedback, while enabling them to produce coherent tonal melodies, also confined musical opportunities to the vernacular by requiring a 'sensible tune' (Bamberger 2006). It is obviously possible to choose the layer in which we function. For example, walking a very familiar route from the train station to the office, the author hardly ever calls up higher levels of cognitive functioning but slips into sensory-motor auto-pilot which frees up the mind, perhaps to think about writing this chapter. On the other hand, walking in a strange city requires more analytical thinking about the direction of travel, looking for street names and perhaps having recourse to the notation of a map. Similarly, predictable vernacular common-places may be apposite when music functions as background, for example, when driving or providing a comfortable or socially affirming ambience. Speculation or surprise may wrench the music inappropriately into the foreground of our attention. It can be argued though that bringing music to the foreground of attention is a major aim of music education and that as many layers as possible should be involved.

It is not at all clear that formal education (schooling) will always necessarily provide the optimum environment for musical development. Much work remains to be done on musical learning outside of instructional programs as part of lifelong enculturation and on the effect of different levels of instructional framing, especially on less-directive and more loosely sequenced or informal teaching and learning. The future development of music education may depend not so much on schools as we know them but on opportunities in local communities and the various musical communities of the 'web'. Musical development is likely to take place within increasingly pluralized contexts and we may expect existing assumptions and theories to be further challenged by this plurality. Indeed, it may be argued that we should look for quite different theoretical perspectives. For example, David Hargreaves and others (Hargreaves, Marshall *et al.*, 2003) have focused on the concept of musical identity and four levels of social interaction; the individual, the interpersonal, the institutional and the cultural. It seems likely though that, even in a world where music learning and musical encounters take multiple forms, there will still be a need for broad generic theories of music and musical development, rooted in inter-culturally shared concepts of the value and function of music and continually tested by evidence. Without such theories, however contested they may be, music education becomes fragmented, while isolated pieces of research may lack coherence and struggle to find professional relevance.

Reflective questions

1   Listen to some student compositions and performances. How useful are cumulative criteria outlined in this chapter for evaluating them? Give reasons for any judgements that you make.
2   Does the developmental theory presented in this chapter answer the question raised in the title?

References

Bamberger, J. (2006), 'What Develops in Musical Development?' in G. E. Macpherson (ed.) *The Child as Musician: a Handbook of Musical Development* Oxford: Oxford University Press.

Barrett, M. (1997) 'Invented Notations: A view of Young Children's Musical Thinking', *Research Studies in Music Education*, 8: 2–14.

Barrett, M. S. (1999) 'Children and Music Development Perspectives', *International Music Education Symposium*, University of Tasmania.

Bentley, A. (1966) *Measures of Musical Abilities*. London, Harrap.

Bunting, R. (1977) *The Common Language of Music, Music in the Secondary School Curriculum*, York: York University Press.

Burnard, P. (2007) 'Routes to Understanding Musical Creativity', in L. Bresler (ed.) *International Handbook of Research in Arts Education*, Dordrecht, Springer.

Cheung-Yung, J. W. Y. (2001) 'The Effects of Computerised Music Instruction on the Attitude and Achievement of Children: with Special Reference to Strong and Weak Framing', *Music and Drama*, London, Institute of Education, University of London.

Christensen, C. (1992) *Music Composition, Invented Notation and Reflection: Tools for Music Learning and Assessment*, New Jersey: Rutgers.

Crain, W. (1992) *Theories of Development*, New Jersey, Prentice Hall.

Davidson, L. and Scripp L. (1988) 'Young Children's Musical Representations: Windows on Cognition', in J. A. Sloboda (ed.) *Generative processes in Music: The Psychology of Performance, Improvisation, and Composition*, Oxford, Clarendon Press.

Davies, C. (1992) 'Listen to My Song: A study of Songs Invented by Children aged 5 to 7 years', British Journal of Music Education, 9(1): 19–48.

Gardner, H. (1973) *The Arts and Human Development*, New York, Wiley.

Green, L. (2001) *How Popular Musicians Learn: a Way Ahead for Music Education*, London and New York: Ashgate Press.

Gromko, J. E. (1994) 'Children's Invented Notations as Measures of Musical Understanding', *Psychology of Music*, 22(2): 136–47.

Hargreaves, D. J. (1986) *The Developmental Psychology of Music*, Avon, Cambridge University Press.

Hargreaves, D. J., Marshall, N. A. and North, A.C. (2003) 'Music Education in the Twenty-First century: a Psychological Perspective', British Journal of Music Education, 20(2): 147–63.

Hargreaves, D. J. and Zimmerman M. (1992) 'Developmental Theories of Music Learning', in R. Colwell (ed.) *Handbook of Research on Music Teaching and Learning*, New York, Macmillan.

Hentschke, L. (1993) *Musical Development: Testing a Model in the Audience-Listening Setting*, London: University of London, Institute of Education.

Hentschke, L. and Ben L. D. (1999) 'The Assessment of Audience-Listening: Testing a Model in the Educational Setting of Brazil', *Music Education Research*, 1(2): 127–46.

Hentschke, L. and Oliveira A. (1999) 'Music Curriculum Development and Evaluation based on Swanwick's theory', *International Journal of Music Education* 34(1): 14–29.

Markea, G. G. (2003) 'Evaluation in Music Education in Greece', *Educate* 3(1): 39–45.

Marsh, K. (1995) 'Children's Singing Games: Composition in the Playground?', *Research Studies in Music Education*, 4.

McPherson, G. E., Ed. (2006) *The Child as musician: a Handbook of Musical Development*, Oxford, Oxford University Press.

Meyer, L. B. (1956) *Emotion and Meaning in Music*, Chicago and London: University of Chicago and University of California Press.

Moog, H. (1976) *The Musical Experience of the Pre-School Child*, London, Schott.

Piaget, J. (1951), *Play, Dreams and Imitation in Childhood*, New York: Norton and Co.

Serafine, M. L. (1980) 'Piagetian Research in Music', *Council for Research in Music Education Bulletin* 62: 1–21.

Silva, M. C. C. F. (1998) *Composing, Performing and Audience-Listening as Symmetrical Indicators of Musical Understanding*, London: University of London, Institute of Education.

Sloboda, J. and Deliège I. (eds) (1996) *Musical Beginnings: Origins and Development of Musical Competence*, Oxford: Oxford University Press.

Stavrides, M. (1995) 'The Interaction of Audience-Listening and Composing: A study in Cyprus schools', *Music and Drama*, London: University of London, Institute of Education.

Swanwick, K. (1979) *A Basis for Music Education*, London: Routledge.

Swanwick, K. (1983) *The Arts in Education: Dreaming or Wide Awake?* London: University of London Institute of Education.

Swanwick, K. (1991) 'Further Research on the Developmental Spiral', *Psychology of Music*, 19: 22–32.

Swanwick, K. (1994) *Musical Knowledge: Intuition, Analysis and Music Education*, London and New York: Routledge.

Swanwick, K. and França C. C. (1999) 'Composing, Performing and Audience-Listening as Indicators of Musical Understanding', *British Journal of Music Education*, 16(1): 3–17.

Swanwick, K. and Tillman J. (1986) 'The Sequence of Musical Development: a Study of Children's Composition', *British Journal of Music Education*, 3(3): 305–39.

Tafuri, J. (2009) *Infant Musicality*, Bologna: Ashgate.

Tillman, J. (1987) 'Towards a Model of the Development of Musical Creativity: a Study of the Compositions of Children aged 3–11', *Institute of Education*, London: University of London.

Upitis, R. (1992) *Can I Play You My Song? The Compositions and Invented Notations of Children*, Portsmouth, NJ: Heinemann Educational Books.

Uricoechea, A. S. (2003) 'Rethinking Music Therapy With the Mentally Handicapped', *Voices* 3(2).

Vygotsky, L. S. (1978) *Mind in Society: the Development of Higher Psychological Processes*, Cambridge, Mass: Harvard University Press.

Part II

Political Perspectives

Chapter 6

Music education and social justice

Towards a radical political history and vision

Paul Woodford

Introduction

Although music teacher educators in the United States and other western coun-tries have long expressed concern about issues relating to social (in)equality, including class, ethnicity and, more recently, gender and disability, those and similar terms are increasingly being subsumed in the professional literature and at academic conferences under the rubric of social justice. The latter term functions in a variety of ways including, for example, as a rallying cry for those on the left of contemporary politics in support of various groups perceived as marginalized or otherwise disadvantaged, as a convenient shorthand for those sharing similar interests and concerns and, for some academics, as a goal for all education. The general idea is that teachers should be responsive to all students' needs and seek to accommodate those from diverse backgrounds while being more inclusive with respect to curricular content. The latter is usually interpreted to mean that teachers should ensure 'fair and equitable representation of musics' in the classroom (Sands 2007: 47; Wright 2001; Karlsen and Westerlund 2010). This implies that they should be careful not to inadvertently relegate any particular music or genre – and thus also the people who are invested in that music, or whose values it represents – to secondary status by treating them as 'exotic' or somehow deficient and therefore of only limited interest. This approach to curriculum is thought to be transformative because it challenges students to rethink their own understandings of music while also developing in them those qualities, dispositions and habits of mind that are needed if they are to contribute to a more just and equitable society (Elliott 2007).

This of course is a political goal. It thus seems strange that proponents of social justice in music education often emphasize musical diversity and inclusivity while neglecting to explicitly teach students how music and music education relate to politics and other forms of experience. This should be a cause for concern, for as philosopher John Dewey (1933a) once said, if teachers and students are to avoid complacency and contribute to the creation of a better world then they will need to know their own histories and be challenged to explore the often contentious social and political issues of the day. Teachers and teacher–educators have a responsibility to defend education by becoming politically informed and by taking 'social action that will improve conditions' (p. 47), otherwise they will be more susceptible to manipulation by the rich and powerful or rendered 'passive tools of antiquated traditions' (p. 45). Historians and philosophers of education can assist in this regard by discovering and allying themselves with 'the social forces which promote educational aims' and by uncovering and opposing 'the vested interests which nullify ideals and reduce them to mere flourishes or to phrases on paper' (p. 48).

My purpose in the following pages is to provide a larger historical context for understanding the politics of social justice in music education by revealing how much of the profession's thinking during the past half century (including a tendency towards political avoidance in curricular and other professional matters) was profoundly influenced by early Cold War politics in America and the growth of neoliberalism. As readers will learn, the aesthetic education movement in music, which arose in the United States during the 1940s and 1950s and subsequently became the dominant music education philosophy there and in Britain for much of the remainder of the century (Rainbow and Cox 2006; Swanwick 1979), was shaped by right-wing democratic elites and members of the American military–industrial complex wishing to stifle political dissent through education reform. Beginning in the late 1930s and continuing to the present day, the latter rejected Dewey's socially progressive ideas of equality and participatory democracy as utopian and as contributing to social instability (Westbrook 1991: xv). Whether American music educators in the 1940s and 1950s realized it or not, their rapid and enthusiastic rallying 'under the banner of aesthetic education' made them complicit in a larger effort by the political right wing to unify and mobilize the country so that it could better flex its military, economic and cultural muscles worldwide (McCarthy and Goble 2002: 20; White 1992). By declaring that music should be taught for its own sake, divorced from the world and its problems, music teachers were aligning themselves with democratic realists who believed in rule by social elites and experts and who were deeply suspicious of notions of social justice that attempted to go beyond negative rights such as equality of opportunity.

This decision may well have helped American music educators to preserve their school programmes during the Cold War but at the cost of discouraging professional controversy that might be perceived as threatening to capitalism and to the religious right (Tanner 1988). Henceforth, and continuing until the present day, mainstream music education in schools and universities was conceived as involving technical and musical 'problems of excellence' (Zinn 2003: 8) and not, as Dewey would have had it, as preparing students to become informed moral agents of social change. Music teacher education became a matter of training undergraduates as expert pedagogues and musicians who could teach children how to perceive and appreciate music's formal properties. Musical experts and connoisseurs were deemed 'the only reliable source of standards' and thus the measure of educational success (Broudy 1958: 84). Given this understanding of the profession's history in America, it is perhaps only to be expected that many of today's music teachers in that country, but also in Britain and elsewhere, 'are loath to engage in their task politically or to conceive of their role in political as well as musical terms' (Jorgensen 2004: 5). This chapter accordingly seeks to reveal some of the historical roots of vested political interests that have long opposed social progress in education, music education inclusive, by silencing teachers or diverting their attention away from political matters affecting them but that they will need to know and confront if their calls for social justice are to be more than just romantic rhetoric.

'No half-way house' vs 'the American way'

In order to understand the early history of the aesthetic education movement in music, one first needs to know something about politics in America during the Great Depression and the Second World War. As historian Howard Zinn (2003: 339) explains, before the Second World War, 'there was an idea in the air, becoming clearer and stronger, an idea not just in the theories of Karl Marx but in the dreams of writers and artists through the Ages: that people might cooperatively use the treasures of the earth to make life better for everyone, not just a few.' Many Americans had suffered through the deprivation and social instability caused by the Depression and were committed to achieving social progress. The best known advocate of this kind of thinking was Dewey (1859–1952), whose ideal of participatory democracy was based on a faith in the ability of the common man and woman to contribute intelligently to society, politics and culture. Intensely critical of capitalism, which he blamed for many of society's problems, including art's segregation from the masses, Dewey called for a radical restructuring of American society along the lines of what was then being proposed by social democratic parties in Europe. This would entail the redistribution of social and political power and of the country's resources and wealth, including art (Dewey 1934a). Art had to be made more accessible to the masses because 'any revolution that stops short of affecting the imagination and emotions of man' was bound to fail (Dewey 1934b: 344). 'The first stirrings of dissatisfaction and the first intimations of a better future,' he observed, 'are always found in works of art' (pp. 345–46). Art fostered imagination, empathy and moral judgement, all of which were necessary to the improvement of society, and was thus far from only peripheral to Dewey's social democratic politics. Indeed, according to Westbrook (1991: 401), his 1934 book *Art As Experience* remains 'one of the most powerful statements' of his radical politics. During the 1930s, Dewey argued vociferously that social democratic reform was the only way to ensure 'a decent standard of living for more than a fraction of the American people' (Dewey 1934a: 289). Politics, art and education should all have a democratic and thus also a moral and meliorative purpose insomuch as they empowered the masses to reclaim ownership over the design and direction of their lives and to enjoy the fruits of their labour (Dewey 1933a; Dewey 1933b).

All this was anathema to rich capitalists and democratic realists who believed that the masses were incapable of participating intelligently in public life, including in art and music, and who conceived of democracy and education as 'means of social control rather than liberation' (Crist 2003: 458). Social stability and effective government were the goals, not participatory democracy, as the latter would only lead to chaos and weakness. Given that much of the world at that time was subject to totalitarian regimes, rule by corporate elites and experts was seen as the only realistic policy for society, and after the Second World War this policy was promulgated to the world through the Central Intelligence Agency, the United States Information Agency, the State Department and American-controlled international institutions such as the World Bank and the International Monetary Fund. To cut a long story short, these democratic realists – who much later would be called neoconservatives and neoliberals – conflated the real and ideal, arguing that American democratic elitism should constitute a regulative ideal for the free world. Democratic society, according to this realist way of thinking, was virtually synonymous with a 'corporate capitalist economy regulated by a centralized state directed by administrative experts, which, even when it works, betrays an identification of the good with the goods' (Westbrook 1991: xv). The concept of democracy itself was reduced to a set of negative rights (e.g., equality of opportunity) and procedural rules governing competition for the popular vote and not, as Dewey had envisioned it, as an ethical ideal and way of life motivated by concern for the common weal.

Wary of Dewey's politics, right-wing political pundits mounted an aggressive public campaign aimed at undermining him and other social progressives by blaming them for many of the failings of American education and society. It is difficult for us today to appreciate the politics of the late 1940s and 1950s, but growing anti-communist hysteria during those years made it increasingly dangerous for American artists, musicians and public figures to espouse socialist or social democratic causes in their work, as they would likely be subjected to surveillance by the FBI, as actually happened with Dewey in his dotage (Zimring 1984), or summoned to testify before Senator Joseph McCarthy's Senate Permanent Subcommittee on Investigations, as happened with socialist sympathizer Aaron Copland in 1953 (Crist 2005). During the early years of the Cold War, so-called serious music and art were valued by government and by many democratic élites on both the political left and right as a defence against middle and low-brow culture, and because they were useful to the latter as propaganda demonstrating the superiority of the 'American way' of life (Saunders 1999: 1, quoted in DeLapp 2004: 318). But while the serious arts were encouraged, prominent right-wing leaders were fearful of populist composers and musicians such as Copland and Pete Seeger whose music espoused socially progressive ideas, and those right-wing leaders attempted to shape public opinion by denigrating accessible music. During the 1950s, musical inaccessibility became a 'political virtue' as serious composers and performers retreated for their own safety into formalism and academia and generally avoided talk of politics (Ross 2007: 401; Crist 2003).

Bruner: 'after John Dewey, what?'

It was no accident that aesthetic education came to the fore in the late 1940s and 1950s, as democratic élites on the extreme right of American politics also set the terms for music education during the Cold War. Music teacher educators during the late 1940s and throughout the 1950s were aware of the persecution of musical social progressives like Copland and Seeger and, further, realized that some sort of unifying philosophy was needed to fill the void left by the decline of progressive education, especially given the repeated demands by those on the political right for a greater investment in science and the military. Fearful of Soviet technological advances after the testing of their first atomic weapon in 1949 and the success of Sputnik I in 1957, prominent American educational reformers such as Admiral Hyman Rickover had been calling for greater emphasis on the development of intellectual and other forms of ability over democratic values and citizenship. Leading music educators in the 1950s such as Charles Leonhard, Robert W. House and the young Bennett Reimer (1959) all concurred, arguing that music had nothing to do with politics and that music education should instead focus on developing children's aesthetic potential through exposure to great music, thereby helping them to transcend the real world. They may well have had no choice but to take that position given the politics of the time, as it was clear that the federal government was going to instigate curricular reforms through its new Office of Education (created in 1954) and that business, military and other elites were to have a significant say in any future proposed reforms at the national level. Education, to paraphrase Rickover, 'was too important to leave to educators' (Efland 1988: 262). The country needed the best minds to shape the future of education so that America could fight the Cold War.

This was the beginning of the politicization of public education in the United States. Whereas progressive education had previously provided an umbrella philosophy for all school subjects, each subject now had 'to stand on its own merits and the leaders of the various disciplines had to persuade policymakers [and business and other interests] that their own subjects were truly important enough to remain part of the newly-emerging curriculum' (Mark 1998: 107). From that point onward, business, military and other elites felt that they were entitled to have a strong voice in the shaping of national education policy either through direct access to the Office of Education, and in some cases to the President, and through the shaping of public opinion through private foundations, media outlets, and various think tanks that they owned or controlled. Music teacher leaders saw the proverbial writing on the wall when the 1958 National Defense Education Act called for improvements to the teaching of mathematics, science and other so-called *serious* subjects that were deemed important to national security. They realized that they had to convince government and the military–industrial complex that music education was also a serious subject if they were to preserve a place for music in the nation's public schools and universities. An additional spur to music education reform was the publication in 1961 of a pamphlet by the Educational Policies Commission of the National Education Association (NEA) declaring that the central purpose of American education was to teach children how to think rationally, as that would allow them the freedom to make intelligent choices. This meant that, as in science and mathematics education, the emphasis in music classes had to be on the 'structure of the discipline', that is, the knowledge of structural principles that children needed to 'achieve mastery of a subject matter' (Efland 1988: 263). Music was to be taught 'as an objective and unbiased producer of knowledge for its own sake' (p. 264).

Unfortunately, neither the writers of the NEA pamphlet nor leaders of the Music Educators National Conference (MENC) seemed to realize that this call for educational reform was based on an instrumentalist notion of reason that better served capitalist or totalitarian than democratic interests. Children were to learn how to think rationally for its own sake but without necessarily ever having to grapple with the moral and other complexities and uncertainties of life. As one contemporary educational philosopher warned, without this experience and knowledge of the 'great political, economic, moral and religious issues of our time' thinking remains maddeningly abstract and more likely to indoctrinate children to the status quo than it is to prepare them to critically engage with the world (Brameld 1961: 11). There is also the matter of how this educational scheme favoured the already privileged with the requisite cultural capital to meet curricular objectives and expectations based on that abstract notion of rationality. Even when provided with equality of educational opportunity in schools, children from lower socio-economic classes and from disadvantaged or marginalized groups, or those who were simply unwilling to submit to the authority of the military industrial complex and its doctrinal system – in this case as represented by the classics and related pedagogical practices – were likely to perform poorly compared to their more socially privileged counterparts. This was intentional, for as Dewey (1927/1946: 200) observed, the American education system was never designed to adequately serve the broader educational needs of the masses, as that would be a threat to the 'captains of capitalistic society'. America, Dewey wrote, had rejected 'dynastic and oligarchic aristocracies' only to replace them with an economic class that 'claims to rule, not in virtue of birth and hereditary status, but in virtue of ability'. Then, as now, schools were in significant part intended to sort children according to ability so that the more able could be recruited into 'a shifting, unstable' managing élite (pp. 203–04; see also Zinn and Macedo 2005).

Predictably, MENC followed the lead of the NEA in defining musical rationality purely in terms of abstract perceptual skills and abilities with respect to traditional musical concepts (i.e., harmony, rhythm, melody, etc.) and musical syntax (Hartshorn 1963). In order for music to qualify as an academic discipline, it too had to be taught systematically and sequentially as abstract skills and knowledge divorced from real world problems. Like in science and mathematics education, the aim became 'progress toward abstraction' and 'a weaning away from the obviousness of superficial experience' (Bruner 1962/1970: 121). This was the exact opposite of what Dewey had been proposing, which was that thought should vivify and enrich everyday experience. He would have abhorred the idea of teaching music as an academic discipline because it led to its segregation from politics and other realms of experience that were important not just to under-standing but also to the pursuit of freedom and equality, not to mention personal enjoyment (Dewey 1927/1946). For the next several decades, and following the publication of Leonard Meyer's *Emotion and Meaning in Music* in 1956, music was taught and appreciated for its structural complexity and not, as progressive educators had urged, for its potential to change the world.

One of the more pure historical expressions of the realist worldview in American music education is found in the report of the 1963 Yale Seminar on Music Education which concluded that school music was failing to develop in children the performance skills and understanding of musical structure that they needed to keep up with a rapidly changing society (Palisca 1963). The report similarly recommended that school programs should focus on developing children's musi-cality with reference to the building blocks of musical structure (i.e., melody, rhythm, harmony and form) and syntax. Children needed to develop 'a deeper understanding of musical processes', and this was to be accomplished through exposure to great music (Anon. 1963: 86). Perhaps not surprisingly, given Admiral Rickover's lack of faith in teachers and Jerome Bruner's assertion in his influential book *The Process of Knowledge* (1960) that curricular reform required the involvement of the best minds in each discipline, few music educators were invited to the symposium. The decision to limit the involvement of music teachers was probably based on the belief that music teachers were on the periphery and not at the core of the discipline of music. Bruner, for example, talks in a later book of scholars, scientists, artists and 'men of affairs' coming together 'with talented teachers continually to revise and refresh our curriculums' (Bruner 1962/1970: 125). Teachers, it seems, were perceived as having little knowledge of their own. Their job was only to deliver the curriculum.

Bruner's *The Process of Knowledge* reported on a review of science and mathe-matics education reform held at the 1959 Woods Hole Conference and, in another book published in 1962, entitled *On Knowing: Essays for the Left Hand,* he proposed that similar knowledge structures might be identified and taught in social studies and the humanities. One of the influential people involved in estab-lishing the Yale Seminar for Music Education was physicist Jerrold Zacharias, a member of the Panel on Education Research and Development of the President's Science Advisory Committee, who was interested in music and had served as an advisor to Bruner following the Woods Hole Conference. Zacharias and other panel members had expressed concern that education was becoming too lopsided in favour of science and proposed that arts education would benefit from similar reforms and that, vice versa, an education in music and the arts would help to create better scientists. They were particularly worried about what they considered to be the failure of schools to produce a more musically literate and active society and recommended that the school music curriculum be examined in light of that fact. Also not surprisingly, given this mandate and the backgrounds of participants in the Yale Seminar – most of whom were university-based musicologists, performers, music critics, orchestra conductors and other faculty who were trained under and indebted to the German analytic tradition – their report concluded that schools were not keeping up with 'twentieth century musical developments' (Mark and Gary 2007: 400). They were referring to *serious* contemporary music such as serialism and not, with the exception of jazz, recent developments in popular music. The fact that two jazz 'experts' were invited to the seminar suggests that academics were by then beginning to recognize that jazz too was *serious* music. Popular music was viewed as degenerative.

The report of the Yale Seminar was essentially calling for greater continuity between school and university programmes and between music education and the professional world of *serious* musicians. Leading music educators agreed with this recommendation and with the general scientific methodological approach to teaching and learning music that was outlined in the seminar's final report. Charles Leonhard (1965), for example, stated in the *Music Educators Journal* that there was growing recognition among music educators of 'the need for emphasis on objectives directly related to music, the need for structure and sequence in the music program [and] the need for systematic evaluation of the results of the music program' (p. 60). From this perspective, and also that of music educators associated with the tradition of aesthetic education in the succeeding years, if school music was to have any political purpose at all it was to 'develop the useful [musical] powers of every individual' (Leonhard and House 1959/1972: 75). As with the NEA's claim with respect to the development of rationality in children, this aim was said to be an expression of democratic values.

But, as already suggested, if children have no idea what democracy means and of its relevance to everyday musical life beyond the school, they might just as easily use whatever powers they develop in pursuit of quite different ends. Further, if children are taught, as Leonhard and House insisted, that only great music represents 'true and enduring values' and can lead to 'true self-realization', and that there is only one educationally valid way to think and learn – sequentially and systematically – then music education too becomes 'a means of social control rather than liberation' (Crist 2003: 458). There can be no significant freedom if the ends are already predetermined or, as already explained, children lack knowledge of and experience dealing with the moral, political or other dilemmas of the day in which music is often implicated. Clearly, the attitude of the academics and other musical elites involved in the Yale Seminar was that all children who were able should learn to think like highly trained classical and jazz experts. From their perspective, and also that of leading music education academics such as Leonhard and House (1959/1972), teaching for democratic citizenship and other 'extrinsic values' would only frustrate that purpose while contributing to 'musical delinquency' (p. 75).

Dewey (1933a), however, would have regarded this conception of music education as the development of highly specialized musical experts as 'colorless, because neutral, in most of the vital social issues of the day' (p. 45) and a danger to society because it contributed to intellectual segregation and political impotence (unless propped up by capitalist or totalitarian interests). In any event, and given the professional backgrounds of the participants in the Yale Seminar, their stated interest in achieving greater continuity between school and university, and their proposal to create publicly-funded academies and schools for the exceptionally talented, they were probably less interested in educating and musically empowering the masses than they were in ensuring that future music and music education majors were prepared for university. There was no recognition that school and university music programmes might serve somewhat different educational and social purposes.

In the end, the Yale Seminar had little direct effect on school music in the United States not only because few music educators were involved and practicing teachers resented some of the criticisms levelled against them, but also because they regarded some of the recommendations as self-serving and thus suspect. It was also evident to them that the seminar's participants were remarkably out of touch with the social realities and needs of public schools. The chief value of the seminar was that it contributed to 'a climate conducive to change' the ends of which were already to some extent predetermined by government (Mark and Gary 2007: 400). If nothing else, and given that music educators were not adequately represented among the seminar's participants, it must have contributed to a sense of professional vulnerability among them, because the seminar literally had the ears of government. It had been sponsored by several major science organizations, the US Office of Education and elements of the military–industrial complex and was observed by a specialist for music education from the Cultural Affairs Branch of the Office of Education. More than ever before, music teachers must have felt a need to justify themselves not only to government and to the military–industrial complex but also now to music academics. The Yale Seminar was probably an important stimulus to the growth of the aesthetic education movement in music in that it provided additional incentive for music educators to develop philosophical rationales that they could use to convince academics and politicians that teaching music was a discipline in its own right that could contribute to the Cold War effort.

McCarthy: 'the past in the present'

Throughout much of the world today, while the Cold War is a thing of the past, we can observe many interesting parallels with the America of the 1940s and 1950s, including calls after 9/11 for surveillance and possible suppression of musicians, actors and academics on the political left and the consequent retreat of the latter into 'discourses that threaten no one' (Hedges 2009: 91); a belief in objectivity and absolute truths among many on the extreme political right; a corresponding educational emphasis on the development of job-related skills, factual knowledge and national standards at the expense of democratic values;

calls for the elimination of music and other so-called 'frills'; and a general climate of uncertainty and fear attributable in part to the War on Terror but also to the economic instability brought about by neoliberal market fundamentalism that discourages political involvement among the masses (Ginsberg and Lyche 2008).

State education systems and Dewey also continue to be blamed for all of the economic and social ills of the western world, which is ironic considering that many of our economic and military problems and dilemmas experienced during the past half century – including the wars in Iraq and Afghanistan and the recent economic recession – were in significant part caused by unbridled capitalism and/ or political and military hubris. As was the case with President Franklin Roosevelt's New Deal program during the Great Depression, today's economic stimulus programmes and reforms, including massive cuts to social services and education in the United States and England are necessary to save capitalism from itself! It was for precisely these reasons that Dewey (1927/1946) warned that the masses were more in danger of its leaders and experts than the other way around. But he was not as influential as his critics often suppose. Although a leading philosopher of the twentieth century, many of his educational ideas were never actually put into practice because, as already explained, they were considered a threat to rich capitalists and to the religious right. And even when teachers drew on his work for inspiration, they often bastardized it by stripping it of its moral and political dimensions or, in the case of curriculum developers, by re-packaging and marketing it as 'ready-made' lessons (Tanner 1988: 477).

Not all that much has changed in American music education since the Yale Seminar, probably in significant part because music teacher education remains divorced from the study of politics, economics and other subjects that can contribute to students' understanding of the teaching profession and its problems. Students enrolled in university undergraduate music education programmes, as Colwell (in press) says, 'gain little or no competence in liberal (general) education' where they might 'encounter the big, tough questions about themselves and their place in the country and in the world' and thereby also gain a better under-standing of their own professional roles and responsibilities. Nor have music education historians paid sufficient attention to the 'painful or difficult dimen-sions of music education – for example, the ills of competition, lack of recognition and participation of minority groups in mainstream practices and institutions, or tensions between the music industry and the practices of music teaching and learning' (McCarthy 2003: 125). In consequence, music teachers often have a distorted sense of their own history as apolitical and unproblematic and thus fail to realize that the profession's energies are increasingly being 'harnessed to the services of power' as its leaders look to the corporate world for leadership and financial partnerships (Phenix 1959: 270). As Eklund-Koza (2006) argues, MENC's collaboration with the corporate world has shaped the profession, and music teaching and learning, by 'keeping obsolete [and consumer-driven] musical practices alive in schools' and by contributing to a culture of high stakes testing and assessment that may be antithetical to critical thinking and thus also to the pursuit of equality and social justice (p. 32). This is perhaps only to be expected since teachers and the public have by now been subjected to decades of relentless propaganda from corporate leaders, conservative think tanks and politicians insisting that 'business knows best' and that standardized tests should 'dictate what is taught' (Zakaras and Lowell 2008: 101). As is demonstrated shortly, this de facto policy has serious implications for multicultural music education and related notions of musical diversity, inclusivity and social justice in general.

Thus far, American and other music teachers have not been enthusiastic about the idea of standardized testing, but political pressure seems to be mounting for its adoption. Arkansas governor Mike Huckabee (2009), for example, recently admonished delegates at the MENC Centennial Conference to emphasize competition and standardized testing in their programmes, 'because what we keep score on, we consider important' (p. x). This was echoed in a Rand Corporation report warning that if music education is to have an important place in the school curriculum teachers will have to develop 'standards-based assessments' (Zakaras and Lowell 2008: 101). This is all couched in the language of educational excellence and democracy, but it is really about supplyside economics. Music educators are told to band together with business leaders, other arts organizations and state policymakers to create greater demand for fine art and music by 'cultivating the capacity of individuals to have aesthetic experiences with works of arts' (p. xvi). This is a throwback to the democratic realism of the 1950s and to a lesser extent to the discipline-based arts education model of the 1980s, when aesthetic education was at its peak. Then, as now, the idea was to democratize fine art and music by training children as future connoisseurs and consumers of fine art and music. But of course, and as already explained, this model of music education was never intended to serve the broader social and educational needs of the masses for the reason that connoisseurship, like talent and the pursuit of excellence, is by definition 'rare and approachable by only the few' (McMurray 1991: 65). Similarly, and although standards and standardized testing are often touted as promoting greater educational equality, their real purpose is to transform education into a competitive race in which the privileged 'rise to the top, and all others must learn to accept their humble place' (p. 65).

This gives new meaning to the popular slogan 'music education for all children' and the related notion of musical inclusivity, which is that music education should also play a supporting role in promoting a musical class system based on ability and privilege while contributing to the shaping of future workers, consumers and entrepreneurs, all of whom are necessary to economic success in a highly competitive world. Even multiculturalism, which during the 1960s and 1970s was valued in western schools because it was thought to contribute to the formation of democratic citizens who could 'work with others to find sites of commonality, despite differences', has been 'replaced with a meaner, harder logic of competition on a global scale and of a strategic, outward-looking cosmopolitanism' (Mitchell 2003: 392). It is important to understand that multiculturalism has always been closely aligned with capitalism and that, during the Cold War, it was even used by the American government to justify its own political and economic expansionist goals. If America was to have any credibility in promoting demo-cratic capitalism abroad it had to 'adopt the language of inclusion' (p. 391). But whereas the earlier conception of multiculturalism in education was based on progressive notions of egalitarianism, social welfare, personal fulfilment and the 'ethical self', the new and ideal neoliberal citizen has little to do with democracy or ethics. Rather, he or she is 'the superior footsoldier of global capitalism' (p. 400). If terms like multiculturalism, diversity, inclusivity and equality of opportunity in education have meaning at all for the neoliberal state it is in terms of facilitating global economic competitiveness and not democratic citizenship as a means of creating a more just and humane society. As should be clear by now, neoliberals and neoconservatives don't particularly believe in the ideal of education as the pursuit of personal fulfilment and social justice, viewed as they are as impediments to the pursuit of educational excellence and economic success. Throughout much of the world today, the neoliberal solution to the problem of low achievement in schools is 'the erasure of difference, and assimilation to the norms and codes of American "excellence" ' (p. 399).

All of this should give music teachers pause when responding to calls for stand-ardized testing and increased competition while also seeking greater musical diversity and inclusivity in the classroom, for as already suggested at the beginning of this chapter, unless teachers and students are historically informed and politi-cally aware they might not realize that calls for greater inclusivity and equality of opportunity in music education might serve to gloss over real differences and social inequities by contributing to the myth that their country 'tells one story: the unbroken, ineluctable progress of freedom and equality' (Bloom 1988, quoted in Zinn 2003: 629). The reality is something quite different. Since the earliest days of European settlement, and certainly during Dewey's lifetime, the United States has been controlled by a rich élite representing only a tiny fraction of the population that owns 'a third of the wealth' and most of the mass media (Zinn 2003: 632). The country is 'divided … into classes of extreme wealth and extreme poverty, separated by an insecure and jeopardized middle class' (p. 629).

Similar observations can be made with respect to the United Kingdom, where about five per cent of the population owns 40 per cent of the wealth, poverty has been on the rise for some time and powerful media moguls have direct access to government. And in the absence of socially and politically informed and engaged music teachers and curriculum and other materials that can counter the propa-ganda of the corporate–state education system by challenging students to think more critically about musical society and its problems, then the latter are not likely to see through the myth that they live in 'a successful society and that … if you work hard and get educated, you will be prosperous and successful' (Zinn and Macedo 2005: 33–4). This, as McMurray (1991) insists, is the democratic mission of schools, which is to help children identify the often vested interests that shape their understandings of the musical and wider world and thereby to also help them gain some modicum of control over their own destinies, and not the creation of expert performers, composers or connoisseurs!

Among the lessons that all of us in music education (whether in Canada, the UK or elsewhere) can learn from the American experience are that policy and practice are inseparable from politics and that the teaching of music and other school subjects is often from the perspective, or in the interests, of the privileged and powerful and is thus ideological and one-sided (Zinn 2003; Cox 2002). Nor are educational history and philosophy free from, or immune to, political interest and influence. Given my all too brief history of the music teaching profession in America during the early Cold War and around the turn of the present century, it seems clear that what is needed to help counter the global neoliberal economic educational imperative are more overtly political histories and philosophies of music education that seek to tell not just the 'who, what and when' of educational reforms but also the 'why' by identifying and critiquing the ideologies and social agendas of vested interests who would place their own needs above those of children, teachers and the public, or who would assume that they have a monopoly on truth. There is a desperate need for alternative and radical histories and curricula that challenge conventional accounts, policy, philosophies and pedagogies by tracing their historical roots while also presenting relevant political or other information so that teachers and students realize that their own understandings are sometimes built on a foundation of lies, or that they have been operating under the erroneous impression that music's only *legitimate* meaning is to be found in 'the quality of its making' rather than also in its relation to politics and other forms of experience that are vital to its understanding (Taruskin 2004: 33).

This, however, is not to say that traditional histories are necessarily deliberately distorted or completely inaccurate. This chapter is indebted to, and would have been impossible without, the work of prominent American music education historians. It is just that historical work is inevitably ideological and thus distorted for the reason that historians must choose 'facts' from among a welter of often conflicting information and that 'any chosen emphasis supports (whether the historian means to or not) some kind of interest, whether economic or political or racial or national or sexual' (Zinn 2003: 8). Historians traditionally prize objectivity, but that is an impossible standard, the pursuit of which better serves the rich and powerful by either masking their social and political agendas or by glossing over atrocities and issues of power and control, thereby making them appear more acceptable. In the end, historians are perhaps inevitably forced to take sides and, like Zinn, I prefer to be on the side of the unwashed masses, the poor and the otherwise disenfranchised and under-represented who are often ill-served by business and by school, university and government programmes.

This is something that British and other music educators should consider in this time of economic recession and increasing poverty as their governments continue to divert vast sums of public money from social to corporate welfare. Now, more than ever before, all of us in the arts and humanities need to become politically engaged and outspoken in defence of our programmes lest, as happened during Dewey's own time during the height of the Great Depression, political leaders declare them educational frills and therefore expendable. This already appears to be occurring at the university level in England, where Prime Minister Cameron recently announced drastic cuts in funding of arts and humanities programmes compared to ones thought to be more important to economic growth, and teacher education programmes relocated to special teacher schools. Dewey's (1933b) characteristic response to those calling for the elimination of music and other so-called frills 'in the interest of economy' was that it made no economic sense to cut programs that contributed to the life of the mind, school and community by developing the imagination, and that stripping state schools of the arts would be a socially regressive move that would render schooling a drudgery and result in the creation of 'a docile peasantry' that was easily manipulated (pp. 141, 146). Anyone who calls for their elimination from state schools, he said, is either rich and 'sends his own children to a private school or else one who disbelieves in the whole democratic endeavour' (p. 142). The wealthy would never tolerate those school conditions for their own children! A similar argument applies to the relocation of teacher training programmes from universities to special schools, that education will likely become 'wholly technical and abstract' and schools 'tools of private advantage and material success' because teachers-in-training will be even more distanced from the liberal education they need to understand society and its problems. When that happens, Dewey said, teaching is likely to become 'aimless and confused' and result in 'conformity to and duplication of the existent with all its limitations and evils' (Dewey 1933a: 59).

This chapter thus presents a radical idea and vision for music education insomuch as it calls for a return to a more socially progressive conception of music education as empowering teachers and students to reclaim ownership over the design and direction of their musical lives by helping them to see and hear the world with critical eyes and ears (and all of the senses). And if this is to happen – if calls for social justice in music education are to be more than 'mere flourishes or phrases on paper' – then, as Dewey (1933a: 48) might say today, music teachers and teacher educators must discover and ally themselves with others who are also disposed to challenge the neoliberal economic imperative for education with its codes of excellence and equality of opportunity which are intended to privilege the few at the expense of the many. The last thing that the rich and powerful want, and notwithstanding Prime Minister Cameron's rhetoric about educational excellence and equality, is a state school system that seeks to develop the intelligence of the great masses of students, as that would require a more truly equitable redistribution of the country's wealth and educational resources and the development of politically savvy teachers and politicized curricula, all of which would threaten the privileged status of social and economic élites and their private schools. And as Dewey (1934a) similarly warned during the height of the Great Depression, in the continued absence of any significant challenge to the prerogatives of the rich, the kinds of government social, educational and economic reforms already instigated or planned in response to the recent market meltdown are likely to be at the expense of democracy and social justice.

Accomplishing education reform in the name of social justice will therefore be no easy task, especially since our state education systems have long operated as almost subsidiaries of the corporate world and are designed to protect us, our students and the wider public 'from seeing what we observe, from knowledge and understanding of the world in which we live' (Chomsky 1987: 136). That is why all of us who believe in music education's potential for contributing to a better world will need to do more than just lecture and publish academic papers. If we are not to be mere dilettantes and therefore complicit in the neoliberal agenda for education – by confining our 'radical critiques' to the classroom, thereby teaching political passivity to students – then we will have to become more socially and politically active both within and beyond our own institutions and the very narrow confines of the teaching profession (Zinn and Macedo 2005: 64).

Reflective questions

1   A key idea of this chapter is that historical work is inevitably ideological and therefore to some extent distorted because historians are guided by their own beliefs, values and assumptions. Analyse a music education history textbook for evidence of ideological bias and try to trace the roots of the author's particular ideology or set of assumptions with reference to contemporary politics and educational philosophy.

2   This chapter has documented and analyzed some of the ways that music education has been, and continues to be, 'harnessed to the services of power.' What do you think are some other ways that music education today is unduly influenced, or is subject to co-option, by politicians, business or special interest groups to serve purposes that might be antithetical to education?

References

Anonymous, (1963) 'Seminar on Music Education: Musicians Meet at Yale University', *Music Educators Journal*, 50(1): 86–7.

Bloom, A. (1988) *The Closing of the American Mind: How Higher Education has Failed Democracy and Impoverished the Souls of Today's Students.* New York: Simon & Schuster.

Brameld, T. (1961) 'What is the central purpose of American education?', *The Phi Delta Kappan*, 43(1): 9–14.

Broudy, H.S. (1958) 'A Realistic Philosophy of Music Education', in N. B. Henry (ed.) *Basic Concepts in Music Education*, Chicago: National Society for the Study of Education.

Bruner, J.S. (1960) *The Process of Knowledge*, Cambridge, MA: Harvard University Press.

Bruner, J.S. (1962/1970) *On Knowing: Essays for the Left Hand*, New York: Atheneum.

Chomsky, N. (1987) 'The Manufacture of Consent', in J. Peck (ed.) *The Chomsky reader*, New York: Pantheon Books.

Colwell, R.J. (in press) 'Pride and Professionalism in Music Education', in G. McPherson (ed.) *Oxford Handbook of Music Education*, London: Oxford University Press.

Cox, G. (2002) *Living Music in Schools, 1923–1999: Studies in the History of Music Education in England*, Aldershot: Ashgate Publishing Limited.

Crist, E.B. (2003) 'Aaron Copland and the Popular Front', *Journal of the American Musicological Society*, 56(2): 409–65.

Crist, E.B. (2005) *Music for the Common Man: Aaron Copland During the Depression and War*, New York: Oxford University Press.

Delapp, J. (2004) Review of *Music on the Frontline: Nicolas Nabokov's Struggle Against Communism and Middlebrow Culture*, by I. Wellens, 2002. Burlington, VT: Ashgate, *American Music*, 22(2): 317–19.

Dewey, J. (1927/1946) *The Public and its Problems: an Essay in Political Inquiry*, Chicago: Gateway Books. First published by Henry Holt and Company.

Dewey, J. and Childs, J.L. (1933a) 'The Social-Economic Situation and Education', in W. H. Kilpatrick (ed.) *The Educational Frontier*, New York and London: Century Co; re-printed in J. A. Boydston (ed.) (1989) *John Dewey: the Later Works, 1925–1953, vol. 8: 1933*, rev'd edn, Carbondale and Edwardsville: Southern Illinois University Press.

Dewey, J. (1933b) 'Shall We Abolish School 'Frills'? No', *Rotarian*, May, 42: 18–19, 49; reprinted in J. A. Boydston (ed.) (1986) *John Dewey: the Later Works, 1925–1953, vol. 9: 1933–1934*, Carbondale and Edwardsville: Southern Illinois University Press.

Dewey, J. (1934a) 'No Half-Way House for America', *People's Lobby Bulletin*, November, 4: 1; reprinted in J. A. Boydston (ed.) (1986) *John Dewey: the Later Works, 1925–1953, vol. 9: 1933–1934*, Carbondale and Edwardsville: Southern Illinois University Press.

Dewey, J. (1934b) *Art as Experience*, New York: Perigee Books.

Efland, A.D. (1988) 'How Art Became a Discipline: Looking at Our Recent History', *Studies in Art Education*, 29(3): 262-74.

Eklund-Koza, J. (2006) ' "Save the Music"? Toward Culturally Relevant, Joyful, and Sustainable School Music', *Philosophy of Music Education Review*, 14(1): 23–38.

Elliott, D.J. (2007) '"Socializing" Music Education', *Action, Criticism, and Theory for Music Education*, 6 (4): 60–95.

Ginsberg, R. and Lyche, L.F. (2008) 'The Culture of Fear and the Politics of Education', *Educational Policy*, 22(1): 10–27.

Hartshorn, W.C. (1963) 'The Study of Music as an Academic Discipline', *Music Educators Journal*, 49(3): 25–8.

Hedges, C. (2009) *Empire of Illusion: the End of Literacy and the Triumph of Spectacle*, Toronto: Alfred A. Knopf.

Huckabee, M. (2009) 'Forward: Excerpts from Governor Mike Huckabee's speech to the Centennial Congress', in J. R. Barrett (ed.) *Music Education at a Crossroads: Realizing the Goal of Music for All*, Lanham, Maryland: Rowan & Littlefield Education in partnership with MENC: The National Association for Music Education.

Jorgensen, E.R. (2004) 'Pax America and the World of Music Education', *Journal of Aesthetic Education*, 38(3): 1–18.

Karlsen, S. and Westerlund, H. (2010) 'Immigrant students' Development of Musical Agency – Exploring Democracy in Music Education', *British Journal of Music Education*, 27(3): 225–39.

Leonhard, C. (1965) 'Philosophy of Music education', *Music Educators Journal*, 52(1): 59–61.

Leonhard, C. and House, R.W. (1959/1972) *Foundations and Principles of Music Education*, New York: McGraw Hill Book Company.

Mark, M.L. (1998) 'Public policy and the Genesis of Aesthetic Education', *Philosophy of Music Education Review*, 6(1): 107–12.

Mark, M.L. and Gary, C.L. (2007) *A History of American Music Education*, 3rd edn, New York: Rowan & Littlefield Education in partnership with MENC: The National Association for Music Education.

McCarthy, M. (2003) 'The Past in the Present: Revitalising History in Music Education', *British Journal of Music Education*, 20(2):121–34.

McCarthy, M. and Goble, J.S. (2002) 'Music Education Philosophy: Changing Times', *Music Educators Journal*, 89(1):19–26.

McMurray, F. (1991). 'Part 2: Variations on a Pragmatic Theme', in R. J. Colwell (ed.) *Basic Concepts in Music Education, II*. Niwot, CO: University of Colorado Press.

Meyer, L.B. (1956) *Emotion and Meaning in Music*. Chicago: University of Chicago Press.

Mitchell, K. (2003) 'Educating the National Citizen in Neoliberal Times: from Multi-cultural Self to the Strategic Cosmopolitan', *Transactions of the Institute of British Geographers, New Series*, 28(4): 387–403.

Palisca, C.V. (1963) *Report of the Yale Seminar on music education*, Yale University, New Haven, CT: United States Department of Health, Education and Welfare, Office of Education.

Rainbow, B. with Cox, G. (2006) *Music in Educational Thought and Practice: a Survey from 800 BC*, 2nd edn, Woodbridge, Suffolk, UK: The Boydell Press.

Reimer, B. (1959) 'What Music Cannot Do', *Music Educators Journal*, 46(1): 40–45.

Ross, A. (2007) *The Rest is Noise: Listening to the Twentieth Century*, New York: Farrar, Straus & Giroux.

Sands, R.M. (2007) 'Social Justice and Equity: Doing the Right Thing in the Music Teacher Education Program', *Action, Criticism, and Theory for Music Education*, 6(4): 43–59.

Saunders, F.S. (1999) *Who Paid the Piper? The CIA and the Cultural Cold War*, London: Granta Books.

Swanwick, K. (1979) *A Basis for Music Education*, Windsor, Berks, UK: NFER Publishing Company Ltd.

Tanner, L.N. (1988) 'The Path Not Taken: Dewey's Model of Inquiry', *Curriculum Inquiry*, 18(4): 471–79.

Taruskin, R. (2004) 'The Poetic Fallacy', *The Musical Times*, 145 (1886): 7–34.

Westbrook, R.B. (1991) *John Dewey and American democracy*, Ithaca: Cornell University Press.

White, D.W. (1992) 'The American 'Century' in World History', *Journal of World History*, 3(1): 105–27.

Wright, R. (2001) 'Addressing Individual Needs and Equality of Opportunity in the Music Curriculum', in C. Philpott and G. Spruce (eds.) *Learning to Teach Music in the Secondary School: a companion to school experience*, London: Routledge.

Zacharas, L. and Lowell, J.F. (2008) *Cultivating Demand for the Arts: Arts Learning, Arts Engagement, and State Arts Policy*, Santa Monica, CA: The Rand Corporation.

Zimring, F. (1984) 'Notes and Documents: Cold War Compromises: Albert Barnes, John Dewey, and the Federal Bureau of Investigation', *The Pennsylvania Magazine of History and Biography*, 108(1): 87–100.

Zinn, H. (2003) *A People's History of the United States: 1492–present*, New York: HarperCollins.

Zinn, H. and Macedo, D. (2005) *Howard Zinn on Democratic Education*, Boulder: Paradigm Publishers.

Chapter 7

The National Curriculum as manifest destiny

Cathy Benedict and Patrick Schmidt

> So much of the education debate in this country is backward looking: have the standards fallen? Have exams got easier? These debates will continue, but what really matters is how we're doing compared with our international competitors. That is what will define our economic growth and our county's future. The truth is, at the moment we are standing still while others race past.
>
> (Prime Minister David Cameron, Deputy Prime Minister Nick Clegg, The Schools White Paper 2010: 3)

> The search for scientific bases for confronting problems of social policy is bound to fail, because of the nature of these problems. They are 'wicked' problems, whereas science has developed to deal with 'tame' problems. Policy problems cannot be definitively described. ... Even worse, there are no 'solutions' in the sense of definitive and objective answers.
>
> (Rittel and Webber 1973: 155)

Introduction

We open this chapter with two quotes. The first is a call to arms in no uncertain words and is intended to bring fear into the hearts of the *true* citizen of a great nation state. Clearly, not 'the' great nation state Britain could be but that is, of course, what '*really* matters' and what *counts* in terms of rhetorical provocation of political incitement. At least, it's what matters on the surface. As the speech is uttered, indeed, as this is stated, the message is made clear 'through a logic that presumes the efficacy of modern democratic ideals' (Lyon, 1999: 3). One does not deserve the moniker 'citizen' if one cannot see how the educative system has failed its children and by extension its nation. Undoubtedly the need for reform is fierce and the time for 'urgent thorough going reform' (Gove 2010) – is now. Always now.

In the second quote, through their interrogation of the attempts that have been made at solving problems through the 'scientific management movement' and its modernist belief in efficiency, Rittel and Webber (1973) direct our attention to those ways problems have traditionally been formulated and 'solved.' The term *wicked* is coined in the context of social policy and planning and is a direct attempt to highlight and challenge the failure to address the 'juncture where goal-formulation, problem-definition and equity issues meet' (p. 156). Political discourse and action does not result by accident or from fortuitousness. Rittel and Webber suggest the possibility that 'failure' might also be connected to deliberative practices.

> We do not mean to personify these properties of social systems by implying malicious intent. But then, you may agree that it becomes morally objectionable for the planner to treat a wicked problem as though it were a tame one, or to tame a wicked problem prematurely, or to refuse to recognize the inherent wickedness of social problems.
>
> (Rittel and Webber 1973: 160)

While educational reform is a complex and nuanced endeavour, when analyzed historically it is not absurd to suggest that governments have often spoken of education and the educative process as a problem with a solution. Nor would it be absurd to suggest that education has been the basis for political platforms and used as a vehicle for the reform and redemption of the Nation-State. As such, while the creation of the National Curriculum, and its external establishment through hard copies and the at once pervasive and elusive presence of a website that hosts it, both suggest and reflect complexity. The presentation of the National Curriculum also makes indelible the impression that the British Government has 'not abandoned the hope that the instruments of perfectibility can be perfected' (p. 158).

Perpetual clarion calls

The call to reform education is hardly new. Indeed, in the UK, every decade has produced a re-examination of the educational system: previous to the establishment of the current National Curriculum there were subsequent 'reform milestones' including the 'falling standards, in the early 1960s' and the 'economic downturn of the mid-1970s' (House of Commons 2008–09: 10). And while these milestones have often produced the instinctual effect of 'Oh no, not again,' Lawson's *et al.* (1994) depiction of a troubling view of the state of music education at the particular historic juncture of the creation of the National Curriculum articulates the recognition of diminishing programmes, parent contribution for funding becoming more pervasive, lack of specialists, unequal offerings and time availability for music instruction, etc. The reality that government intervention and the establishment of pervasive policy delineating the imperative of music in schools has had a stabilizing effect – in terms of establishing and equalizing distribution – seems therefore undeniable. What remains more open is the next step. Being that education, in music and otherwise, is established as a right, in what ways is that right *de facto* implemented and developed? And to what effect?

At the core of this chapter is the belief that since the late 1980s, when the process of creating a National Curriculum began in the UK, the development of this endeavour has reflected a rhetorical progression much like those of revolutionary movements of the past. These movements or departures, that signal both a break from the past and revolutionary beginnings, have often been marked by what we can call the *manifesto*. Lyon (1999) examines the concept and construct of this idea by addressing the manner in which manifestos are used in the creation of public spaces. One such very 'public' contemporary space is the delivery of the National Curriculum, whether through the website that houses it, or hardcopies that can be accessed, each of which we assert are not just simple platforms for the distribution of information, but rather sites of identity formation, including the construction of 'we' and 'them.'

We therefore build on Lyon's work by arguing that while the National Curriculum and extant documents are never referred to as manifestos, they function as such. We further her thinking and posit that – as a departure from more traditional or historical forms – the most recent iteration of the document has co-opted the rhetoric of the revolutionary discourse of oppressed populations, to underscore and further a particular ideological value system that provides the conservative discursive conditions under which support for the National Curriculum can exist. In other words, the National Curriculum is not a representation of the work a government develops alongside and on behalf of its citizens, but rather, a discursive tool in the actualization of political goals and ideological wants.

We further contend that politically it is important and significant that music educators attend to this so that a strong authorial voice may be developed and made present. If we choose to disregard development and reform intricacies of documents such as the National Curriculum, as well as the ways in which language is utilized, we cannot enter the process of manoeuvering educative processes that address the concerns of arts educators. As a set of texts the National Curriculum is fixed and defined. Although it is ostensibly left open as to how one can 'teach' the curriculum, it is in essence a document that is taught (and subsequently measured)[1] and not a 'thing in the making, continuously evolving through our understanding of the world and our own bodies' experience of and participation in that world (Ellsworth, 2005: 1).

Curriculum, of course, always seems like good policy. At the micro level of the classroom, it provides needed guidance, and at the macro level of politics it offers a complete vision of the educational enterprise that can be *translated* into accountable aims. But is 'good' policy akin to quality in educational terms? Specifically, do systems such as National Curriculum skew the notion that 'schools are complex webs of human activity' where 'input-output models are inapplicable' (Orchard, 2002: 166)? Is the framework of structures such as the National Curriculum in fundamental contradiction to the jostling for space enacted by alternative and innovative practices? From these questions we argue, in the latter part of this chapter, that a lack of attention to *localities* as fully capable of curricular development is connected to a preoccupation with *improvement* that is defined as capacity to perform acts rather than development of a *life in music* or dispositions toward *making up music*.

Serious critique of the Music National Curriculum is clear to anyone looking carefully at the literature. Lawson, Plummeridge and Swanwick (1994) reported the view of headteachers that 'in some instances arts presentations are being regarded as necessary public relations exercises within the context of an increasingly competitive educational service' (p. 5). Cooksey and Welch (1998) argued that 'the National Curriculum poses serious problems to teachers because of the assumption that pupils, regardless of age, stage of physical/emotional/cognitive/social maturation, and socio-cultural status will follow a univariate, linear paradigm of development' (p. 101). Kushner (1994) pointed out the manner in which a curriculum that failed to start from where pupils were, impaired their judgment and undermined their development. Our examination, however, focuses on the intersection between the political language (manifestos) with policy (the totalizing element of how that political language is transformed into policy) and then into practice – and their effects on the local capacity to develop curricular structures – which places the teacher as a full professional. And while government parties come and go, if we choose to disregard how documents such as the National Curriculum are developed and delivered, as well as the ways in which language is utilized, we cannot aid in the process of manoeuvering educative processes that address the concerns of arts educators.

Manifestos

> This White Paper signals a radical reform of our schools. We have no choice but to be this radical if our ambition is to be worldclass. The most successful countries already combine a high status teaching profession; high levels of autonomy for schools, a comprehensive and effective accountability system and a strong sense of aspiration for all children, whatever their background. Tweaking things at the margins is not an option. Reforms on this scale are absolutely essential if our children are to get the education they deserve.[2]
>
> (David Cameron Prime Minister and Nick Clegg Deputy Prime Minister)

In this section we focus on the force and impact of language and the structure of the National Curriculum. We consider the correlation to legitimacy that allows for reinforcement of that structure and how this limits those ways curriculum can be reentered, adapted and changed. We do so by viewing the National Curriculum and its extant documents as manifestos and contend that its website, as a 'commoditized infrastructure' (Van Dijck and Nieborg, 2009: 856) furthers a nearly indisputable discourse and ideology of global competition and the inevitability of market-based development.

Directly related and in fact predicated on this discourse, is a secondary discourse that focuses on: basics, privatization, 'a tighter, more rigorous, model of ...

knowledge', self-surveillance or 'blowing the whistle on weak schools,' and 'order' in classrooms (Gove 2010). This in turn presents a simplifying process of delineating education as a series of *problems* with *tangible* and, in fact quite direct solutions which is supported by an over-focus on *measurable* results. All of which directly impacts pedagogy and learning to such an extent that methods of teaching, while seemingly neutral and apolitical, are influenced by rigour, order and measurement. Consequently, it is of no surprise that the National Curriculum and the processes of Ofsted push teachers to teach to the curriculum. It would be then feasible to argue that:

> those … who choose methods of production which maximize profits will survive and flourish; those who make different choices will lose their capital and the social power it represents.
>
> (Woods 2004: 47)

Most of us have never thought through what makes manifestos 'manifestos' but we probably have a sense of their purpose and intent; one usually recognizes them to involve a rallying call of revolutionary purpose. While there is certainly not one template for the manifesto, Lyon (1999: 2) suggests there are characteristics that delineate and designate the form of a manifesto that 'addresses and at the same time elicits an entity called the People'. Through the use of such characteristics as a rigid definition of 'we' and 'them', the formation of the universal subject, pronouncements of urgency in the moment, the use of 'highly selective' historical evidence that supports the need for reform, and an unmediated style of rhetoric that is designed to prevent interrogation or dissent, a manifesto names and demands allegiance.

In doing this, however, the manifesto also reduces the complex social context into a rigid structure that as Lyon describes:

> … creates audiences through a rhetoric of exclusivity, parceling out political identities across a polarized discursive field, claiming for 'us' the moral high ground of revolutionary idealism, and constructing 'them' as ideological tyrants, bankrupt usurpers, or corrupt fools.
>
> (Lyon 1999: 3)

What both fascinates and concerns us is that the manifesto to which we are referring is not one that emerged from the disenfranchised, or disempowered. The State isn't a marginalized group; there is little oppression which it needs to chronicle. It does not need to 'yield an alternative historical narrative' (Lyon 1999: 15), it *is* the historical narrative. As political winds shift, ideological leadership comes and goes in such consistent fashion that it probably does not surprise any of us that with each re-visitation of the National Curriculum what was once valued becomes immediately suspect, and that documents developed through and based on research can, overnight, be repackaged as a 'straitjacket which stifles the creativity of our best teachers' (Gove 2010). Throughout current documents the rhetoric of creativity, participation, social skills and social justice are unabashedly and 'intimately wedded to the rhetoric of capitalism' (Van Dijck and Nieborg 2009: 867) and unapologetically used to argue economic benefits. Consider the 24 September 2010 Press Notice for the announcement of the Review of Music Education document. (The following quotes are presented in order as they appear in the two-page document):

> Research shows that quality music education improves behaviour, attention and concentration, and has a hugely positive effect on numeracy and language skills.
> Evidence suggests that learning an instrument can improve numeracy, literacy and behaviour.
>
> (Gove, Review of Music Education)

> I am looking forward to delivering to ministers a report which outlines how we can ensure that every child in England benefits from a *world-beating* music education system.
>
> (Darren Henley, leader of the independent review of music education; italics added)

> Immersion in music can lead to improved social skills and educational success, with behaviour, wellbeing, confidence, team-working and concentration skills all proven to improve with good music provision.
>
> (Minister for the Creative Industries, Ed Vaizey September 2010, Review of Music Education)

Hardly surprising rhetoric, but it is menacing and intimately connected to teaching methods that reflect a retrenchment that is tied to the most basic forms of functional literacy skills.

Providing a description and the underlying rhetoric of *The Schools White Paper*, or public notices of the *Review of Music Education*, or any of the other supporting documents, is fairly simple and straightforward. Providing a 'brief' description, however, of the National Curriculum or of the website – as one is an extension of and inseparable from the other – is virtually impossible (and if the music standards are to remain part of the UK educational vision, the National Curriculum will most assuredly be housed on a website). Simply thinking about the length of the hard copies of the *National Curriculum Key Stages 1 and 2: Handbook for Primary Teachers* (188 pages) and *The National Curriculum Handbook for Secondary Teachers in England* (222 pages) is overwhelming.[3] Consequently we highlight the over-structure of the National Curriculum and its manifestation, in terms of the totalizing language that it presents, because as Rowe argues 'the sentences we form are the structures which create the world of meaning in which we live' (Rowe 1991). In different terms, the formation of a language that is established and legitimized becomes the nature of a *social contract* in the face of which alternatives are restricted. The result might be 'a curriculum concerned with transmitting rather than receiving, centered around subjects, not the learner' (Bray 1998: 334).

Considering the work of Debord, Merrifield (2005: 60) reminds us of capitalism and the tautology embedded in what Debord refers to as spectacle: 'That which appears is good, that which is good appears'. In turn, we are reminded of one of the characteristics of the manifesto: 'The syntax of a manifesto is so narrowly controlled by exhortation, its style so insistently unmediated, that it appears to say only what it means, and to mean only what it says (Lyon 1999: 9). Far from being a set of neutral documents or a neutral site that simply presents content, the totalizing rhetorical persuasion of both curriculum and website deflects the complexity of education as a wicked problem and supersedes and perhaps deters efforts toward autonomy of local curriculum and the positioning of teachers as full professionals that can indeed engage with curriculum development. In the following section we address possible pathways to create a closer relationship between the requirements of the State and the needs of local insight, by proposing a shared agenda and a national models bank.

The locality in music curriculum design and development

At the time of writing no National Curriculum exists in the US. There is, however, movement toward this end in the form and guise of the *Common Core State Standards Initiative*. Indeed, the Obama Administration has linked competitive education grants (including the 1.35 billion dollar budget for Race to the Top challenge funds) with the adoption of these standards. Consequently, over 45 States have voluntarily adopted the core English Language and Mathematics Standards as the basis for their State standards. While the core standards only comprise English and Mathematics, the arts education community is pushing forward its own agenda referred to as the National Arts Standards 2.0.

This push forward 'to be next' (Shuler 2010) in the US has historical precedence in the American 1995 National Standards movement. In the mid 1990s, the US music education community, led by the authority and direction of Music Educators National Conference (MENC)[4] presented its initial reaction to the movement toward Standards in the early 1990s, and contrary to the more collective engagement taking place in the UK, *ad hoc* committees were formed and charged with writing a document – de facto speaking for the music education field. The *National Standards for Arts Education* would be subsequently adopted by 21 States, with the remaining States modelling their own standards for the arts on that 1994 document. John Mahlmann, then CEO of MENC, nicely articulates the role of MENC in *streamlining* the process of establishing the National Standards and its *undeniable* benefits:

As a result [of the national standards], school systems *saved* almost a year of analysis and planning. More important, teachers and administrators found that the arts standards strengthened their advocacy of the arts in the overall curriculum.

(Mahlmann, Purcell, Salisbury Wills, and Hatfield 1996)

Schmidt (2011: 93) argues that through a limited participation process and as a representation of a vision sponsored by MENC, the National Standards became 'in the words of Mahlmann, a proxy for the investigation of needs and curricular parameters of whole States'. Thus, it was not difficult to argue that 'political and moral' rather than curricular foci became a priority and consequently 'efficiency [was] clearly placed in a privileged position over local inquiry.' A more cynical interpretation of Mahlmann's position would even argue that:

> the National Standards and its ensuing policies have become not the mani-festation of the will and agency of a constituency, but rather its substitute. In Mahlmann's words, 'the standards articulated a vision for arts education that many teachers had felt but had been unable to express.'
>
> (Schmidt 2011: 91)

What seems interesting is that the pathway currently chosen in the US – param-eters for a revision have been discussed without any national conversation – both mirrors the 'limited engagement' process of the early 1990s in the UK, as well as the aim to achieve over-articulation of unified scope and content. Thus, it is significant that despite the vast differences between the US and British realities, there are pervasive similarities in terms of a concern with language and advocacy, placement of music as a core discipline, as well as qualification of teachers as agents of curricular delivery, and not development. Lastly, the *restrictive* role and value of professional judgment seems an impactful presence on both sides of the Atlantic, while serving – rhetorically and practically – as the main qualifier for curricular policy that is *obligated* to function in terms of external accountability.

We know, however, that external accountability neither needs to be paramount in the maintenance of standards of quality, nor must be in contradiction with strong local curricular design and development. Indeed, Gane (1996: 55) argues that, 'the value of a curriculum determined by teachers themselves with and for their pupils obviates the necessity for expensive external validators of standards'. Unfortunately, the author fails to address the interactive nature that local goals, programme structure and curriculum development can (and perhaps ought to) have with macro, State-sanctioned, guidelines. Several models in education and music education articulate and support the manner in which such interactions can foster both autonomy and accountability; in fact they articulate the benefits of a co-dependence between the two (see Ball 2003; Schmidt 2009; Weaver-Hightower 2008).

Before moving forward, it is important to clarify that when referencing *local-ities* or *local engagements,* we are not equating it to the political re-dressing of a conservative discourse that aims at smaller government. Of course, the Thatcherian liberalism of Cameron has its mirrored opposite on the left, whose zealous concern with the particular, unitary or the marginal often obstructs attention to macro conditions and necessities. At this political juncture, however, we are concerned with the normalization of rhetoric that seemingly uses communal potential for political gain. For example:

> We plan to strip away these stifling bureaucratic burdens and offer local authorities the space they need to be more daring and imaginative in how they provide services and deploy resources to the benefit of every child in their area. In particular, local authorities will be free to develop new and innovative ways of supporting the vulnerable.
>
> (David Cameron, December 2010)

Quite differently, notions of locally developed curriculum structures – fully conceptualized in context and with themes that connect curriculum to in-the-world realities – seem to be in synchrony with notions of standards of quality and considerations of range which 'take into account musical activity across a variety of working conditions' and can 'only be acquired over time and are only revealed in time' (Swanwick 1997: 213). While we do not share Swanwick's concern with range as an experience of 'musical styles,' range could be differently defined in terms of varied 'working conditions' and thus inserted into notions such as *musical entrepreneurship*, which could work as an example of *vertical curricular design*. We exemplify what we mean by vertical design later on, but first it is important to articulate that this conceptual notion situates local autonomy as *the* agent leading the application of broader – indeed national – curricular guidelines. We would submit that modelling quality of engagement 'in time and revealed by time' requires a curricular understanding that goes beyond managerial elements and thus beyond the mere distribution of something prepared externally and *a priori*. Thus, we favour a notion of 'shared agendas,' where local – or teacher-driven – curricular engagements place managerial delivery and evaluation not as anathema but as elements aiding in the operationalization of vertical design. In other words a notion of subsumed aspects, albeit part and parcel, of conceptual construction and design, implementation and assessment of curriculum.

Key in understanding and enacting an agenda that 'shares', and brings together, macro imperatives and micro needs, is modelling how local attitudes and values can become 'explicit' considerations as well as formal structures interfacing with the National Curriculum apparatus. Ball and Bowe (1992) in fact mused that the Curriculum Act in Britain could 'exaggerate diversity of practice in the sense that teachers construct their own version of the National Curriculum in accordance with their individual philosophies' (p. 339). While in retrospective we know that evaluation and the increased performativity of the State (Ball 2003) has prevented the unfolding of these 'individual philosophies,' we argue that an engagement with local knowings, today, seems not only a significant but a necessary response to the overwhelming presence – virtual and real – of the National Curriculum.

At issue then is a central re-positioning of the question of effectiveness and accountability. A first step is to highlight and enforce differentiations between 'assessment (informed but nevertheless *subjective judgment*) and evaluation (definition of a precise – and, therefore, presumably, indisputable – value)' (Paynter 2002: 216; italics in the original). But that is insufficient. It is also necessary that we offer legitimate spaces where efficiency is more than 'the manipulation of human beings into compliant patterns of behaviours' (MacIntyre 1981: 71). This then points us to a larger, and perhaps systemic, problem, namely: the degree to which curriculum development and implementation is framed by limited and limiting conceptions of assessment/evaluative capabilities. Addressing this conundrum – for evaluation is necessary, but so is professional agency – requires a rethinking of how accountability is construed and the spaces it may generate for *professional* action.

Possible futures and practices

Imagine for a moment that one of the initiatives connected to the National Curriculum in England or the National Standards in the US, would be a focus on developing a *Portfolio* of program structures. A national data bank – a *models bank* to be more precise – charged with presenting examples of the processes that successfully *adapted* music curricula to the needs, interests and capacities of local constituents. The goal here is not to cater to 'traditions', grouping students based on ability, nor to vocational needs. The goal is to think of music in-the-world, manifested in pathways of study. For example a Key Stage curriculum that functions around the theme of *music entrepreneurship*, or a year-long focus on *music and digital media*, or studies framed from the stance of *music and communities of learning*.

While the National Curriculum currently offers 'exemplifications for foundation subjects' they retain a focus on delivery and remain atomistic in nature.[5] Differently, we are arguing for in-depth studies of thematic ideas or concepts that have a direct application and that students can recognize as a possibility into their lived world. These would serve as full examples of a structure of thought and practices that teachers could attempt to engender on their own, re-tooling their curriculum in relation to their local community's interests, while making use of the atomistic and managerial elements abundant in the current National Curriculum. The intent is to consider *vertical conceptions* of curriculum by which we mean fully developed understandings that thematically guide curricular connections between skill and action in the world. In other words, a curriculum that, designed by teachers, presents musical practices that have social, cultural or economic value and impact as the leading element in interconnecting skill development, theoretical underpinnings, and practical applications. A vertical construction of the curriculum would present critical reflection of musical practices in-the-world and would introduce different ways for musical and pedagogical tasks, actions, and conceptualizations to bring students to fully understand and experience said practices.

We suggest that there is a symbiotic relationship in the process of strengthening the National Curriculum by way of empowering professional action. One way to start would be to rethink the possible role of *portfolios* as aiding teachers to conceive curriculum in localized and vertical ways. As educational portfolio research demonstrates (Fullan, 2001; Herman and Winters 1994) necessary elements in this concept are the notions of internal validity as well as construct validity. That means that portfolios are assessed/evaluated departing from the standpoint of a coherent structural design developed by the proponent of the portfolio. Such structural design (vertical) must present an internal logic or cohesion that clearly organizes the elements of the portfolio according to central conceptions. Further, a well-conceived portfolio must connect to established external parameters and delineate possible applications of the work developed.

Portfolios are indeed part of the language of the National Curriculum, but framed as what we would call a collectors tool; the extent of the process is the atomist agglomeration of tips and good or best practices. While we are not opposed to these, in the absence of the larger, critical-thinking-based elements of a *portfolio* architecture, what becomes emphasized is dependence and compliance. Consequently, the State is not a partner to its *subjects*, but indeed plays the *pastoral* role of the protective patriarch.

So what can be done? Imagine then that a school's curriculum of study for music – year-long, focusing on Key Stage 4, with a theme based on what Paynter (2002: 217) called 'the immediacy of the [musical] experience' and supported by a national focus on portfolios; a school that decides that 'immediacy' is a valid, necessary, and appropriate theme for its community – would develop its own curriculum and form its own programme while focusing on two elements: the internal cohesiveness of the programme; and the external responsibility to meet curricular guidelines. Imagine now a fully-fleshed programme modelled after the initiative that Savage and Challis (2002) present where a larger conceptual notion – in this case that of the development of a digital arts curriculum – is the guiding element or theme. Inside it, we find projects such as *Reflecting Others*, where 'the idea of representing oneself and others through sound and image' (p. 8) is a guide for pedagogical engagements as well as the skill-based requirements emphasized in the National Curriculum.

What we are suggesting is that, in time and through the proliferation of interactions between autonomy and accountability, a few things might occur: a) centralized government would be able to amass a *models bank* of programs developed in music which offer a complex picture of the ways in which school music can be structured; b) contrary to case studies, units or projects, models of how those structures are organized and conceptualized would be highlighted, without relegating the ways they connect to larger national guidelines; and c) these would provide examples of how each model frames music as action in-the-world, pertinent to the local context, placed in socio-creative parameters, and understood as clearly economically and academically viable sources of opportunity. The shift would be, in simple terms, to place content in the service of learning and experiencing *ways of being*. That is, what does the lifeworld of music entrepreneurs look like both locally and nationally? What are the differences? Why are certain patterns clearly present? Why might certain musical idioms be absent?

While this is merely an outline, we use it to highlight our initial comment: school curricula and programs in music, at the local level, do not need to 1) be at the mercy of constricting evaluation – in the US much instruction and curriculum structure has *de facto* been swallowed by teaching-to-the-test parameters; 2) become the *management* or implementation of State or centralized design; 3) relegate music teachers (and teaching labour in general) to enforcing or executing global – read universalized and impersonal – ideals and practices; 4) become a site for the delivery of factual knowledge.

Indeed we can have it both ways. The National Curricula or National Standards could become more porous guidelines while still reminding professionals of qualifying and necessary parameters in the education of school children of various ages. We could have global directories, but also amplify them and in the process make them more meaningful and humane through local adaptation.

Concluding thoughts

While we diverge from a number of the outcomes articulated by Paynter, we are sympathetic to the notion that the music curriculum has at its basis, the conceptual notion of '*making up music*' (Paynter 2002: 219); to which we would add *making up musical lives*. Both notions, combined, lead then to the question: can teachers engage with practices fully committed to the idea of *making up music* or *musical lives* when they are not capable of fully *making up* their own curriculum? The question that perhaps precedes this one is: is there a necessary relation between fully understanding the capacities, needs and expanse of the curriculum one is teaching, and developing a complex manifestation of this same curriculum in practice? More specifically: is it possible for a teacher to model critical thinking out of an engagement with a curriculum that denies local insight, input or possibility for adaptation?

A discussion of the possible relationship – which we tend to dismiss – between larger policy frameworks and the impactful role of people's everyday agency, brings the frame of diverse democratic practices to the discussion of a National Curriculum or to National Standards in the US – and reminds us of Swanwick's statement that 'however the new structure is rebuilt we can be sure of one thing: in diversity is survival' (Peggie 1994: 181). Further, this discussion leads us to reconsider the impact and significance of language at a time when the public face of the National Curriculum, its website, is continually being redacted and changed.

Ranciere (2010) calls the 'paradox of democracy' the relationship between democracy as a form of government in tension with democracy as a social practice. This tension arises, according to him, from governmental need for political legitimacy, usually constructed by means of policy directives that clearly 'resolve' contentious social issues. Samuel Huntington's radical, and amply subscribed, assertion exemplifies this point:

> Democracy leads to an increase in demands [by its citizens], and this puts pressure on governments, undermines authority and renders individuals and groups unresponsive to the necessities of discipline and sacrifice associated with ruling in the name of common interests.
>
> (Ranciere 2010: 47)

That is the somewhat perverse logic for a pastoral representation of government, one which arguably could be placed at the centre of the disposition toward a *National Curriculum* structure. At issue then, in the case of education, is how a call for democratic deliberation by one's peoples can 'entail an excess of political activity that encroaches on the principles and procedures of 'good policy, authority, scientific expertise and pragmatic experience' (p. 47). Is there no space for serious interaction between State and the individual?

We understand the challenges of a local emphasis on curriculum, particularly in the face of questions such as: 'given the real difficulties head teachers have in similar schools managing reducing budgets, and having colleagues with little musical experience, how can all children in their charges be given a real musical entitlement?' (Hitchcock, in Peggie 1994: 182). What seems worth considering, however, is that a school music programme that concerns itself with the full fleshing of its ideals and their interaction with National *guidelines*, might be a fundamentally different programme than one where the concern is how to manage an outside structure with no local interface, and no local professional demand other than that of *delivery*. Locality, as a central partner in educative enterprise, as we see it, is not about *private autonomy* in the sense of market directed liberalism. What we have argued is simply the fact that neither the left nor the right has attempted a model that asks for constructive accountability.

Since we began writing this chapter *Music Education in England – A Review by Darren Henley for the Department for Education and the Department for Culture, Media and Sport* has been published. As Henley outlines recommendations he returns time and again to reinforce the need for music organizations to not only work together, but to work at the local level as well.

> 1.12 Where Music Education is delivered at its best, money from central government and Local Authorities is harnessed together alongside imaginative use of school budgets and exciting collaborations with arts organizations. The best Music Education comes about through partnership; no one teacher, performer, school organization, group or body has all of the requisite skills to deliver every part of a rounded Music Education to every child. Instead, when interested parties work together, with funding invested carefully to deliver the right level of expertise at the right moment in the education process, we see strong results.
>
> (Music Education Review 2011: 5)

Indeed, the recently published national music plan 'The Importance of Music' provides the framework for hubs (2011, p. 3) which could be quite instructive in breaking down the often rigid structures of schools. This would be quite positive as long as it is not enacted in a market-driven, outsourced fashion which empties the still powerfully democratic role schools have to play in the lives of students and communities.

In closing, we return to Ranciere (2010: 54) who emphasizes that 'those who want the government of cities and states to be grounded on the simple and unequivocal principal of community' find contextually-based or locally driven practices such as those articulated here 'unacceptable'. To be clear, the notion of portfolios or *model banks,* where sharing and 'borrowing' can be done, is not aimed simply at presenting 'a perspective, sensitive and critical response to music of different styles in a cultural and historical context' as the National Curriculum currently suggests. Rather, the notion is more radical. It is to suggest latitude for exclusion of this universalist requisition, and trade it for in-depth structures, based upon full conceptions of *ways of being with and through music.* The proposition is that these actions would maintain a capacity to transfer learned knowledge to other contexts, provide less abstract or disconnected experiences, while exploring the plurality or webbing of musical engagements through the lenses of a particular thematic practice.

Reflective questions

1   In what ways do you think the development of the National Curriculum has shaped the ways in which music education is viewed in the UK?
2   Consider how curriculum development may be tied to advocacy and policy efforts. In what ways might this impact on how an education in and through music has (and continues to be) perceived and developed?
3   Read several of the White Papers published over the years in the UK. How has the purpose of general education been addressed during each government and how has this shaped the goals established for music education?

Notes

1 'Teaching to the test' in the UK has in many ways come to mean teaching to Ofsted.
2 The UK is not alone in expressing similar pronouncements. A cursory examination of several government websites suggests that the web provides the space to proclaim to the world that one is a serious player in the market-based economy and education is the vehicle for such competition.
3 This page-count does not include the 598 pages of the 12 *National Curriculum Subject Booklets* which 'set out the legal requirements of the National Curriculum in England for each subject and provides information to help teachers implement each subject in their schools,' nor the 368 extant publications that come up using the search terms National Curriculum (see the website of the independent UK book retailer, Langton Info Services, England: www.langtoninfo.com).
4 As of September 2011 MENC has officially changed the name of the organization to National Association for Music Educators, or NAfME.
5 Examples can be found in the *Exemplification of Standards* (SCAA 1996).

References

Ball, S.J. (2003) 'The Teacher's Soul and the Terrors of Performativity', *Journal of Educational Policy*, 18(2): 215–28.

Ball, S.J. and Bowe, R. (1992) 'Implementation of National Curriculum Policy', *Journal of Curriculum Studies*, 24(2).

Bray, E. (1998) 'Uncovering Music in the National Curriculum – a Social Semiotic Approach to the Title Page' *The Curriculum Journal*, 9(3): 333–40.

Burnard, P. (2000) 'How Children Ascribe Meaning to Improvisation and Composition: Rethinking Pedagogy in Music Education', *Music Education Research*, 2: 7–24.

Burnard, P. (2007) 'Reframing Creativity and Technology: Promoting Pedagogic Change in Music Education', *Journal of Music, Technology and Education*, 1(1): 37–55.

Cameron, D. (April 2010) *The Conservative Manifesto 2010*. Online www.conservatives.com/Policy/Manifesto.aspx

Cameron, D. (December 2010) *The Importance of Teaching: White Paper Equalities Impact Assessment*. Online www.education.gov.uk/b0068570/the-importance-of-teaching

Cooksey, J. and Welch, G. (1998) 'Adolescence, Singing Development and National Curriculum Design', *British Journal of Music Education*, 15(1): 99–119.

DES (1991) *National Curriculum Music Working Group*, Interim report.

DfE (1995) Music in the National Curriculum, England. London: HMSO.

DfE (2010) *The Importance of Teaching – The Schools White Paper 2010*. Online www.education.gov.uk/publications/standard/publicationdetail/page1/CM%07980

Ellsworth, E. (2005) *Places of learning: media, architecture, pedagogy*, New York, NY: RoutledgeFalmer.

Finney, J. (2000) 'Curriculum Stagnation: The Case of Singing in the English National Curriculum', *Music Education Research*, 2(2): 203–11.

Fullan, M. (2001). *The new meaning of educational change*. New York: Teachers College Press.

Gane, P. (1996) 'Instrumental Teaching and the National Curriculum: A Possible Partnership?', *British Journal of Music Education*, 13: 49–65.

Gove, M. (2010,) *Oral statement on the schools White Paper* [General article], UK: Department for Education. Online www.education.gov.uk/schools/teachingandlearning/schoolswhitepaper/a068680/oral-statement

House of Commons: Children, Schools and Families Committee. National Curriculum. Fourth Report of Session 2008–09. Retrieved from UK Parliament website http://www.publications.parliament.uk/pa/cm200809/cmselect/cmchilsch/344/34402.htm

Herman, J. and Winters, L. (1994). Portfolio research: A Slim Collection. *Educational Leadership*, 52(2), 48–55.

Kushner, S. (1999). Fringe Benefits: Music Education out of the National Curriculum. *Music Education Research*, 1(2), 209–218

Lawson, D., Plummeridge, C. and Swanwick, K. (1994) 'Music and the National Curriculum in Primary Schools', *British Journal of Music Education*, 11: 3–14.

Lyon, J. (1999). Manifestos: Provacations of the Modern Era. Ithaca, NY: Cornell University Press.

MacIntyre, A. (1981). *After Virtue: A Study in Moral Theory*. Notre Dame, Indiana: University of Notre Dame Press.

Major, A. (1993) A matter of skill, *Music Teacher*, 72(8): 8–11.

Merrifield, A. (2005) *Guy Debord*, London, England: Reaktion Books.

Mills, J. (1994) Music in the National Curriculum: The First Year, *British Journal of Music Education*, 11: 191–6.

Orchard, J. (2002) 'Will the Real superhero Stand Up? A Critical Review of the National Standards for Headteachers in England', *International Journal of Children's Spirituality*, 7(2): 159–69.

Paynter, J. (2002) Music in the School Curriculum: Why bother? *British Journal of Music Education*, 19(3), 215–26.

Peggie, A. (1994) A Report of a National Conference for Head Teachers, Education Officers, Governors, Parents, Teachers and Heads of Music Services organized jointly by Music for Youth and the Music Education Council', *British Journal of Music Education*, 11: 181–190.

QCA (2000) *The Arts, Creativity and Cultural Education: An International Perspective*, London: Qualification and Curriculum Authority/NFER.

Ranciére, J. (2010). *Dissensus: On Politics and Aesthetics*. London: Continuum.

Rittel, H. and Webber, M. (1973) 'Dilemmas in a General Theory of Planning', *Policy Sciences*, (4): 155–69.

Rowe, D. (1991) *Wanting Everything*, London: HarperCollins.

Savage, J. and Challis, M. (2002) 'A Digital Arts Curriculum? Practical Ways Forward', *Music Education Research*, 4(1): 7–23.

SCAA (1996) *Exemplification of Standards in Music: Key Stage 3*, London: School Curriculum and Assessment Authority.

Schmidt, P. (2009) 'Reinventing From Within: Thinking Spherically as a Policy Imperative in Music education', *Arts Education Policy Review*, 110(3): 39–47.

Schmidt, P. (2011). Living by a Simple Logic: Standards and Critical Leadership. In Paul Woodford (Ed.), *Re-thinking Standards for the Twenty-first century: New realities, New Challenges and New Propositions*. (Vol. 23). London, Ontario, Canada: University of Western Ontario Press.

Shuler, S. (2010). National Arts Standards 2.0 Planning Meeting. November 10, 2011. Retrieved from http://nelae.wikispaces.com/SEADAE+Meeting+with+Partners-+Reston%2C+VA

Swanwick, K. (1997) 'Assessing Musical Quality in the National Curriculum', *British Journal of Music Education*, 14(3): 205–15.

Terry, P. (1995) 'Accomodating the History of Music within the National Curriculum', *British Journal of Music Education*, 12: 29–43.

Thomas, R. (1997) 'The Music Nation Curriculum: Overcoming a compromise', *British Journal of Music Education*, 14(3): 217–35.

Van Dijck, J. and Nieborg, D. (2009). Wikinomics and its Discontents: a Critical Analysis of Web 2.0 business manifestos. *New Media and Society, 11*, 5, 855–874.

Weaver-Hightower, M. (2008) 'An Ecology Metaphor for Educational Policy Analysis: A Call to Complexity', *The Educational Researcher*, 37(3): 153–67.

Chapter 8

Musical ideologies, practices and pedagogies

Addressing pupil alienation through a praxial approach to the music curriculum

Gary Spruce with Francesca Matthews

Introduction

If at surface level only, two features most obviously distinguish contemporary, formal music education from that of say, 30 years ago. The first is the presence in many classrooms of digital technologies and the second is the diversity of repertoire represented in the music curriculum of many schools: schemes of work will typically refer to Indian, Balinese, African popular and jazz musics, and it is not uncommon for children to have access (sometimes within the school) to instruments associated with those musical cultures and traditions.

Resources – including recordings and scores, and ICT (e.g., high quality, sequencer-based, digitized sounds of non-western instruments) – are readily available to support the teaching of a whole range of musics and support for 'musical diversity' is expressed through statutory national curricular and policy documents; the 2007 English National Curriculum refers to 'a range of live and recorded music from different times and cultures' and music that reflects 'cultural diversity and a global dimension' (The National Curriculum for England 2007: 183). Lucy Green (1998) conducted research which showed that teachers considered popular music to be the most important music in the curriculum with non-western and world musics holding equal second place. All of this then might lead to the assumption that western classical music is no longer the dominating presence in formal music education that it once was. That it is now simply one of many musical traditions to be chosen, as appropriate, by the teacher from a kind of 'menu of musics' all of which are considered as being of equal value. However, as Green points out, 'the mere entrance of a wider variety of musical styles into an education system does not simply halt the construction and perpetuation of ideologies[1] of musical value' (Clayton *et al.*, 2003: 268) – ideologies which can result in the alienation of many children from music in school.

This chapter falls into three sections. In the first we argue that despite the introduction into the music curriculum of music from a much broader range of musical traditions and cultures than hitherto (including musical traditions and cultures from within our own society) the musical values inherent in western art music continue to be promoted as self-evidently defining 'good' music and consequently 'high status' musical knowledge, resulting in the alienation of many pupils from the formal curriculum. We then go on to consider how – despite the introduction into the curriculum of music from other traditions and cultures to try to address such alienation – the way in which these musics are typically presented sustains and reinforces rather than counters the western art music rooted conception of high status music knowledge. Following this we explore the nature of music as praxis. We argue that a curriculum that takes as its starting point not just the cultural artefacts of music but also its musical practices has the potential to address issues of alienation through the development of a critical pedagogy. Here, young people engage with music not as an objectified and fixed phenomenon, existing independently of them, but rather as something which can be acted upon and changed. Such an approach challenges, as Hess puts it, the myth that, 'there is only one way to learn and only certain content worth knowing' (Hess 2011: 2).

Western art music, high status knowledge and musical alienation

In *Classical Music and Postmodern Knowledge*, Kramer writes:

> As Leo Treitler observes, 'If there is a single word that can express what is for the modern period the essential attribute of "western music" … that word is "form", flanked by all its qualifiers (rational, logical, unified, concise, symmetrical, organic, etc.)'. Form is associated with closure, unity and – perhaps above all – structure, 'the idea that every note is necessary to the whole and no note is superfluous to it'. By this account, form is a dynamic principle of containment or regulation, a contingent foreclosure of contingent or excessive sonority. And as such is opposable both to 'oriental' luxuriance and to Western 'decadence' and 'effeminacy'.
>
> (Kramer 1995: 35)

Within this short paragraph Kramer (and Treitler) succinctly expose the post-Enlightenment western art music view of the primary (and perhaps exclusive) focus of musical engagement being the musical artefact.[2] The emphasis on form and the association of form with 'closure and unity' and 'containment and regulation' points both to musical objectification and thence to the ideology of musical autonomy. Musical autonomy is the belief that 'good' music expresses its meaning solely through the relationships and interplay of its sonic materials and means the same wherever and whenever it is presented. 'Good' music is typically performed in a socially *decontextualized* context such as concert halls, leading to what Lydia Goehr (1992) refers to as the creation of an 'Imaginary Museum of Musical Works' which is attended to view, at a distance, the cultural objects of the western art music tradition.

For those brought up in western society – and particularly within the tradition of western classical music – this way of thinking about music – this musical 'ideology'– appears so self-evident that it is unquestioningly accepted. The discourse of western art music centres on the ideology of objectified music both generically ('pieces of music' or 'musical works') and specifically (sonatas, songs, symphonies and string quartets). Social capital, which proceeds from this conception of high status musical knowledge, is gained from the *production* of a musical artefact through performing and/or composing, the *appreciation* of an artefact at a concert, or the *study* of an artefact through the analysis of the 'musical score' and/or recording. The conception of music as artefact allows for music to be characterized as a commodity to be bought and sold. One could argue that the dominant narrative of western art music in post-Enlightenment western society is that of comodification through the production of scores and recordings and the removal of music from its original social spaces to places where access to it can be controlled through entrance charges.

Spruce (2002) argues that the attributes and values of western art music are conceived as synonymous with those of high status music and by implication those of high status musical knowledge. Drawing on the work of Michael Young (1999) he shows how knowledge in schools is stratified into high and low status knowledge which is then reflected onto social structures and hegemonies. In such a way 'education is integrally involved in producing and perpetuating social arrangements including their unjust and exclusionary features' (Wright 2010: 264). Spruce demonstrates how, through a process of *abstraction*, *decontextualization* from social context and *commoditization*, high status knowledge is objectified into 'bodies of knowledge' which are thought of as existing independently of the knower. High status knowledge is often perceived as being synonymous with literary or scripted forms as it is through such forms that knowledge can be most easily objectified. Objectified knowledge is, by definition, readily open to objective assessment which then legitimates its use as a tool of selection. The possession of this high status knowledge then becomes a form of social capital through which is gained access to, and membership of, dominant social groupings.

Philpott suggests that high status knowledge is characterized by 'reification'. Reification can be defined as the act of perceiving as an object something that is intrinsically abstract. From such a perception derives the semantically obtuse, but commonly held, belief that one can 'read music'. Philpott argues that reification '… emphasizes knowledge as a commodity as a 'thing' distinct from the knower …' and that: 'This is exemplified in school music by the autonomous existence of 'good' music quite apart from the experience of and values of the pupils themselves' which results in the alienation of children from the music curriculum as they perceive (consciously or subconsciously) a '… disjuncture between … how learning and the development of knowledge naturally takes place, and how it is experienced as part of a socially mediated school music curriculum' (Philpott 2010: 83).

The myth of musical diversity and educational inclusion

One of the oft-expressed intentions of bringing into the curriculum music from a broad range of traditions and cultures, is as a means of addressing the alienation of children from the music curriculum in schools; the assumption being that the presence of such music will, by definition ensure a more inclusive curriculum. However, despite the inclusion of such music, the ideology of high status music knowledge as manifest through western art music continues to be promoted through the way in which these musics are presented and taught in the classroom. In other words, the presence of a culturally diverse musical repertoire in classrooms has not significantly challenged the musical and cultural values that previously were explicitly articulated through the dominant presence of classical music in the curriculum. The relationship between the knower and what there is to be known remains the same and the ideological values of western art music – of autonomy, objectification, abstraction and decontextualization – remain unchallenged.

An ideology is at its most powerful when it is 'invisible' and this invisibility is typically achieved through being cloaked by values which are perceived (particularly by those social or cultural groupings whose interests it does not promote) as objective, self-evident, neutral and – especially – universal. Lucy Green (2003) argues that one of the ways in which this is achieved is through the process of *legitimation*, the purpose of which is to make an act or process appears morally and/or logically justified.

When faced with music from other traditions and cultures, western art music asserts its ideology by imposing on these musics the attributes and characteristics of high status knowledge through a process of objectification, commodification and social decontextualization which is then legitimated in three ways.

Firstly, by suggesting that the original intention of bringing these musics into the curriculum has not been compromised by the process of being turned into a form of high status knowledge. This is achieved through promoting the idea that musical artefacts of themselves, despite being disconnected from the social practices, structures and relationships which brought them into being and which give them meaning, say something about the culture of their provenance. That through enabling children to engage with these musical artefacts they consequently gain a greater understanding of that culture thus addressing issues of diversity, cultural understanding and inclusion. However, in many cultures and societies, musical meaning is evinced not through its musical artefacts but its musical practices– its *practices* are what give music its meaning.

Secondly, legitimation occurs through promoting the idea that the categorizations of music into style and genre types that proceed from objectification and commodification, is the natural and only way of thinking about and classifying music. Step into any record store or log on to iTunes, Napster or any other online downloading site – the marketplaces of commoditized music – and one can see how music is organized into its commoditized and objectified forms, with sections devoted to 'classical', 'rock', 'film', 'pop' and 'jazz' musics and – inevitably – a mopping-up category of 'world musics'. The music curriculum is then typically organized to reflect the underpinning structure of this musical market place with discrete units on jazz, opera, Indian music, Chinese music, etc.[3], with, however, little indication of how these form a progressive pathway to greater musical understanding.

However as Rogers points out:

> Commodification *abstracts* the value of an object (or action) so it can enter the system of exchange. In this process, then intrinsic use-value and the spec-ificity of labor invested in the commodity are lost: it becomes in practice equivalent to all other commodities ... In order to create the appearance of difference (and hence value) amidst this equivalence, additional meanings are attached to the commodity.
>
> (Rogers 1999: 12–13)

Many musics therefore lose any authentic meaning through the process of commodification, with this meaning being replaced by meanings which promote and sustain the dominant musical ideology.

An enlightened and inclusive music education is then conceived of as one which enables engagement with as many artefacts from as many musical cultures as possible. This results in a curriculum which simply tours the world's music in a whirlwind of musical speed-dating, collecting musical artefacts as it goes but ignoring the musical practices that underpin the creation of these artefacts and which are central to the understanding of many of these musics.

Thirdly, having legitimated the process of musical objectification on musics for whom practices are of central importance, the characteristics and attributes of high status subject knowledge which are projected through such objectification are then used as the means of asserting the relational superiority of western art music. This is realized through a process of musical 'othering'. In educational arenas, musical 'othering' occurs where schools, teaching methodologies and/or curriculum documents promote the dominant musical culture (western art music) as the 'norm' with music from 'other' cultures viewed relationally in terms of how they differ from this norm – i.e. as the 'other. These 'other' musics are then evaluated in terms of the extent to which they act differently from the ideological norm of western art music (autonomous, objectified music with strong formal and structural framing). Bohlman points out how the 'othering' of music results in the construction of binary opposites between 'high' and 'low' culture, 'literate' and 'oral'; 'élite' and 'popular' (Bohlman 2002: 36–7) and, as he further observes, '...all these terms and the conceptual pairs they form have distinctly Western origins' and that 'within the pairs one term is available for the observer, trans-forming the other into a place occupied by the observed'.

The dominant status of western art music means that its values are almost always cast in the role of observer and consequently 'other' musics are 'judged' by the extent to which they conform to the ideology of music as autonomous and

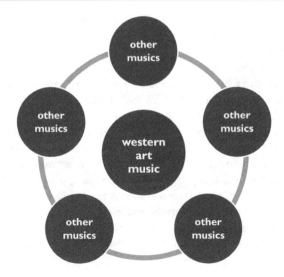

Figure 8.1 The dominant ideology of western art music.

objectified artefact. However as we have argued, for many other musical cultures and traditions the focus is not on the production of an artefact *per se*, but rather on musical practices, with artefacts being, in a sense, simply a by-product of these practices. Consequently, when these artefacts are evaluated exclusively in terms of their formal properties they are inevitably found to be lacking and this is taken as evidence of their essential inferiority. This is how western art music articulates its seemingly self-evident superiority over other musics.

The impact of musical 'othering' on music education is significant. The binary opposites referred to above strengthen the dominance of high status musical knowledge through pedagogies which promote and value notated (literate) musical forms over oral forms, 'high' culture music over 'low' culture and 'élite' musical forms over 'popular' musical practices. Furthermore, through the process of objectifying music from 'other' cultures and conceptualizing it as artefacts rather than practices, the dominant ideology of western art music is actually reinforced in that it is perceived as the 'core' music with other musics simply as planets around its axis (see Fig. 8.1).

Therefore, the focus on artefacts in the teaching of music from different cultures does not *counter* the hegemony of western art music but rather acts as a kind of musical prophylactic protecting western art music from the musical values and ideologies of these cultures.

Western art music sustains its influence on what is defined as high status musical knowledge – and consequently the way in which music is taught and learned – not so much then through the presence in the curriculum of its own artefacts, but rather through promoting the idea that the values, practices and beliefs and ways of thinking about music that underpin it can be applied with equal validity to the music of other cultures and traditions (*legitimation*). Consequently the teaching of music from 'other' cultures focuses on the production and study of musical artefacts rather than the development of musical practices. Such teaching fails to recognize, reflect or value the fact that the music with which most children are involved in outside of school, the focus of musical endeavour is not on the artefact but rather on musical practices. This then results in the alienation of young people from the curriculum as they perceive a fundamental disjuncture between school music and how they engage with and experience music in the world outside of school.

In the following section we argue that the alienation experienced by many children from a curriculum dominated by the values of western art music can be countered through a curriculum which is predicated upon musical practices. We argue that a focus on practices – or music as praxis – affords teachers a potentially much richer panoply of approaches to musical learning and leads pupils to a deeper understanding of the nature and purposes of music. More especially however it can address the hegemony of high status knowledge as the root cause of alienation from the curriculum.

Music curriculum as praxis

Music as 'praxis' is rooted in the belief that music is understood not simply through the examination, exploration and 'appreciation' of the artefacts of music as autonomous objects, but also that of equal, and perhaps greater, importance is how people engage with music: how they produce, transmit (and who does the transmitting) and receive (use) music (Green and O'Neill 2001).

David Elliott argues that a 'praxial concept of music has four major aspects' (Elliott: 1995: 129). These concepts challenge the prevailing concept of high status musical knowledge as promoted through the ideological values of western art music. In Table 8.1 we take each of these aspects in turn and briefly describe the way in which they counter these values.

A praxial view of music holds that what is understood by the term music, the purposes for which music is used both individually and collectively, what is musically valued and how musicality and musical expertise is defined, recognized and expressed, are all culturally and socially rooted and vary across and often within cultural groupings.

Drawing on Bourdieu's idea of fields of practice, Turino proposes a different but complementary perspective on music as praxis positing the idea that music should be thought of not as a 'single art form subdivided into various styles and status categories' but rather that we should 'conceptualize music making in relation to different realms or *fields* of artistic practice' (Turino 2008:25). Turino's ideas offer a more detailed working out of music as praxis and a potential way forward for a praxis-based music curriculum.

Turino suggests that there are four broad fields of musical practice which are characterized and defined by 'the values, power relations, and types of capital (e.g. money, academic degrees, a hit song, athletic prowess, the ability to play a guitar) determining the social roles, power relationships and status of actors and activities within a field' (Turino 2008: 26).

Table 8.1 Aspects of praxial music and implications for the ideology of high status knowledge.

Aspects of praxial music	Implications for the ideology of high status knowledge
'Music is human endeavour. It is people who make and listen to musical works in deliberate and culturally patterned ways. Musical practices, musical works and musicianship that they depend on for their existence are social-cultural constructions'.	If music is human endeavour and meaning is socially and culturally patterned then musical knowledge cannot meaningfully exist independently of the knower as the knower plays a key role in the mediation and construction of that knowledge.
'Music is never a matter of works alone, and musical works are never a matter of formal elements, auditory designs, or sound patterns alone'.	High status musical knowledge is predicated upon the belief that music is fundamentally about autonomous works. This aspect of praxial music challenges this conception of music.
'Music is meant to include such related actions as moving, dancing and worshipping that people may engage in as part of, or in addition to, musicing and listening'.	This aspect broadens the definition of music from just its sonic materials to associated activities and responses. In doing so it presents another challenge to the notion of music as an object.
'This [the above] concept of music acknowledges that musical sounds can be made for a variety of purposes and functions across cultures' (*Ibid.*).	Music is not understood simply through formal properties or sonic materials. Its meaning lies in the uses to which it is put.

The fields of practices Turino proposes are:

- Presentational
- Participatory
- High Fidelity
- Studio Art.

Turino suggests that each of these fields reflects a particular paradigm of musical practice with distinctive modes of musical production, transmission and reception and consequently different relationships between 'composer', 'performer' and 'listener'.

The broad characteristics of these practices and their implications for music education are as follows.

1. Presentational practices

The focus of presentational practices is on the *presentation* of music to another and *separate* group of people – typically an audience. In presentational practices, music is 'presented' as an 'object for attention'. Consequently the focus of its production, transmission and reception is on its formal properties. Music that is produced for presentational practices will typically be 'complete' in that it will have a clearly defined beginning and ending and may be 'scripted' through notation or recorded form. Its scripted nature allows for complexity of form which is highly valued.

Because the focus of attention is on the music's formal properties, textural clarity is important in allowing those formal properties to be heard. Presentational practices therefore typically focus on uniformity of presentation in terms of tuning and ensemble and meticulous realization of the score: skills commonly, but not exclusively, associated with western art music. In presentational practices musical roles tend to be clearly delineated between composer, performer and listener. Events which are focused on presentation practices typically occur in places such as concert halls where there are minimal external distractions.

Implications for music education

Although the practices of western art music are most closely reflected in presentational practices, it does not follow from this that presentational practices are exclusively represented by and within western art music. Aspects of presentational practices can be found in, for example, Indian classical music and some jazz performance events. This is an important point, because to assume that presentational practices are synonymous with, and exclusive to, western art music, is to collude in their appropriation and manipulation in the construction and legitimation of high status knowledge.

The focus of presentational practices on the formal properties of music has, however, made such appropriation relatively easy and resulted in a shift of focus from the practices themselves to the *products* of these practices, in order to facilitate objectification, abstraction, reification of the music and its perceived existence as independent of the knower. Such knowledge then often takes the form of 'music to be learned' or 'appreciated' – to be consumed – for its own supposed, autonomous value, independent of the needs or desires of the learner and unrelated to their own musical lives. Presentational practices in school then become but a poor shadow of their out-of-school, unmediated forms as they lack the presence of 'self' which, in the world outside, gives meaning to these practices for those involved. Because the musical objects with which they are required cannot contribute to what Kramer refers to the 'cultural construction of subjectivity' (1995: 21) they experience an alienated relationship with that music.

There is here an absence of what Kramer describes as 'hermeneutic windows, sites of engagement through which the interpreter and the interpreted animate one another' (1995:21). In order for presentational practices to reconstitute themselves authentically within the classroom and resist ideological appropriation they need to construct sites of engagement where such animations can take place. Key to the efficacy of these sites is learners' ownership of, and consequently non-alienated relationship with, musical knowledge and the possibilities that this holds for a dialectical relationship with that knowledge. In order to achieve this, sites of engagement need to counter the decontextualized character of high status knowledge and reconnect with learners' lived realities. Such sites of engagement perhaps exist at present within the domains of informal learning and in those classrooms where the principles of informal learning are at play; most notably in those *Musical Futures* classrooms where these principles are firmly established and integrated into teachers' pedagogical approaches. Pupils work in self-selected groups, choose their own music to work with, learn through listening and imitation. The pedagogy emerges from the pupils' practices as a means of supporting those practices and is not imposed upon them in furtherance of political and ideological goals. Here pupils have ownership over musical knowledge and consequently an unalienated relationship with it.

2. Participatory practices

Participatory practices differ from presentational practices in two ways. First, the primary focus of participatory practices is not on presenting an artefact but rather facilitating and encouraging involvement.[4] Second, the roles of composer, performer and audience are much less clearly delineated, being characterized by 'no artist –audience distinctions, only participatory and potential participants ... the primary goal is to involve the maximum number of people in some performance role' (Turino 2008: 26).

Music making in participatory practices involves a process of constant evolvement where music remembered from previous participatory events is 'refashioned anew in each performance like the form, rules and practiced moves of a game' (p: 59). So, for example, traditional musicians do not conceive of folk music as '... a set of songs and tunes ... [but] more of a working practice. People take available musical resources and develop strategies to make good use of them. Behind this work lie aims, reasons for giving music its share of your life and energy' (Slobin 2011: 3). The repertoire and key musical aspects form a 'palette' from which the musicians can pick and choose.

Rather than focusing on precise and uniform tuning and ensemble to achieve clarity of texture, participatory practices aim to produce more opaque textures which result from wider tuning parameters and 'constantly shifting heterophonic approaches to the performance of specific melodies' (Turino 2008: 45) all of which provides a 'cloaking function that helps inspire musical participation' (p. 46).[5]

Participatory practices are formed of two sub-fields: 'simultaneous participation' and 'sequential participation'. In the first of these everyone performs simultaneously whilst in the second participants perform in turn for each other so that in the course of a session participants will be both performers and audience. As Turino points out, in sequential participation there are 'features of presentational music making' (Turino 2008: 48).

Implications for music education

The focus of participatory practices on 'involvement' and their typically 'unscripted' nature means that music roles are less sharply delineated and consequently performing, composing and responding emerge naturally from these practices as unified and integrated, thus acting as a resistant to objectification. Further challenges to western art music-orientated high status musical knowledge are manifest through the conception of musical artefacts, not as fixed and objectified – and thereby existing independently of the knower – but as resources that can be reworked and refashioned anew. The absence of 'a script' enables children's engagement with, and immersion in, the materials of music to be more immediate as they 'refashion' musical materials within the practices and conventions of the musical tradition within which they are working. Building on participatory practices enables teachers to develop pedagogies which enable such immersion and create a context in which children demonstrate their musical understanding through 'doing and making'. For example in *Samba Batucada* music children learn together as a group. This acts as 'a cloaking function' (Turino 2008: 59) which promotes simultaneous participation practices. As the children gain in confidence they have opportunities to become the 'leader' and play individually to create their own rhythms against the groove.

The very process of 'refashioning' music anew and the fundamental importance in participatory practices of musical understanding through 'doing' – reflecting Elliot's view that 'our musical knowledge is in our actions; our musical thinking and knowing are in our musical doing and making'(Elliott 1995: 57) – promotes a 'oneness' between the knowledge and knower in a dialectical, unalienated relationship.

3. High Fidelity

High Fidelity practices are typically concerned with the use of recording technology to 'capture' presentational and participatory events. Through acting as the means by which music is decontextualized from its social context and commodified through the production of CDs and digital downloads, it can be argued that High Fidelity practices promote the ideology of music as artefact. Indeed it can be argued that High Fidelity practices can 'make presentational' what were participatory events. Such is the strength of the ideology of music as autonomous artefact that, particularly in western art music practices, many believe that to possess a recording of a musical event is virtually synonymous with being there; or possibly even better as the absence of others ensures that the listener's direct and unmediated engagement with the sonic materials of music remain undisturbed. In order not to disrupt this illusion, high fidelity practices strive first and foremost to make invisible or 'silent' the technological mediation that is taking place so that the illusion of a recording is virtually synonymous with being present at the event.

Turino also acknowledges that for many the notion of High Fidelity as a musical practice is potentially problematic in that it does not involve the creation of sonic materials and can therefore be seen as 'parasitic on and secondary to, the "actual" music making'(2008: 68). However, as he demonstrates, High Fidelity practices involve making *some* musical decisions through, for example deciding the relative balance between participants and clarity of parts, selecting the best 'take' and sequencing the order of tracks on a CD to achieve variety and contrast.

Implications for music education

High Fidelity practices are an important element in many vocational qualifications and as Turino points out, the High Fidelity practices do require musical decision-making. For example, a student working in the classroom in the role of a recording engineer will be required to make ongoing evaluations of performance 'takes' against negotiated criteria and work with performers to draw out the best performance. They will need to make musical decisions about the balance between parts and the recording ambience and then evaluate how effectively the recording is representative of the live performance – if that kind of representation is what they wish to achieve. However for this practice more than perhaps any of the others, the principle interest resides in its relationship to the other practices and the implications of the products of this practice for music education.

High Fidelity practices as perceived through the ideology of high status musical knowledge perform the function of objectifying music through recordings so that it can become an object of attention. In school contexts these recordings have traditionally played central roles in musical appreciation and listening lessons, examinations, and tests of musical perception – thus reinforcing the idea of musical knowledge existing independently of the knower. However High Fidelity practices have the potential to have a much more enriching impact on music education. Not only do they make available rich resource of music for young people at the click of a mouse or flick of a switch but, returning to the idea of Kramer's 'hermeneutic windows' and 'sites of engagement' (*op. cit.* 21), recordings can allow a self-modulated, 'distanced' relationship with music allowing the opportunity to recognize and reflect 'on an expressive act' and thus to 'empower the interpretive process' (1999: 9). Kramer is referring to 'interpretive process' here in the context of listening to music and he is postulating the idea of the listener not as a passive receiver and processor of sonic information – as in the school examples above – but rather as an active constructer of musical meaning. Again, within the context of praxis there is manifest here an unalienated relationship between knowledge and knower.

4. Studio Art

The distinction between Studio Art practices and High Fidelity practices is that in Studio Art practices the technology is *foregrounded* and made audible/visible. An important feature of many Studio Art practices is the possibility of generating sounds which are not imitative of acoustic or conventional electronic instruments and thus allow the creation of unique sound worlds. Studio Art can take a number of forms and reflect and promote a range of 'ideologies'. Compositions which are exclusively electronic, such as Stockhausen's *Kontakte* (1958–60) can be said to represent the *ne plus ultra* of music as artefact as the music is fixed in its electronic form and not subjected to mediation by a 'performer'. However, Studio Art practices can also interact with 'live' performance as in, for example Gabriel Prokofiev's *Concerto for Turntables and Orchestra* (2008). Performed by DJ and orchestra, combining live orchestral performance with sampled extracts of both orchestral players and electronic instruments woven together in time by a DJ at the turntables.

Implications for music education

The hardware and software of studio practices – computers and mobile technologies – provide children with the tools for the relatively unmediated production, transmission and reception of music. The easy access to the means of musical production and reception subverts the separation of knowledge from the learner which lies at the heart of decontextualized, high status knowledge. Studio Art practices, and particularly digital technologies, also provide the means for recontextualizing musical practices to social spaces where young people can engage in dialogue about their music and co-construct musical knowledge.

The development of social networking sites has encouraged people – especially young people – to draw on both Studio Art and High Fidelity practices to engage in participatory practices via the internet. For example, there are now many music-sharing sites online which provide 'safe' places for young people to share with others the music they create. Audio or video recordings of performances can be posted which can then be commented on by others. More especially however these sites provide the opportunity for the collaborative development of compositions. In inland Australia, for example, where there are great distances between schools, these techniques are used to enable pupils in inner city and rural schools to work together on their compositions. Criteria for co-composition are agreed, and then using sequencing software, pupils work on their composition, post it back online for others to contribute to, and the process goes on. The musician Brian Eno, speaking in a television interview,[6] speaks of such sites and practices as being the first step to an 'open source' musical world. He argues that digital technologies have fundamentally changed the nature of music and musical roles arguing for example that a 'a composer is more like a gardener than an architect – planting sets of musical seeds and seeing how they will evolve'.

A final point

It is important to note that Turino's fields of practice are 'ideal types'. Particular musical cultures and traditions and their practitioners are likely to reflect and inhabit more than one practice. For example, the jazz practices exhibited at New

York's Lincoln Centre reflect more of the presentational practices of the concert hall than the participatory features of a traditional jazz club, and the floor-to-ceiling glassed room, overlooking central Manhattan, is as much a temple to the presentation of musical artefacts as is Carnegie Hall. Similarly, where music originating from participatory practices is recontextualized into spaces which emphasize presentational practices, audiences can experience a form of split personality where some audience members act in accordance with the presentational context and treat the music as an 'object for attention' whilst others continue to engage with it – often much to the annoyance of the former group – as participatory music. The important point here is that practices are as much about 'reception' as 'production' and 'transmission'.

Conclusion

Our suggestion therefore is that by locating the music curriculum within a framework of musical practices, we can begin to address the alienation of children from the formal music curriculum. Children's understanding of music as praxis can lead them to recognize musical ideologies not as immutable 'givens' but rather as belief systems that can be engaged with and challenged. Teaching music as praxis makes musical ideologies more visible and thus open to challenge. Furthermore, the focus on praxis shifts the focus from content which is open to being controlled, to one of pedagogy. The 'making visible' of ideologies and the foregrounding of pedagogy over content is central to the notion of a critical pedagogy in music as children are no longer distanced from music as objectified knowledge, existing independently of them but rather are immersed in music as active participants in the construction of musical knowledge.

Within the context of music as praxis, a broad and inclusive musical education will be predicated not on the acquisition of cultural capital in the form of musical artefacts (either as performer, composer or listener) but rather on the opportunities that it offers for children to engage and act musically and progress within the full range of music practices and *to know them as practices*.

A consequence of a curriculum based on music as praxis is that there is no longer a need to tour the world's music cultures and traditions collecting artefacts as cultural capital. Rather, examples of music are drawn upon as an exemplification and working out of musical practices within a particular culture or tradition. The use of the plural form (practices) here is important in that it acknowledges that, as demonstrated by Turino and through the examples given in this chapter, although musical traditions and cultures might be located predominantly in one practice field, they will almost always also inhabit other fields of practice; as will their practitioners. A key aspect of understanding music will be exploring it from the different dimensions that Turino proposes.

Pedagogies then emerge naturally as reflections of the musical practices rather than being artificially imposed as manifestations of a particular ideology. So for example, integration occurs as a natural outcome of engagement with most participatory practices, whilst those skills and understandings related to western art music are manifested as characteristics of (primarily but not exclusively) presentational practices. Musical judgements and assessments are then located within the values of different practices and negotiated with young people as an integral part of their role as co-constructors of knowledge.

Finally, a music curriculum predicated on music as praxis can begin with, and focus more meaningfully on, the range and diversity of musical practices within young people's own society and cultural groups and thus enable students and teachers to come to understand these communities more deeply. As Goble says, 'through exploring more deeply the music of their respective cultural communities and engaging with the musics of their own regions and countries (gradually expanding their focus outward) students will be able to discover what makes different music important to different people who undertaken them' (Goble 2010: 23).

Reflective questions

1   Consider your personal experiences of music making. How might they be described in terms of the four practices outlined in this chapter? Are you more involved with one practice than others, and is this related to a style or genre you participate in the majority of the time? Do you think this has an influence on your approach to music teaching?
2   In what ways do you feel that a praxial approach might support the development of a critical pedagogy within your own teaching context?
3   How might the four musical practices challenge the prevailing western art ideology of treating composing, performing and listening as separate musical disciplines?
4   Do you agree that a common approach to world musics in the curriculum is one of 'speed dating'? How might a teacher provide a more authentic, praxial approach to classroom music teaching, drawing on the characteristics of the four fields of practices?

Notes

1   This chapter adopts Keller's definition of ideologies as being ' a coherent set of ideas brought together not for strictly intellectual purposes but, rather, in the service of some strongly held beliefs or values'. (Keller 2007: 93)
2   Prior to the beginning of the eighteenth century the primary purpose of the practice of music was to create or contribute to a social event; not the production of a score.
3   Often preceded (typically in the first year of secondary schooling) by a study of the musical elements (rhythm, texture, timbre, pitch etc.) – the 'building bricks' of music – which further emphasize the abstraction of musical knowledge in school.
4   This involvement can be musical, movement, dancing or engaging in the social event of which the music is part.
5   Turino cites examples from Peruvian, Central African Pygmy singing and Balinese Gamelan as examples of how some music practices tune 'unison' instruments

slightly apart to create the 'dense' textures which can encourage and facilitate participation (2008: 45).
6 Interview on BBC Newsnight, 5 October 2011.

References

Bohlman, P.V. (2002) *World Music: A Very Short Introduction*, Oxford: Oxford University Press.

Elliott, D.J. (1995) *Music Matters*, Oxford: Oxford University Press.

Goble, J.S. (2010) 'Not Just a Matter of Style: Addressing Culturally Different Musics as Social Praxes in Secondary School Music Classes', in *Action, Criticism and Theory for Music Education*, 9(3), http://act.maydaygroup.org

Goehr, L. (1992) *The Imaginary Museum of Musical Works*, Oxford: Oxford University Press.

Green, L. (2003) 'Music Education, Cultural Capital and Social Group Identity' in M. Clayton, T. Herbert, and R. Middleton (eds) *The Cultural Study of Music*, London: Routledge.

Green, L. (2003) 'Why "Ideology" is Still Relevant for Critical Thinking in Music Education', *Action, Criticism and Theory for Music Education*, 2(2), http://act.maydaygroup.org

Green, L. and O'Neill, S. (2001) 'Social groups and Learning in Music Education' in *Mapping Music Education Research in the UK*, Southwell: British Educational Research Association.

Green, L. (1998) 'From the Western Classics to the World: Secondary Music Teachers' Changing Attitudes in England, 1982 and 1998', *The British Journal of Music Education*, 19(1): 5–13.

Hess, J. 'Tokenism in the Classroom: Decolonising Music Education', Paper presented at the Research in Music Education Conference, Exeter, April 2011.

Keller, M. (2007) 'Why is Music So Ideological, and Why Do Totalitarian States Take It So Seriously? A Personal View from History and the Social Sciences', *Journal of Musicological Research* 2: 91–122.

Kramer, L. (1995) *Classical Music and Postmodern Knowledge*, California: University of California Press.

Kramer, L. (1990) *Music as Cultural Practice 1800–1900*, Berkeley: University of California.

Philpott, C. (2010) 'The Sociological Critique of Curriculum Music in England: Is Radical Change Really Possible?', in R. Wright (ed.) *Sociology and Music Education*. Farnham: Ashfield.

Qualifications and Curriculum Authority (2007) *The National Curriculum for England*, Crown Copyright.

Rogers, R. 'World Music: Commodification, Imperialism and Resistance', paper presented at the Western State Communicative Association Annual Conference, Vancouver, February 1999.

Slobin, M. (2011). *Folk Music: A Very Short Introduction*, Oxford: Oxford University Press.

Spruce, G. (2002) 'Ways of Thinking About Music: Political Dimensions and Educational Consequences', in *Teaching Music in Secondary Schools: a reader*, London: RoutledgeFalmer/Open University.

Turino, T. (2008) *Music as Social Life: The Politics of Participation*, Chicago: The University of Chicago Press.

Wright, R. (2010) 'Democracy, Social Exclusion and Music Education: Possibilities for Change' in R. Wright (ed.) *Sociology and Music Education*, Farnham: Ashfield.

Young, M. (1999) 'The curriculum as socially organised knowledge', in R. McCormick and C. Paechter (eds) *Learning and Knowledge*, London: Paul Chapman.

Part III

The Pedagogy of Music

Integrity and autonomy for music in a creative and cross-curriculum

Jonathan Barnes

Introduction

Music, creativity and collaboration

In this chapter I discuss ways in which music can continue to be fully included in the statutory curriculum. In particular, I outline arguments for the inclusion of music in creative cross-curricular work and answer some of the criticisms from those who argue that music can only survive in a separate and autonomous subject setting.

The starting point is that music is so fundamental to human beings that it must remain part of the formal education of every child. Music is a distinct mode of thought and action with its own vocabulary, history and skills; music clearly contributes to our understanding of the world. It is not simply a successful aspect of the 'window dressing' of many schools but has a special place in all cultures. Donald Brown's research into these 'human universals', (Brown, in Pinker 2002: 435-439) showed that no less than ten different aspects of music are culturally universal: including special music for children, music seen as an art, music as essential for ceremonial/religious purposes, musical repetition and music following the rhythms and cadences of language.

Music is probably the most universally recognized discipline after language. In our own society, researchers (see e.g., Hoskyns and Bunt 2002; Justlin and Sloboda 2009) have demonstrated the dominance of music in lives outside school, often helping us manage and express emotions. Music is with us throughout our days from our ringtones, through private listening on the way to work, its canned varieties in lifts and supermarkets, to the TV and films we watch in the evenings.

Following on from this, creativity is at the heart of music as a discipline. Creativity happens at the meeting point of two or more different thought systems (Koestler 1964; Csikszentmihalyi 1997; Pope 2005). It is more often a collaborative than a lone activity (John-Steiner 2001) and under current definitions is evident in the lives of all people (Barnes and Scoffham in DCSF 2008). Though creativity is often divided into its 'little c' and 'big C' (Craft 2000; Boden 1990), many commentators observe that in its everyday form it is abundantly present in the lives and actions of children (Wyse and Rowson 2008; Barnes 2010; Robinson 2010; Demos 2010). I have argued elsewhere (Hope, Barnes and Scoffham 2008; Barnes 2011b), that the discovery of the self as a creative being is an important element in the sense of deeper wellbeing for both teachers and children. Such creativity of course has its dark sides, its struggles and disappointments, but as Csikszentmihalyi argues it is 'a central source of meaning,' for many (1997:3).

Given the centrality of music to humanity and its inherently creative and collaborative nature, the discipline is ripe for cross-curricular work in schools. Those who look beyond simply serving the economy towards enhancing human wellbeing as an educational aim have increasingly championed music in a cross-curricular and creative context as providing an essential ingredient of a broad, balanced and inclusive approach to the curriculum. Indeed, under pressure from statutory changes in education those in music education may increasingly need to turn to cross-curricular work to ensure its survival as the birthright of every child.

Cross-curricular approaches to education have a long history. They are implicit in aspects of ancient Greek and Chinese education where drama, music and literature were usually combined. Cross-curricular experiences, at least for younger pupils, reappeared in the writings and work of eighteenth and early nineteenth century progressives like Rousseau, Pestalozzi and Froebel. In the UK cross-curricular approaches were re-examined in the twentieth century a number of times prior to their last outing in the 1960s and 1970s after the Plowden Report (1967). In Scotland and Northern Ireland music has been subsumed within cross-curricular themes like 'Creative and Expressive Studies', and 'cultural heritage', (e.g., Northern Ireland *Common Curriculum* 1991). UK government legislation and independent advice in the first decade of the twenty-first century has secured its re-examination in widely different contexts, across the Key Stages (DfEE/DCMS 1999; Ofsted 2002; DfES 2003; QCA 2003; DfES 2008). Recent curriculum reviews (Rose 2009; Alexander 2010) have proposed that music should lie within generic curriculum categories like 'place and time' and 'arts and creativity', as a perception of curriculum overload grew. Furthermore, music has become central to many successful cross-curricular and creative projects (Roberts 2006; DCSF 2008; Creative Partnerships 2006; Cape UK 2008; Ofsted 2010).

Successful educators have shown how music can be easily integrated into any theme, adding both depth and breadth to the learning experience. Used sensitively and given its personal, wordless, emotional and collaborative nature music has been made accessible across a wide spectrum of students. This chapter will draw upon experience and research in music education to examine how music as a discrete language and discipline can be sustained, developed and flourish within a broad, balanced, creative (and cross-) curriculum. Creativity does not necessarily imply a lack of specific subject rigour. Indeed as students' confidence in the disciplined knowledge, skills and understandings of music increases the potential to use them creatively increases.

There is no necessary conflict here between 'playful' and 'rigorous' approaches to music education. It is true that 'creative' modes of teaching and learning have been criticised as causing the loss of the rigour necessary for progression (Barnes and Shirley 2005), and have made learning vulnerable to an over-emphasis on low level knowledge. However, taught well, creative cross-curricular work can promote deep, transferrable and lifelong learning (Rogers 2003). Depth and transferability in music education involve encouraging purposeful and progressive musical play, musical compositions of increasing complexity or subtlety and the development of a broad range of listening and evaluative skills. Each aspect needs practise and each may be more profoundly understood when combined with the thought processes of another discipline. Indeed, creativity flourishes in such challenging circumstances (see Nachmanovich 1990; Csikszentmihalyi 1997).

So far I have argued that both music and creativity are important in the holistic development of all individuals. Since music is a highly creative and collaborative medium, it suits those seeking to develop wider creative and cross-curricular responses in students and teachers. Working together on shared and meaningful projects that involve music connecting with other ways of thinking stimulates social and interpersonal progress and can be at the heart of the process of education. However, in arguing for both musical creativity and the inclusion of music in wider cross-curricular creative projects I am aware of the risks of compromising the integrity and autonomy of music itself. I address these risks in the following discussion on music within cross-curricular approaches.

Cross-curricular approaches to musical learning

To maintain the emphasis on the integrity of music as a discipline in a cross-curricular setting I suggest we need to look more carefully at several different modes of cross-curricularity. I have identified five contrasting modes (Barnes in Driscoll *et al.* 2011). Each kind of cross-curricular practice would tend to use music in a different way and for different purposes. If music is to retain its distinctive character within thematic or project work it is important that teachers understand these differences.

These forms of cross-curricular teaching and learning I have called:

- hierarchical
- multi-disciplinary
- interdisciplinary
- opportunistic
- double focus.

Hierarchical cross-curricular teaching and learning

Music is often used in cross-curricular contexts for its associations or supposed authenticity – providing little more than an atmospheric backdrop to the 'main activity'. The personal, expressive potential of music and its ability to express beyond the level of words, is usually absent in such appearances. Typically music is used to commit rules, tables or grammars to memory in English, Maths or Foreign Languages, reduced to an illustrative aspect of a distant place, a suitable backing for a P.E., Art or Science theme or evoking a distant time in a history study. In this way music plays the handmaiden's role, humbly serving another 'more important' subject. This subservient, or hierarchical role is, sadly the most common one for music in cross-curricular teaching and learning.

The hierarchical mode uses one subject to enhance understanding in another (see Fig 9.1). It is probably the most common context in which music combines with other subjects. A class rendition of *Greensleeves* might form the music element of a cross-curricular study of the Tudors, *Frère Jacques,* the musical contribution to Modern Languages or a simple chant in mathematics to help children remember the two times table (see Box 9.1). Alternatively recorded music may be used as a soothing background to work, reflect or converse against. In each instance music serves another subject, and little musical progression is likely – music is instrumental in the teaching of something considered more important. The danger is that school music may be cast forever in this subservient and submissive role.

Music, however also shows some of its particular strengths when used in a hierarchical cross-curricular context. Music making involves participants on emotional and physical levels which often generate greater participation and satisfaction than more didactic teaching situations (see Barnes in Evans and Philpott 2009). Used in a hierarchically weaker context new music skills may not be learned but the strength of music as a medium of communication, motivation and enjoyment may be enhanced. Music may be the route through which the child understands difficult concepts (see Gardner 1993; 1999), or simply provide

Figure 9.1 Hierarchical cross-curricular learning. *Learning in the 'superior' subject (Subject A) is enhanced with help from an 'inferior' subject in this case music.*

the enjoyment which motivates other learning. Occupying a hierarchically inferior position is the least challenging way to include music in an overcrowded curriculum. The many primary students and teachers who feel insecure in their ability to teach the elements or ensure musical progression find it relatively unthreatening to use a song or musical game to consolidate learning in another subject. See Box 9.1 for an example of this.

BOX 9.1: HEADS AND SHOULDERS

Three student teachers visiting a class in a rural school in India, used the song *Heads, shoulders, knees and toes* to teach Tamil children the English terms for parts of the body. With the help of the children they translated the song into Tamil and by the end of the lesson the English students sang to the class in Tamil.

Clearly in a hierarchical context music also can be the 'superior' discipline. Particularly in a secondary school setting where themes from subjects like English, Maths or Art may be used to enhance the musical experience. However, such reversals in the pecking order serve to perpetuate similarly limited learning, beyond the serendipitous, in the 'inferior' subject.

In other forms of cross-curricular teaching and learning it is more easily possible to ensure musical progression and a challenging, coherent and lasting musical experience.

Multidisciplinary cross-curricular teaching and learning

As with all learning approaches, multidisciplinary projects best arise from powerful and emotionally significant experiences for the children and teachers (Perkins 1992) (see Fig 9.2). Multidisciplinary cross-curricular approaches occur when several subjects are called upon *separately* to bring understanding to a theme, experience or idea. A topic may be introduced (usually by the teacher) and a variety of subject responses linked to the theme, but with *no intention of combining* them. ITE students often say they find linking subjects to themes is highly motivating for children. Effective multidisciplinary work in schools relies upon high degrees of teacher knowledge and confidence (see Roth in Wineburg and Grossman 2001). When the participating subjects are treated equally, multidisciplinary approaches can result in progress in all subjects, but when more than two subjects are used to serve a single theme it can become much more difficult to ensure progression in all.

Multidisciplinary modes offer a chance to develop musical skills and knowledge within a wider context. But learners usually require the motivation of personally engaging, and memorable experiences to generate deep, transferrable learning (Perkins in Sternberg and Williams 1998; Barnes in Driscoll *et al.*, 2011). Engaging, relevant, meaningful experiences have been argued to be fundamental to learning since the days of Plato and educational 'progressives' like Rousseau or Dewey, but are looked upon with suspicion by more conservative elements in education. Powerful experiences do not need to be high profile, whacky or time-consuming events. The effective single subject teacher will daily utilize a wide variety of engaging techniques to motivate, enhance, illustrate and summarize learning. Some of these experiences are so powerful that for a time they fully engage the whole class. Similarly, significant experiences in a cross-curricular context do not need to be sophisticated or complex to be effective. A story well-read, an interesting visitor from the community, a visit or an engaging focus exercise may be as powerful as a spectacular event. As Gardner reminds us:

> ... the brain learns best and retains most when the organism is actively involved in exploring physical sites and materials and asking questions to which it actually craves the answers. Merely passive experiences tend to attenuate and have little lasting impact.
>
> (Gardner 1999:108)

The second Case Study illustrates how progression in musical understanding was generated by a powerful experience. It is unlikely that imagining a journey would have been motivating for all children, notwithstanding the astonishing skill of some teachers to provoke the imagination. Box 9.2 records students learning ways of capturing their real experience on a visit to a nature reserve. Using experience as a motivator, the teacher taught (and children learned and used), musical structure words like: *rondo, theme, repetition* and *episode*. After the students had presented their first musical thoughts, the teacher suggested each composition group could work on applying one or more structures to their compositions. Students were introduced to new skills in changing the timbre of classroom

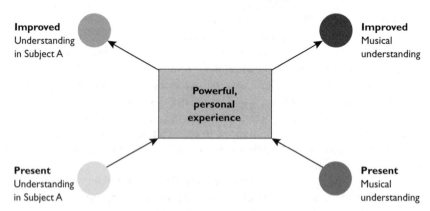

Figure 9.2 Multi-disciplinary cross-curricular learning. *Discrete learning in two or three subjects is enhanced through a shared and powerful experience.*

instruments learning to make three or four different sounds by striking and holding them in different ways. As a result of the same visit, specific and progressive skills in geography were also developed by all.

BOX 9.2: MUSICAL JOURNEYS

In an east London primary school Year 4 pupils took a short journey through a nature reserve with a 'journey stick' (a 15 cm strip of card with a band of double sided sticky tape attached). Children were directed to collect five tiny objects which caught their eye on their journey. On return to class each child made a sketch map of their journey, using recently taught geographical skills in map making. They used symbols to represent where they found each of their objects. Their maps were discussed and displayed in the classroom

Separately the children were given a musical challenge in the nature reserve. In groups of five they were asked to gather a collection of sounds from five different places using sound recorders. Back at school the groups made musical versions of their found sounds and strung them together with a repeated, whole class, 'Rondo' theme which represented their walking. Their musical journey was performed to the rest of the school in the following week.

Children's geographical learning was founded upon previous teaching and their musical learning on structure and timbre in music was part of an ongoing programme on these aspects of music. Teachers reported that the experience took children to higher standards than expected in both subjects.

(Website: http://www.engagingplaces.org.uk/teaching+and+learning/art69235)

Interdisciplinary cross-curricular teaching and learning

The prefix *inter* indicates joining, sharing or combining. The aim of interdisciplinary teaching and learning is *creatively to combine* the approaches of two or more subjects (see Fig 9.3). Research has suggested that creativity flows from situations where the disciplines are brought together to address a need or solve a problem (Csikszentmihalyi 1997). Interdisciplinary work often leads to some kind of joint outcome – a presentation, performance or product. Student teachers report this method of cross-curricular teaching generates creative responses and encourages creative teaching, but is also the most difficult to plan and assess. If creativity truly involves originality and imagination then how can a teacher foresee what an outcome will be in order to assess it? The answer lies in assessing progress in the two subjects as in multidisciplinary learning, but also assessing such aspects as the degree of originality.

Startling musical originality is all around us. Music in popular culture, TV, film, video games, promotions or advertising campaigns may be in the background, but is composed in highly sophisticated ways which take full account of the medium and the intended listener. Composers use standard musical structures and clichés – sequences, suspensions, cycles of fifths, *ostinati*, pedal notes, repetitions, tension and release to enhance images and words, but combined with the thought processes of other disciplines these familiar musical ideas often take on the feel of originality. Film music becomes less comprehensible without the images and the film less affecting minus the music: both disciplines have equal and complementary status. Educational examples of such combinations of disciplines grew with the successes of the Creative Partnerships scheme in the UK and related research and practice sponsored by independent arts organizations (e.g. CapeUK 2008).

Combining subjects in an interdisciplinary mode is more challenging than multi-disciplinary teaching. Equal confidence is required in both subjects. Subjects are not just applied to a single experience, theme or event but are combined in responding to that experience. Understanding in the separate subjects should be increased through thinking about the synthesis of ideas or materials, but we know that increased understanding does not always result from interdisciplinary work. Studies (e.g., Roth in Wineburg and Grossman 2000; Barnes and Shirley 2005; 2007) have shown that applying two, three or four subjects to the same theme can easily produce a 'bland broth' of half-understood ideas and new misconceptions. Some (see Hirsch 1998), use this argument to counsel against cross-curricular approaches altogether. Interdisciplinary cross-curricular teaching needs therefore to arise from confident subject knowledge, clear learning intentions and meaningful challenges for each subject if it is to be successful in taking learning forward. Box 9.3 illustrates this mode of cross-curricular work through an exploration of the Blitz.

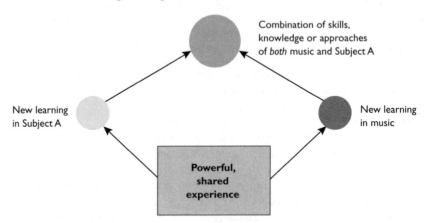

Figure 9.3 Inter-disciplinary learning. Learning in two subjects is taken forward as a result of a shared learning experience and then brought together in a presentation or application to a shared problem.

BOX 9.3 THE HARSH REALITIES OF THE BLITZ

Year 7 were involved in a topic on the blitz of London in the Second World War. As part of their preparation they spent the morning in a powerful simulation, *The Blitz Experience*, in the Imperial War Museum and collected thoughts and images that struck them most strongly. In discussion the teacher linked the horrors of seventy years ago with those currently being suffered in Palestine, Afghanistan and Iraq and led the class to think about the suffering of war. On return to school and on the same day as the museum visit, sections of Benjamin Britten's *War Requiem* were shared with the class and children discussed how the composer had expressed his anti war sentiments. This was contrasted with original newspaper coverage of the events of 1940. Both music and newspaper articles comprised historical evidence relating to the Second World War and the class evaluated these opposing views in the light of their modern understanding of the issues involved in today's wars.

Following this powerful experience the class embarked upon a music project that at first ran alongside their history work. The brief was to write a group composition of three minutes, to express a key emotion: Fear, anger, sadness or peacefulness. This music was to become the backing track of a dramatic empathy-based video capturing an event in the blitz. Students had to use digitally enhanced sounds, subtly and with a consciousness of the role of music in the video. They were asked to combine a range of music technology software with acoustic instruments and plan the compositions within recognizable, musical structures websites.

The final fusions of historical understanding, enhanced video technique and music for a special purpose were presented to parents and friends at a school open day six weeks later.

A further example of this popular and important approach can be found in Box 9.4.

BOX 9.4 MUSICAL HAIKUS

Each student in a Year 7/8 group in Canterbury wrote their own Haiku (A Japanese poetry form consisting at its simplest of three lines: five syllables, seven syllables and five syllables long) arising from an 'insignificant' detail of the local Cathedral. They had to find an object, describe it in detail and then say how it reminded them of something on a much higher philosophical/spiritual plane. In groups of five or six they shared their Haikus and agreed on one which might most suitable to put to music. After instructions to compose one minute of music with a distinct structure and the subtle use of timbre and dynamics, each group chose instruments, voices and/or found sounds to make their compositions. Students experimented with the words of the haiku, repeating, patterning, emphasising and generally playing with, silences and sound. Though inspired by the words and feelings of their Haiku, sometimes words entirely disappeared from the final products. After five minutes students were asked to present their 'work in progress' (none had finished) to the rest of the class. Their fragmentary pieces already avoided simple 'sound effects' because the proposed minute of music was far longer than their haikus. Most partial compositions suggested a mood generated by the words; some abandoned words and relied on sound only to tell their three line stories. After brief and positive but focussed feedback from the rest of the class each group was given just three minutes to pull their presentation together and mount a proper performance.

Opportunistic cross-curricular teaching and learning

Opportunistic approaches to cross-curricular learning are child-led, unpredictable and include an element of risk. The experienced and creative primary teacher is relaxed about building upon chance happenings in class and generating deep learning in any subject (see Austin 2007; Cremin, Barnes and Scoffham 2009).

Sometimes children's musical responses come unplanned and unexpected. Teacher confidence and good subject knowledge is crucial to maximize such child-led modes of cross-curricular learning. They must also feel empowered to follow the lead given by children, knowing that they have the support of colleagues and school leaders. In the current 'high accountability' school culture it may not be easy for teachers to feel this degree of professional trust. Successful teachers throughout time and culture have however been able to craft the unpredictable responses of creative learners into subject specific progress. They have done this first by acknowledging the subject 'home' of particular ideas, then by identifying particular elements within that subject that the idea exemplifies and third by suggesting improvements along a clear and disciplined trajectory. The Case Study in Box 9.5 is an example of opportunistic cross-curricular work.

BOX 9.5 OPPORTUNISTIC CROSS CURRICULAR WORK

One teacher heard two year one girls singing an improvised song whilst they were painting a decorative wall for an outdoor classroom the class was making. She said, '....that's lovely music, you've even got a verse and a chorus in your song.' This short comment was enough at the children's level, to establish both subject home and the element of structure in the minds of the children. When later in the day the class was singing a class song, the teacher reminded them that this was a bit like Maisy and Dori's song because it had a chorus too.

On a more ambitious scale, opportunistic cross-curricular learning has been a successful feature of many projects sponsored by Creative Partnerships between 2002 and 2011 in England (see Roberts 2006; Department of Culture Media and Sport (DCMS) 2006; HC 2007).

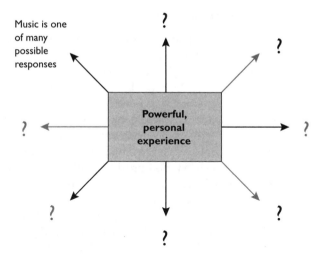

Figure 9.4 Opportunistic cross-curricular learning. *Unpredictable and child-led learning opportunities arise from a powerful and shared experience.*

Partly as a result of the UN Convention on the Rights of the Child the child's voice has become more prominent in planning the curriculum – opportunistic methods are thus discussed more often at both primary and secondary levels. They have always dominated at Foundation stage. At the same time as the pupil voice movement gathers pace, restrictive and over-assessed curricula are becoming more dominant (see Alexander 2010). These conflicting agendas again raise the issue of how best to motivate children towards lasting learning in music whilst maintaining music's status as a scholarly discipline.

In the UK the training of non-specialist primary teachers requires specific approaches to the teaching of reading and mathematics but students' preparation for the teaching of music is often left to chance (Rogers 2003). The two-tier approach to curriculum subjects has implications for both teacher education and opportunistic methods of teaching. In a musical context, novice teachers need opportunities to play with sound themselves and develop an appropriate musical vocabulary before they can effectively ensure progression in a child's musical learning. This argues for a broad and balanced education for our teachers where they develop confidence in a range of subjects in order to be able to build upon children's responses to real experience. In our cash-strapped schools and local authorities it may be similarly difficult to find accessible sources of in-service training for teachers and support staff – especially in music. Music requires a good measure of confidence to teach effectively and such confidence rarely comes from websites and resource books. Increasingly ITE institutions that still teach music will need to provide the training and development and confidence-building needed by serving teachers.

Double focus cross-curricular teaching

Double focus approaches relate more specifically to the ways teaching is organized. This approach treats music and all other subjects in two distinctive ways: first as a separate discipline with its own rules, language, skills and knowledge, second in combination with other subjects. In a double focus system each curriculum subject should have equal importance as recommended by Robinson (1999).

The skills, knowledge and attitudes of each established discipline provide powerful lenses through which we have traditionally made sense of experience (see Gardner 1999 and 2004). The aim in double focus teaching is to ensure subject progression through separate subject teaching but also provide regular opportunities for the creative application of subject skills and knowledge in a cross-curricular context.

Double focus approaches may be the solution if both music and creativity are valued. As in all good teaching, cross-curricular references will be part of normal separate subject teaching. Good music teaching relies on experiential approaches in the same way as effective cross-curricular or creative activity. The distinctive character of double focus teaching is that whilst separate subject teaching dominates, carefully planned and extended opportunities creatively to combine subjects punctuate the school year perhaps six or eight times.

Combinations should not be random in a double focus approach; progression in subject learning must remain the centre of attention. In order to provide an appropriate level of challenge and progress, standards remain at the core of both single subject studies and cross-curricular opportunities.

BOX 9.6 THE DOUBLE FOCUS APPROACH

A primary school linked to the *Room 13* project (2011) in Poptahof, Delft, Holland has two major curriculum foci; sustainability in the environment and music. The standard curriculum of language, mathematics, science, history, geography, music continues throughout the year using exciting and principled methods but when children have finished their work or can persuade their teacher that they may leave the class to work elsewhere, they are given a ticket to go to *Room 13*. Here a professional musician/composer is based to help the children in groups and singly to apply their classroom knowledge to real projects. In *Room 13* they work on authentic communal compositions and improvisations, exploring the possibilities of sound and how they can be combined. Many of these compositions arise from themes involving the ecology of the surrounding area and recently they composed the soundtrack for a book festival where their music arose from a story about aliens.

The timetable below shows what a week in a double focus curriculum might look like in a primary context. Each of the 11 curriculum subjects are core; each has its dedicated time but, in this instance, music, science and English have extra time devoted to a cross-curricular theme. Next term's cross-curricular theme may focus on different subjects.

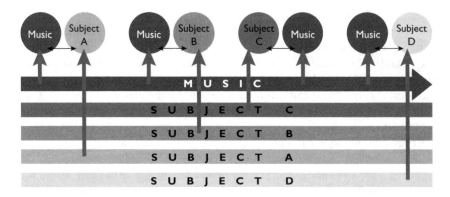

Figure 9.5 Double focus cross-curricular learning. *Learning in each curriculum subject continues separately throughout the year but is regularly joined with one or two others and applied to a shared experience.*

Table 9.1 An example of a double focus weekly timetable showing both separate subject studies and a cross-curricular project.

Monday	**Core Literacy/ English**	**Core Numeracy/ maths**	**RE** (Core learning)	**Music** (C-C theme)
Tuesday	**Core History**	**Literacy/ English** (C-C Theme)	**Cross-curricular** (C-C-theme, music and sci. focus)	**Cross-curricular** (C-C theme)
Wednesday	**Core Numeracy/ maths**	**Core Design and technology**	**Core PE**	**Core Art**
Thursday	**Science** (C-C theme)	**Science** (C-C theme)	**Core MFL**	**Core Geography**
Friday	**Core Literacy/ English/MFL**	**Ongoing Investigative Numeracy/ maths**	**Cross-curricular** (C-C theme, Music and science focus)	**Cross-curricular** (C-C theme Music and Sc focus)

Conclusion

The English national curriculum as conceived in 1988 made music education statutory, to be inspected and evaluated as other subjects, seen as essential to the well-rounded individual. For the first time a full, regular, well-thought-out and resourced music experience became the right of every child. The national curriculum also enshrined the right to music centred on creativity rather than simply knowledge and skill-based features. Thus it was envisaged that all children until 14 years of age had structured and regular opportunities to play with sound and organize it in imaginative and creative ways, just as art involves playing with and shaping colour and line. This was a hard-won battle. At the time of writing the debate on the status and nature of curriculum music has been renewed. Once again enthusiasts for progressive music education are arguing not only for its continued inclusion in every school's curriculum but for an honoured place in creative and integrated curricula of all education institutions.

The main argument of this chapter has been that creative cross-curricular approaches are an important part of the debate for the future of music education. Such approaches can demonstrate music to be an inclusive, life-enhancing, community-building, health-giving and spiritually satisfying subject. Furthermore, they will not weaken the integrity of music so long as musical progression is protected. Music will only be considered a worthy discipline if these values are clear to the general population as well as enthusiasts. This has important implications for teacher education. For music to survive as a curriculum subject, teachers will need to understand its importance and pedagogy as a single and cross-curricular discipline such that they can argue for and provide plentiful opportunities for *all* children to find and develop their musical voice.

Reflective questions

1   In what ways can pure music teaching include cross-curricular references?
2   Do cross-curricular and creative approaches inevitably 'dumb down' music education?
3   How can separate music teaching exist alongside regular opportunities for the cross-curricular application of musical knowledge?

References

Alexander, G. (2010) *The Cambridge Primary Review*, Cambridge: University of Cambridge Press.
Austin, R. (ed.) (2007) *Letting the Outside In*, Stoke on Trent: Trentham.
Barnes, C. (2009) 'Special Music', in *Primary Music Today*, Spring 2009.
Barnes, J. (2001) 'Creativity and Composition in Music,' in C. Philpott and C. Plummeridge (eds) *Issues in Music Education*, London: Routledge.
Barnes, J. (2009) 'Music in Cross Curricular Context Particularly the Arts', in C. Philpott and J. Evans, *A Practical Guide to Music in the Secondary School*, London: Routledge.
Barnes, J. (2010) 'The Generate Project: Curricular and pedagogical inspiration from parents working with their children', in *Improving Schools*, 13(2): 143–57.
Barnes, J. (2011a) in P. Driscoll, A. Lambirth and J. Roden (eds) *The Primary Curriculum*, London: Sage.
Barnes, J. (2011b) 'What Sustains a Fulfilling Life in Education?', paper presented at the ESREA Conference, Geneva, March 2011.

Barnes, J. (2011c) 'Music in Primary School ITE Placements', *NAME magazine*.

Barnes, J. and Shirley, I. (2005) 'Strangely Familiar; Promoting Creativity in Initial Teacher Education', Paper presented at British Educational Research Association (BERA) conference, September 2005.

Barnes, J. and Shirley, I. (2007) 'Strangely Familiar: Cross-Curricular and Creative Thinking in Teacher Education', *Improving Schools*, 10(2): 289–306.

Boden, M. (1990) *The Creative Mind: Myths and Mechanisms*, London: Abacus.

Brown, D. and Pinker, S. (2002) *The Blank Slate*, London: Penguin.

CapeUK (2008) Online at www.capeuk.org/> (accessed 20 February 2011).

Craft, (2001) *Creativity in the Primary School*, London: Routledge.

Creative Partnerships, (2006) Online at www.creative-partnerships.com (accessed 20 February 2011).

Cremin, T., Barnes, J. and Scoffham, S. (2009) *Creative Teaching for Tomorrow*, Deal: Future Creative.

Csikszentmihalyi, M. (1997) *Creativity and the Psychology of Discovery and Invention*, New York: Hodder.

DCMS (2006) *Government Response to the Roberts Report*, London: DCMS.

DCSF (2008) Creative Partnerships and the Curriculum. Online at www.publications. parliament.uk/pa/cm200708/cmselect/cmchilsch/266/266.pdf (accessed 20 February 2011).

Demos (2010) Born Creative. Online at www.demos.co.uk/publications/born-creative (accessed 20 February 2011).

DfEE/DCMS (1999) *All Our Futures*, the report of the national Advisory Committee on Creative and Cultural Education, London: Crown.

DfES (2003) *Developing Children's Social, Emotional and Behavioural Skills: Guidance*, London: Crown.

DfES (2003) *Excellence and Enjoyment*, Primary Education Strategy.

DfES/QCA (1999) *Curriculum Guidance for the Foundation Stage*, London: Crown.

DfES/QCA (1999) *The National Curriculum Handbook for Primary Teachers in England*. London: Crown.

Gardner, H. (1993) *Frames of Mind: The Theory of Multiple Intelligences*, 2nd edn, London: Fontana.

Gardner, H. (1999) *The Disciplined Mind; What All Students Should Understand*, New York, Simon and Schuster.

Gardner, H. (2004) *Changing Minds: The Art and Science of Changing our own and other people's minds*, Boston Mass: Harvard Business School.

Hope, G., Barnes, J. and Scoffham, S. (2008) 'A Conversation about Creative Teaching', in A. Craft, T. Cremin, and P. Burnard, *Documenting Creative Learning 3–13*, Stoke on Trent: Trentham.

Hoskyns, S. and Bunt, L. (2002) *The Music Therapy Handbook*, London: Routledge.

John-Steiner, V. (2001) *Creative Collaboration*, Oxford: Oxford University Press.

Justlin, P. and Sloboda, J. (2009) *Music and Emotion*, Oxford: Oxford University Press.

Koestler, A. (1964) *The Act of Creation*, London: Penguin Arkana.

Nachmanovitch, S. (1990) *Free Play: Improvisation I Life and Art*, New York: Penguin Putnam.

National Advisory Council on Creative and Cultural Education (NACCCE) (1999) *All Our Futures: Creativity, Culture and Education*, London: DfEE.

NIED (1993) Common Curriculum. Online at www.nicurriculum.org.uk (accessed 14 June 2011).

Ofsted (2002) *The Curriculum in Successful Primary Schools,* London: OFSTED.

Ofsted (2010) *Learning: Creative Approaches that Raise Standards.* Online at www.ofsted.gov.uk/Ofsted-home/Publications-and-research/Browse-all-by/Documents-by-type/Thematic-reports/Learning-creative-approaches-that-raise-standards> (accessed 20 February 2011).

Perkins, D. (1992) *Smart Schools,* New York: Free Press.

Perkins, D. (1998) in R. Sternberg and W. Williams, (eds) *Intelligence, Instruction and Assessment,* Mawah, NJ: Lawrence Erlbaum Associates.

Philpott, C. and Evans, J. (2009) *A Practical Guide to Teaching Music in the Secondary School,* London: Routledge.

Plowden, Lady, B. (1967) *Children and their Primary Schools,* London: HMSO.

Pope, R. (2005) *Creativity: History, Theory, Practice,* London: Routledge.

QCA (2002) *Designing and Timetabling the Primary Curriculum,* London: QCA.

QCA (2003) *Expecting the Unexpected,* London: QCA.

QCA (2003) *Creativity Find it Promote It.*

Roberts, P. (2006) *Nurturing Creativity in Young People: a Report to Government to Inform Future Policy,* London: DCMS.

Robinson, K. (ed.) (1990) *The Arts 5–16: A Curriculum Framework,* London: Oliver and Boyd.

Robinson, K. and Aronica, L. (2009) *The Element: How Finding Your Passion Changes Everything,* London: Allan Lane.

Robinson, K. (2010) Online at http://sirkenrobinson.com/skr/rsa-animate-changing-education-paradigms (accessed 20 February 2011).

Rogers, R. (2003) *The Disappearing Arts,* London: RSA.

Room 13 (2011) Online at www.room13scotland.com/index.php> (accessed 20 February 2011).

Rose, Sir T. (2009) *The Independent Review of Primary Education,* London: Crown.

Sternberg, R. and Williams, W. (eds) (1998) *Intelligence, Instruction and Assessment,* Mawah, NJ: Lawrence Erlbaum Associates.

Wineburg, S. and Grossman, P. (eds) (2000) *Interdisciplinary Curriculum; Challenges to Implementation,* New York: Teachers College Press.

Wyse, D. and Rowson, P. (2008) *The Really Useful Creativity Book,* London: Routledge.

Chapter 10

Assessment for self-directed learning in music education

Chris Philpott

Introduction

This chapter explores the role of assessment in the self-directed learning (SDL) of pupils, a theme that is relatively underexposed in the literature and support materials for school practice. It would be fair to say that self-directed learning presents many challenges to current assessment practices, which are not easily adaptable to SDL, rendering the relationship highly problematic. In some seminal and pioneering research on SDL Lucy Green tacitly acknowledges this in noting:

> Another central educational issue that was left untouched, at least from the research point of view, concerns assessment ... teachers found that they could apply their usual assessment methods to the project. It would be fascinating to investigate exactly how they did this, and to develop approaches that combine best practice, or that offer alternative approaches .... This could include considering approaches to assessment based on apprenticeship models of learning, as well as how to give more weight to pupil self-assessment and peer assessment.
> (Green 2008: 184).

While new models of assessment for new 'pedagogies' await further development, it is most likely that teachers will default to what Fautley calls 'bolt-on accessories', (2010: 202). For the assessment of self-directed learning critical questions surround these: Whose music? Whose learning objectives? Whose criteria? Whose intervention? Whose targets? Whose outcomes? Whose assessment?

By way of pursuing a critical perspective on these issues this chapter examines two case study examples from the UK: the *Musical Futures* project and the *National Strategy Key Stage 3 Music Programme*. Self-directed learning is here taken to be an approach to music education exemplified by, but not entirely synonymous with, the *Musical Futures* project. Current assessment practice, especially 'assessment for learning', is taken to be exemplified by, but not entirely synonymous with, the *National Strategy*. While targeted at the self-directed learning of pupils, our conclusions probably have wider implications for music education that warrant further investigation.

This chapter then, aims to show why the 'bolting on' of current assessment practices to SDL is problematic and how the relationship can be reconceptualized. We first need to recap the 'classic' accounts of SDL and current assessment practices to establish the cause of the alleged dissonance.

Self-directed learning

It is worth remembering that SDL was developed as a possible solution to ongoing issues of pupil alienation from school music (see Schools Council 1971; Harland *et al.* 2000). Music has often been reported as the most unpopular subject in the school curriculum (see Chapter 13 of this book) and yet paradoxically the most important to pupils outside of school. The history of music education in the late twentieth and early twenty-first centuries charts various attempts to 'heal' this alienation. For example, SDL as exemplified in *Musical Futures* is aimed at addressing the ownership of school music by focusing on pupils' interests (as opposed to those of the state or individual teachers). In short, the approach privileges pupils as curriculum makers rather than curriculum consumers (see Philpott 2010). Clearly any approaches to assessment employed in such work will also need to aim at supporting all pupils having access to achievement in school music.

For the sake of brevity the classic exemplification of SDL will be taken from the work of *Musical Futures* and in particular the Hertfordshire Pathfinder Project (see www.musicalfutures.org and Green 2008). As part of this project Lucy Green used her work on how pop musicians learn (Green 2001) to research a classroom pedagogy which exploits informal learning processes, i.e. the processes that some popular musicians seem to employ when learning in music.

> Playing music of one's own choice, with which one identifies personally, operating both as a performer and a composer with like-minded friends, and having fun doing it must be high priorities in the quest for increasing numbers of young people to benefit from a music education which makes music not merely available, but meaningful, worthwhile and participatory.
>
> (Green 2001: 16)

The model for self-directed (sometimes called informal) learning and pedagogy devised by the *Musical Futures* research team was based on five principles (see Green 2008: 9–10).

- pupils work with music chosen by themselves that they enjoy and identify with;
- pupils work in the main aurally through listening and copying;
- pupils work with peers in groups chosen by themselves;
- skills and knowledge are gained in a haphazard fashion with whole 'real' pieces at the core;
- listening, performing and composing are integrated throughout the learning process.

Crucial to developing this approach to SDL is the role of the teacher. SDL draws upon and promotes informal learning and thus aims to begin with the musical ideas and knowledge of the pupils themselves. The role of the 'teacher' in the learning process is relatively non-interventionist where teachers are seen as facilitators and a resource for the pupils to draw on. The 'new' relationships outlined in the project (between pupil–pupil, pupil–teacher) are key to ownership of the music and personalisation of the musical learning. The expectation of the teacher is to:

- establish ground rules for behaviour;
- remind pupils of the ongoing task at the start of each session;
- stand back and observe what the pupils are doing;
- empathise with the pupils' perspectives and the goals they set themselves;
- diagnose pupils' needs in relation to these perceived goals;
- offer suggestions and models for pupils to achieve their self-set goals;
- be available for help but not for instructing in the 'normal' way.

While this may be an over-simplified account of SDL, it can be seen that this approach is an antithesis to the 'formal' notion that teachers set learning objectives, communicate them to the pupils, plan and deliver a set of strategies to achieve these objectives and assess (during and after) the extent to which these have been achieved.

However, it would be fair to say that despite a large and excellent output of supporting literature and materials from *Musical Futures*, assessment for SDL is underplayed. If anything (as we shall see) we are encouraged to 'bolt on' use existing strategies that are common to current schooling.

Assessment

There are two broad, albeit highly interrelated approaches to assessment commonly abroad: *assessment of learning* (sometimes called summative assessment) and *assessment for learning* (sometimes referred to as formative assessment).

Assessment of learning (AoL)

Assessment of learning involves:

> tests that are infrequent, isolated from normal teaching and learning, carried out on special occasions with formal rituals … .
>
> (Black *et al.* 2003: 2)

Assessment here might include an *examination; portfolio; written test; aural test; end of unit test; end of Key Stage levelling; and/or test of musical ability*. Such assessment is typically teacher-focused and aims to make judgements about the learning and understanding of pupils at the end of a teaching programme, course or unit of work. While it is common for us all to make judgements about music (we all know what is good or bad!), the basis upon which we make these is highly problematic in the context of pupils' SDL. Issues here surround two related themes (a) the nature of summative assessment criteria used in, for example, the national curriculum and post-14 examination specifications, and (b) the background of teachers/music educators making the judgements in relation to these. What are the critical issues when using summative criteria in SDL and when making judgements about composition and performance?

A wide range of musics arise in the contemporary 'formal' music classroom and this is especially true of SDL. Making judgements about these musics (especially composition) is a challenge for music educators confronted as we are by issues of taste, value and subjectivity. However, there are aspects of assessment criteria that while parading as objective, derive from a socio-cultural construction of what counts as 'good' music. For example, assessment criteria in music education are often shot through with the following features:

- the more complex the music the better, e.g. the 'more' form it has (complexity);
- the more original the piece the better (originality);
- the more difficult a piece is the more worthy it is of higher levels of musicality (difficulty);
- the more diverse the set of influences the better (breadth);
- linear progression of development through these features to attain higher 'levels' (linearity).

When used to judge a wide range of musics such criteria – which appear as transcendental – are problematic. It is clear that the values of complexity, originality and breadth are not necessarily shared by all music's and could prejudice the assessment of some types of musical achievement if summatively applied to work produced by pupils. It is but a short hop to the notion that some musics are better than others and that we learn in a linear and quantifiable way. This is a subtle process and Spruce notes how this has been reinforced by the pervasive values of classical music being taken as both autonomous and universal.

> The hegemony of western classical music is then rationalized by evaluating non-art music (*pop*) on art music's (*classical*) terms: as an autonomous object, detached from its social and cultural context, valued only in terms of relationships between its musical materials. An exercise in which non art music can only come off worse. Thus the bourgeois aesthetic is confirmed as intrinsically superior and, by association, so are its consumers and creators.
>
> (Spruce 1999: 79)

As Green suggests, the implication for assessment criteria is that even when the state and teachers at grass roots level support the notion of 'musics' (as opposed to music) they are written to appeal to 'the very same qualities of universality, complexity, originality, or autonomy upon which the values of classical music rested.'(2003: 266).

The related notion of linear progress and development is also a highly questionable account of how we learn in music. As Cain (2001) has suggested, the metaphor of moving (racing?) upwards in a straight line towards a predetermined point does not best describe how musicians learn. In relation to his experience of 'folk' music he notes that:

> The idea of learning simple music as a preparation for learning more difficult music is alien, as is the notion of mastering scales or other technical exercises in order to play more complicated music.
>
> (Cain 2001: 112)

He suggests that the 'theme park' might be a more authentic metaphor for musical progress where pupils explore the attractions and some 'choose to go on the same ride over and over again'. Given the haphazard learning and progress noted in the *Musical Futures* pathfinder research this is an important counter to the linearity embedded in summative assessment criteria.

A case study example of these issues can be found in the assessment materials written to support the *Musical Futures* project (www.musicalfutures.org/ assessment) where the achievements of self-directed learning are mapped onto the National Curriculum level criteria to show compatibility. These criteria outline quantitative shifts in the musicality of pupils and assumptions about linearity and breadth abound. For example, at Level 4 'pupils are able to improvise phrases as part of the overall structure; while at Level 5 they are able to improvise solos as part of the overall structure of the piece'. By Level 8 an example is given of a composition that not only 'uses the traditional conventions of a ballad, but also challenges those conventions' (p. 22–3). The 'assessment toolkit for informal learning' developed by the project also maps to the National Curriculum levels and perpetuates the notion that 'more of' and complexity is a valid measure of musical achievement. At Level 4 pupils 'explore the relationship between sounds and how music reflects different intentions' while at Level 7 they can 'discriminate and explore musical conventions in and influences on, selected styles and traditions'. Furthermore, a sheet showing difficulty levels for performance suggests that at the 'easy' level the pupil can 'play two to three note melodies... with simple pulse rhythms' while at the difficult level they can 'play...a wide melodic range ... and the melody moves independently of other parts'. Finally, a sheet that is a model for the summative assessment of composition suggests that at Level 4 pupils can compose 'simple musical ideas' and that at Level 7 they can 'compose in different styles'.

Such examples serve to show that for the assessment of self-directed learning the default is a 'bolt on' which perpetuates some of the very assumptions which the *Musical Futures* project aims to challenge, i.e. the pervasive ideology of classical music. They also illustrate the relative immaturity of assessment strategies in relation to SDL compared with other aspects of this approach.

It is understandable that the *Musical Futures* project would want to be seen as compatible with the National Curriculum. However, by sanctioning such criteria it espouses the very values that it aims to address which have the potential to be prejudicial to music exhibiting other characteristics, e.g. music of simple structure, with simple melody, few harmonic shifts and yet composed and performed with sensitivity and musicality. Music with aesthetic values which champion repetition and simplicity of texture and form can be great music. Given that SDL is by definition often haphazard and that it promotes quality of music making above any quantitative measure of difficulty or breadth, it is questionable whether such criteria, derived from the dominant ideology of western 'art' music, are appropriate for self-directed learning (or indeed any musical learning). By way of summary the position here is captured by Swanwick's assertion that:

> Complexity by itself is no virtue. Performing [a] wide range of complex music without understanding would definitely not count as a high level of achievement. And it is certainly possible to perform, compose and enjoy a high quality musical experience without any great complexity.
>
> (Swanwick 1999: 78)

Summative criteria based on the assumptions and values of western art music impinge upon social justice for pupils. Assessment criteria and the practices of AoL have perpetuated the alienation from school music noted earlier. For example, some authors (see Lamont and Maton 2008; 2010) suggest that pupils perceive post-14 music courses to have an 'élite' content based on possessing specialist knowledge against which they are reluctant to be judged. The playing of certain types of instruments (usually learned outside of the classroom) and certain types of musical backgrounds are more likely to predispose a pupil to success here. In short, those who have benefitted from an aesthetic which is consonant with the assessment criteria are most likely to choose and succeed in these courses to the exclusion of others who may have ongoing ambitions in relation to other musical traditions (see Philpott 2001). Furthermore, there is some evidence to suggest that those who play a 'classical' instrument are more likely to opt for music at post-14 (see Bray 2000). Although there is a need for up-to-date research on this theme it is clear that low uptake at GCSE continues to be an issue for music (compared to say those who choose art; see Chapter 13) and thus there are few reasons to suggest that things are currently any different.

Given that one of the main aims of SDL is to heal the paradox of pupil attitudes to (school) music, embracing criteria which perpetuate this alienation is a serious threat to the outcomes of projects such as *Musical Futures*. The criteria of summative assessment are not 'owned' by pupils, but derive from a tradition that has taken on transcendental significance and espouse values that are not fit for the purpose of assessing all musics (if indeed any music). These values have little to say to the assessment of SDL driven as they are by privileging qualities that have a spurious universality.

Finally, there is some evidence to suggest that the backgrounds of music teachers also works to reinforce the ideological issues arising from AoL outlined above. As Green has noted:

> The majority of school music teachers in the UK and most other countries have classical backgrounds.
>
> (Green 2008: 27)

However, this is only part of the problem, as music teachers are also subject to intense socialization as part of their training in 'legal and professional roles and responsibilities' (Green 2008: 142) – namely, the National Curriculum and attendant expectations for assessment. Finney (2007) also notes that the music teachers' backgrounds and training enables them to empathise with and perpetuate the élite 'codes' wrapped up in officially sanctioned assessment criteria.

In summary, there is a threat to social justice when bolting on 'official' assessment criteria to self-directed musical learning that prejudices capturing the learning and achievement of all pupils.

Assessment for learning (AfL)

On the face of things Assessment for learning (AfL) is an altogether more promising strategy for SDL. It has been defined as follows:

> .... any assessment for which the first priority is to serve the purpose of promoting students' learning ... usually informal, embedded in all aspects of teaching and learning ... [it] becomes *formative assessment* when the evidence is used to adapt the teaching work to meet learning needs.
>
> (Black *et al.*, 2003: 2)

Assessment activities which fall into this category are in one sense the most natural and can be recognized in the account of the teacher's role in SDL noted previously. Assessment for learning is about the ongoing dialogue about music between pupils and teachers (and pupils and pupils) and will include *questioning; feedback; target setting; sharing criteria; self-assessment; peer assessment.*

Such assessment is pupil-focused with the aim of developing musical learning and understanding through teacher observation followed by proactive interventions. This appears more hopeful, but is this approach to assessment always suitable for SDL? The application of AfL strategies to SDL also raises critical issues in relation to ownership, for the 'classic' strategies of AfL are highly interventionist. Furthermore, these strategies often employ 'shared criteria' derived from the summative models noted above and are enacted by teachers who have often emerged from particular musical backgrounds. There is, then, a sense that AfL shares similar issues with AoL when applied to SDL.

Self-directed learning in its purest form is initiated by pupils who set their own objectives for learning. In AfL the objectives for the learning experience are fundamental to an interventionist approach and usually assume that objectives are set by the teacher. It is here that the critical issues surrounding the 'bolting on' of AfL to SDL can be found. Box 10.1 provides an analysis of these issues.

BOX 10.1 APPLICATION OF AFL STRATEGIES TO SDL

Setting and sharing objectives
The National Strategy Key Stage 3 Music Programme (NSKSMP) suggests that 'Sharing learning outcomes at the start of the lesson is the first step in helping pupils to recognize the standards they are aiming for' (2006: 9). When applied to SDL we should ask: Who has set the objectives for the lesson, and Who will judge if these have been met and to what extent? Much of the AfL literature makes it clear that this will be the teacher. Teacher-set objectives are most likely to relate to learning outcomes closely allied to the prevailing curriculum (and its ideology of assessment, in this case the national curriculum for music) and the teacher's background. What are the implications for AfL if the pupils set objectives and assess learning outcomes for themselves?

Agreeing and sharing criteria
In AfL the teacher who sets objectives will also set the criteria for what counts as achievement. Given that the act of sharing criteria is at the heart of AfL and underpins most other strategies below, 'ownership' of criteria is a critical issue. Have criteria been developed by the pupils or the teacher? Does sharing mean from the teacher to the pupils or between the teacher and pupils? The non-interventionist assumptions of SDL are challenged by this principle of AfL.

Feedback
The *NSKSMP* outlines the importance of teachers to engaging in 'teacher-led feedback against criteria that promote successful outcomes' (2006: 9). Once again the issue here is Who has set the objectives and criteria for successful outcomes? The *Musical Futures* project recommends that teachers take a watching brief on musical learning (at least initially) for such teacher-led interventions can be out-of-kilter with pupil-driven outcomes. In any AfL there is always a danger of music teachers offering feedback, especially during creative work, that accords with the needs of the curriculum or their own world views on what constitutes a 'good' music. For this reason teacher feedback can be problematic when applied to SDL.

Questioning
Questioning is an important part of AfL as teachers aim to 'know' the understandings of their pupils. If well-handled a teacher's questions can challenge pupils and cause them to think deeply about learning. However, when applied to SDL issues arise around Why a question would be asked?, and How it relates

to a pupil's self-declared objectives? To what extent will it impinge upon the ownership of music and learning if emanating from implicit criteria wrapped up in the teacher's background and demands of the school curriculum?

Modelling

The *NSKSMP* suggests that modelling 'is useful for articulating how some pupils may improve their work ... a key feature of modelling is the way that the teacher "thinks aloud" the processes of learning thereby making them explicit to the pupils' (2006: 9). When applied as an intervention to SDL questions arise in relation to the impact of the models chosen by the teacher on the pupil's self-directed work. Who then owns the direction and nature of the learning?

Scaffolding

According to the *NSKSMP* scaffolds 'can be prepared in advance and effectively used to redirect pupil's thoughts and learning, making sure that the next steps are those that will eventually lead to success' (2006: 9). Clearly the use of scaffolding to 'redirect' learning is a challenge to the assumptions contained in SDL.

Target-setting

The aim of target-setting is to 'close the gap' between what a pupil currently knows and what they are capable of knowing. Given what we have said above, questions arise here about: whose targets? Are they the teacher's? Are they derived from the curriculum or the pupils' self-set objectives?

Self and peer assessment

Self and peer assessment is at the heart of SDL and has much potential if handled well. There are however critical issues when these strategies are based on shared criteria which do not derive from the pupils' own objectives or when structured in a predetermined way by the teacher.

AfL is also known as 'formative assessment' and it is a common expectation that teachers 'form' the learning of their pupils. This is problematic, for teachers acting formatively through interventions that are not consonant with the interests of the pupils can perpetuate alienation from 'school music'. Assessment interventions always throw up issues of ownership and ownership underpins the fundamental philosophy of SDL.

Musical Futures have published a pamphlet that provides a comparative analysis of the project with the *NSKSMP* (http://www.musicalfutures.org.uk/resource/27233) by means of illustrating compatibility. As with the National Curriculum comparison noted earlier it is understandable why the project would want to be politically acceptable to the wider educational community. However, this comparison is not only selective but also compromises the radical implications of SDL; the differences in underpinning philosophies are there for all to see (see Box 10.2). This comparison is further evidence that SDL is in need of research into how assessment can, in Fautley's words, 'be reconfigured afresh' and not 'bolted on' to current orthodoxies.

BOX 10.2 *NSKSMP* AND *MUSICAL FUTURES* NATIONAL
STRATEGY CONTRASTED

NSKSMP: Offer well-prepared, focused feedback to enable teachers to secure
judgements about their pupils' capacity to ... build towards long-term curricular
targets. When spontaneous feedback is used ... it is specific and sharply focused
on the learning objectives and outcomes of the lesson.

Musical Futures: The teacher/leader offers focused and spontaneous feedback
based on the objectives the pupils are setting themselves. Pupils offer spontaneous feedback to one another.

Problematizing the assessment strategies of AoL and AfL does not mean they
have no role to play SDL, and we now turn to what an assessment for self-directed
learning framework might look like.

Towards a framework of assessment for
self-directed learning (AfSDL)

The issues problematised above are unlikely to find much resonance with the
meta-theories of writers such as Swanwick (see 1988). For Swanwick the notion
that 'to teach is to assess' underpins an interventionist philosophy of learning
based on music teachers establishing and planning a productive tension between
musical encounters and musical instruction. The Piagetian model of musical
development he proposes is, he maintains, an invariant feature of the musical
mind and is thus universal and cross-cultural. His model of musical development,
in the form of a celebrated spiral, plots qualitative shifts in the nature of musical
engagement and as such can form the basis of both AoL and AfL. It must be said
that this theory is both intellectually and practically attractive to music teachers. If
it can be shown that the model of musical development/engagement has universal
validity then issues of a musical assessment are solved (see Philpott 2009).

   However attractive this may be, it is not so certain that the model is not shot
through with the tacit assumptions noted earlier. Efforts to illustrate how the
model is compatible with statutory assessment criteria (see Swanwick 1994) have
done little to dispel this impression.

> There was something about translating from the qualitative to the quantitative
> that neutered the underlying principles .... In mimicking ... Level descriptions
> Swanwick also seemed to firm up a sense of one-dimensional linearity in the spiral.
> (Philpott, 2009:69–70)

In the context of SDL, which champions plurality and ownership, Swanwick's
model of development and associated assessment criteria does not transcend the
issues that surround assessment interventions in self-directed learning. For

example, who chooses the encounters and on what basis does planned instruction take place in self-directed learning?

Fautley has noted the need for a new approach to assessment for 'informal' learning where:

> ... a shift has occurred, from teacher to learner, and from teaching to learning...and so assessment has to reflect this. What this means is a shift in approach from assessing how much of a programme of study learners have absorbed, to how much progress they have made on their own terms...with pupil progress being self referentially evaluated against their attainment.
>
> (Fautley 2010: 202)

Fautley goes on to recommend 'privileging formative assessment', although as we have seen this is not necessarily a fresh reconfiguration. This is a complex task and what follows below aims to provide a framework for considering assessment for SDL based on the work of Folkestad.

Throughout this chapter there has been an explicit tension between formal learning (initiated by teachers) and informal learning (initiated by pupils). Indeed, one of the problems to be overcome in developing an assessment for self-directed learning is to unpack the myth that SDL is synonymous with 'informal' learning. Folkestad (2005; 2006) has recognized that the relationship between the formal and the informal is immensely complex and yet subject to popular and simplistic assumptions. For example, both formal and informal learning can take place in any physical space and is not limited to the school – home/ community dichotomy.

> ... it is far too simplified, and actually false, to say that formal learning only occurs in institutional settings and that informal learning only occurs outside of school...what are described as formal and informal learning styles are aspects of the phenomenon of learning regardless of where it takes place.
>
> (Folkestad 2005: 283)

From Folkestad (2006) we will see that many of the problems surrounding the discourse of SDL are related to its common characterization as informal learning. Following an analysis of the research literature he maintains that an understanding of the relationship between the formal and informal is crucial to understanding all musical learning. He proposes the following distinction:

Formal learning can be characterized as the intentional predetermined sequencing of learning activities by 'a person who takes on the task of organizing and leading the learning activity' (Folkestad 2006: 141). Teaching is always part of the formal moment whoever does it.

> Informal learning can be characterized as being 'not sequenced beforehand' and occurs during *self-chosen and voluntary activity*.
>
> (Folkestad 2006: 141).

For Folkestad the crucial issue here is of the intentionality of the learner. Formal learning is found when the minds of pupils and teachers are directed towards learning *how to play music*. Informal learning is found when minds are directed towards *playing and making* music. Furthermore, 'what characterizes most learning situations is the instant switch between these learning styles and the dialectic interaction between them' (2006: 142). We can characterize this switch as 'flipping' – for example, when a band improvises over a riff but then stops while one member teaches the others how to play a chord. Most musicians of all types will have experienced 'flipping' although the 'formal' moment is often so prioritized in music education that this experience often needs to be 'excavated' (see Finney and Philpott 2010). And so for Folkestad, the relationship of formal to informal is not a dichotomy but a continuum 'and that in most learning situations, both of these aspects of learning are in various degrees present and interacting ...' (2006: 143). In line with the continuum of formal and informal learning we can suggest that assessment in music can operate on a parallel and matching continuum.

However, as far as an AfSDL is concerned the crucial ingredient to be added to this analysis of the relationship between formal and informal learning is *ownership*, i.e. what Folkestad characterizes decisions about '*What* to do as well as *How, where* and *when?*' (p. 142).

Issues of alienation from formal learning, pedagogy and assessment have hinged on the ownership of school music. The SDL of Musical Futures was designed to heal this wound in the UK. The point to be made here is that formal learning (how to play) is most likely to be accepted when it is perceived to be needed by the pupils themselves arising out of their interests (focused on playing and making music) and thus *owned* by them. By the same token assessment strategies that arise out of such ownership are more likely to support an unalienated musical learning for pupils. Teaching and most forms of assessment are always part of the formal moment of learning but need to be *owned* by the pupils if they are to support SDL. Figure 10.1 aims to model what we have suggested thus far.

The formal–informal continuum of musical learning is characterized by constant 'flipping' between the orientations of a focus on *how to play* and on *making and playing* music. Teaching (even self-teaching) is always in the formal moment as are most assessment strategies to be found in current orthodoxies.

Self-directed musical learning

Informal moment of learning	'Flipping'	Formal moment of learning
Focused on making and playing music		Focused on how to play music
Self assessment		AoL
Peer assessment		AfL
Learning	Ownership	Teaching

Figure 10.1 A model for self-directed musical learning and assessment.

Teaching and assessment can exist in an un-alienated relationship with the informal moment if there is ownership. What does ownership mean in an assessment for self-directed learning?

An example of this model could be as follows:

> *A group of pupils decide that they will learn and perform a song during their school lunch breaks. After doodling on instruments individually they jam together haphazardly in a broad imitation of the opening of the song. Amy has worked out the main riff and teaches the others to varying levels of approximation to the original. Dan begins to have stab at some of the vocal lines above the riff. The group cannot quite work out the chords (to their satisfaction) that accompany the riff and approach the guitar teacher to ask if he can teach them the two chords they need. They continue to jam on the song with the 'bits' they have both worked out and been taught by others.*

In this example we can see 'flipping' on the continuum and ownership of the musical learning by the pupils themselves. But what of assessment? Strategies associated with AoL and AfL are legitimate practices here when arising out of the pupils' self-directed objectives, criteria for success and outcomes. In the example above summative assessment (AoL) is most likely to exist in an un-alienated relationship with the pupils if they have set and agreed these and 'teachers' (whoever they are) can share their perceptions of progress with pupils on this basis. In relation to AfL the guitar teacher would have made interventions based on a diagnosis of the pupils self-driven needs and would have given them feedback to achieve their self-declared learning outcomes. However, the strategies of self and peer assessment hold a primacy in SDL as these are most commonly integrated into the very act of making and playing music itself. These could have been found in the ongoing development of approximations to the riff as the music is played in the 'jam' or in a simple look that says 'we have nailed it'.

This model provides a framework for considering the context within which AfSDL can take place. There is much potential here for action research that explores the implications of 'flipping' and ownership in self-directed musical learning (perhaps all musical learning) for assessment. Such work is important in developing greater maturity to this fledgling aspect of music education.

Conclusion

We have seen how the classic strategies of AoL and AfL can militate against ownership and perpetuate the alienation that pupils have commonly felt towards school music. If these strategies are to be owned by pupils as they arise out of self-directed learning, then they will need to fulfil the following conditions in the model above (Figure 10.1):

- by promoting the primacy of self-directed work;
- by the use of 'local' criteria that arise out of the self-directed objectives of pupils;

- by promoting the primacy of self and peer assessments using these criteria;
- through teacher/leader assessment interventions (AoL and AfL) using these criteria that are based on the needs of the pupils themselves;
- in an acceptance by teacher/leaders that there are times when no assessment interventions are appropriate but instead trusting that learning will take place.

For teachers and leaders of music this points to a subtle and nuanced pedagogy, a pedagogy that promotes an un-alienated relationship with school music and in which ownership is at the centre of assessment for self-directed learning. This is challenging work for teachers of all types. There will be concerns that leaving pupils to set their own objectives and to establish their own criteria for summative and formative assessment is a tall order. However, there is enough evidence in the rich engagement of pupils arising out of the *Musicals Futures* research, that we can trust pupils to make the most of genuine ownership of their learning when they are presented with the opportunities to do so. There will be concerns from teachers at a non-interventionist approach to assessment in self-directed learning; what is their role as teachers and facilitators of learning? The implications are for teachers to know when to let go, to trust the pupils and to base their interventions on the self-declared needs and interests of the pupils themselves.

SDL as exemplified in projects such as *Musical Futures* has a huge potential to heal the wounds of alienation that have visited music education in the UK, and yet for those who engage with its principles much work remains to be done in researching and developing AfSDL. We have aimed in this chapter to support this process in what is an area of relative immaturity for SDL. However, while the focus and foreground here has been specifically on an assessment for self-directed learning (in order to make specific critical points) there are probably wider implications for music education that are worth investigating.

Reflective questions

1   This chapter takes a view that 'classic' assessment strategies can work against social justice in self-directed learning in music. To what extent do you feel that statutory criteria and teachers' interventions can inhibit the self-directed outcomes of pupils' creative and practical work?

2   Do you feel that there is a case for teachers to abandon orthodox assessment strategies in self-directed learning? Is there a case for no assessment interventions in self-directed work at all?

3   How can the tensions between orthodox assessment strategies and self-directed learning be resolved?

4   Is an interventionist AfL incompatible with pupil 'ownership' of their learning?

5   Can you identify and describe 'flipping' in your own musical learning?

References

Cain, T. (2001) 'Continuity and Progression in Music Education', in C. Philpott, and C. Plummeridge (eds) *Issues in Music Teaching*, London: Routledge.

Black, P., Harrison, C., Lee, C., Marshall, B. and Wiliam, D. (2003) *Assessment for Learning*, Milton Keynes: Open University Press.

Bray, D. (2000) 'An Examination of GCSE Music Uptake Rates', *British Journal of Music Education*, 17(1): 79–89.

Department for Education and Skills (2006) *National Strategy Key Stage 3 Music Programme (Unit 6)*, London: DfES.

Green, L. (2001) *How Pop Musicians Learn: A Way Ahead for Music Education*, Aldershot: Ashgate.

Green, L. (2003) 'Music Education, Cultural Capital and Social Group Identity' in M. Clayton, T. Herbert, and R. Middleton (eds) *The Cultural Study of Music*, London: Routledge.

Green, L. (2008) *Music, Informal Learning and the School: A New Classroom Pedagogy*, Aldershot: Ashgate.

Fautley, M. (2010) *Assessment in Music Education*, Oxford: Oxford University Press.

Finney, J. (2007) 'Music Education as Identity Project in a World of Electronic Desires', in J. Finney, and P. Burnard (eds) *Music Education with Digital Technology*, London and New York: Continuum.

Finney, J. and Philpott, C. (2010) 'Informal learning and Meta-Pedagogy in Initial Teacher Education in England', in *British Journal of Music Education* 27(1): 7–19.

Folkestad, G. (2005) 'Here, There and Everywhere: Music Education Research in a Globalized World', in *Music Education Research*, 7(3): 279–87.

Folkestad, G. (2006) 'Formal and Informal Learning Situations or Practices vs Formal and Informal Ways of Learning', in *British Journal of Music Education*, 23(2): 135–45.

Harland, J., Kinder, K., Lord, P., Stott, A., Schagen, I. and Haynes. J. (2000) *Arts Education in Secondary Schools: Effects and Effectiveness*, Slough: NFER.

Lamont, A. and Maton, K. (2008) 'Choosing Music: Exploratory Studies Into the Low Uptake of Music GCSE', *British Journal of Music Education*, 25(3): 267–82.

Lamont, A. and Maton, K. (2010) 'Unpopular Music: Beliefs and Behaviours Towards Music in Education', in R. Wright (ed.) *Sociology and Music Education*, Farnham: Ashgate.

Philpott, C. (2001) 'Equality of Opportunity and Instrumental Tuition', in C. Philpott and C. Plummeridge, *Issues in Music Teaching*, London: Routledge.

Philpott, C. (2009) 'Swanwick, Musical development and Assessment for Learning in the Twenty First Century', in *Sound Progress: Exploring Musical Development*, Matlock: National Association of Music Educators (NAME).

Philpott, C. (2010) 'The Sociological Critique of Curriculum Music in England: Is Radical Change Really Possible?', in R. Wright (ed.) *Sociology and Music Education*, Farnham: Ashgate.

Schools Council (1971) *Music and the Young School Leaver: Problems and Opportunities*, Working Paper 35, London: Methuen Educational.

Spruce, G. (1999) 'Music, Music Education and the Bourgeois Aesthetic: Developing a Music Curriculum for the New Millennium' in R. McCormick, and C. Paechter (eds) *Learning and Knowledge*, London: Oxford University Press.

Swanwick, K. (1988) *Music, Mind and Education*, London: Routledge.

Swanwick, K. (1994) *Musical Knowledge: Intuition, Analysis and Music Education*, London: Routledge.
Swanwick, K. (1999) *Teaching Music Musically*, London: Routledge.

Websites

www.musicalfutures.org (accessed 8 August 2011)
www.musicalfutures.org/assessment (accessed 8 August 2011)
www.musicalfutures.org.uk/resource/27233 (accessed 8 August 2011)
www3.hants.gov.uk/music.htm (accessed 8 August 2011).

Chapter 11

Those who can, play; those who can't, use Music Tech?

How can teachers knock down the walls between music and music technology?

Jonathan Savage

Introduction

The last 15 years have seen a transformation in classroom approaches to music education with technology. During the early-to-mid 1990s, computers or other digital technologies were seldom seen in music classrooms. Whilst some teachers had been exploring tape-based technologies and other electronic devices (Orton 1981), the majority of teachers had access only to minimal levels of technology beyond basic tape recorders and the occasional Atari computer. Whilst ICT received a mention in the first version of the English National Curriculum for Music, particularly as a way of encouraging musical composition within the classroom, it was not a major part of the majority of music teachers' classroom practice.

As the 1990s progressed into the first decade of this century, we witnessed much greater access to new technologies, both within schools and wider society. Hardly a week now goes by without comment in the international press about a new technological innovation or application related to the production, reception or consumption of music in one form or another. Regularly there appear new virtual pianos, drums and guitars and other instruments to play on hand-held devices such as the beautiful iPad instrument Seline HD (Amidio 2010).

Within the school, things have also changed radically. Music departments today have a much broader range of ICT available. It is not uncommon to see dedicated computer suites for musical activities, interactive whiteboards, a range of smaller pieces of music technology equipment and, at least in principle if not practice, an acknowledgement by many teachers that hand-held devices such as mobile phones or iPods and iPads have potential as musical instruments.

However, as we will discuss below, unlike the technological developments in wider society, the developments within the world of formal classroom music education have not yet exploited the potential of these new technologies to the full. The disjunction between the two worlds has been noted by many authors (Savage 2004: 167; Cain 2004: 217; Ofsted 2009: 34).

Why is this? Many reasons can be suggested. Perhaps there has been a tendency to isolate music education with ICT and consider it as conceptually and philosophically 'different' from music education without ICT? Perhaps this 'difference' has isolated some teachers as ICT 'experts', or even 'music technologists', and disempowered others whose skills, they consider, might lie elsewhere. Perhaps these differences have been overstated by some to reinforce the need for a framework of qualifications, resources and specialist staff that have a particular interest in ICT? But, at a fundamental level at least, is learning to play a virtual instrument really that different from learning to play a traditional instrument? Is using a sampler to create and explore sounds really that different from working with another live instrumentalist? Composing with a pen and paper is different from using a piece of compositional software on a computer (see Adams (2010) for a beautiful and very humorous exploration of this). But these differences can easily be misunderstood and overstated, thereby masking the commonalities in approach and use within particular musical contexts.

Within the music education research community there has been considerable discussion of these issues. Espeland used the opportunity of his keynote address at the Research in Music Education conference in 2009 to explore the tensions between those who support the use of technology as opposed to those who do not (Espeland 2010: 129–30). Many of the arguments he presents for either side are familiar. Perhaps of greater interest, are his comments relating to what he perceives as the effect of using technology in music education. He cites Salomon and Perkins (2005) who describe three different kinds of effect related to learning: effect with, effect of, and effect through technology. He continues:

> Effects with technology, they say, take place when technology makes it possible for the individual to reach a higher level of learning than without technology. Effects of technology mean that technology gives the student experience and practise, which also is useful when technology is not present. Effects through technology mean that the activity in question changes or is being restructured. … Will technology change the essential activities and contents of music education, and if so, will this change mean that music education will move away from its preferred artistic, performing and bodily-based core?
>
> (Espeland 2010: 130)

In his concluding comments, following a broader historical analysis of the role of the gramophone and its affect on music listening, he raises a series of interesting and very pertinent questions:

> What kind of digital skills in music education might enhance analogue skills and vice versa? How do analogue and digital skills interact meaningfully in music education processes of different kinds? In what way and in what kind of considerations and decisions, considering musical ideas, end-results, performance, reception and music education process profiles, will technology contribute uniquely? And finally; when should technology not be used?
>
> (Espeland 2010: 132)

This chapter will seek to provide an investigation into some of these questions. Drawing on several recent pieces of research, it will commence with a brief overview of the current state of ICT in music classrooms across the United Kingdom. Following this, a model of digital literacy will be introduced and applied to the work of music education. It will argue for a broader model of development for music education with ICT that relates, symbiotically, to established models of musical development with which many educators are already familiar.

Recent research into ICT usage in the music classroom

In the introduction we explored, briefly, how music education with ICT within the classroom setting has developed over the last 15 years. We identified broad differences between the speed of technological developments within and outside the school, and questioned why musical uses of ICT have, on occasions, been slower to respond to the various opportunities for alternative models of music education with ICT.

Recent research (Savage 2007; 2010) has explored these issues in significant detail. This research, along with comments drawn from a recent Ofsted report (Ofsted 2009), reveals the following key points.

1. There is an inherent conservatism in musical pedagogies with technology

First, despite these wider and significant cultural changes in the use of digital technologies, music education within the classroom is predominantly still technologically conservative. Observations of classroom practice in numerous schools revealed many basic uses of ICT for MIDI sequencing and score-writing dominating teachers' work at Key Stage 4. Whilst there is nothing wrong with these applications per se, they are characteristic of a previous era of music technology use that, in many cases, has developed rapidly in recent years but has yet to make a significant impact in the classroom. There was a noticeable lack of integration of hardware and software with other classroom resources. In many cases, the use of ICT within the music classroom made little, if any, links to potential musical applications of ICT outside the classroom.

2. Prioritizing the use of ICT in music education for older students reinforces this inherent conservatism

Second, recent research has shown that teachers believe they are more successful in their teaching with ICT as their students get older. They reported a greater degree of impact in their use of music technologies in Key Stage 4 and on post-16 courses than with younger students at Key Stage 3

(Savage 2010: 96–7). This seemed to be because they felt they could judge 'success' with music technology when it reinforced a traditional approach to music education, such as the production of a musical score. There were a number of explanations for this. Some teachers felt that the 'overbearing' and 'rigid' structures of GCSE specifications actively discriminated against the creative use of new technologies. It was interesting that musical performance with any type of ICT was peculiarly absent from the reported observations in both pieces of research. This reinforces the general perception reported by Ofsted, that schools either implicitly or explicitly tend to encourage only students with traditional instrumental abilities to take further their musical studies through the GCSE qualification:

> An over-emphasis on instrumental skills also contributed to lack of conti-
> nuity in Key Stage 4. Music GCSE is not always seen as a natural extension
> to work in Key Stage 3 and the schools surveyed discouraged students,
> explicitly or implicitly, from taking GCSE if they did not have additional
> instrumental lessons or were not already an accomplished performer.
>
> (Ofsted 2009: 52)

3. Student experience with ICT at Key Stage 3 is limited

The prioritisation of ICT in music education within Key Stage 4 and post-16 courses is matched by a limited use of ICT at Key Stage 3. The Ofsted report makes this clear in two places:

> There was insufficient use of ICT in music, even though it is a statutory
> requirement in Key Stage 3. A detailed focus on 22 schools in the survey
> showed the use of ICT to be inadequate in more than half of these; only four
> were good or outstanding in this respect.
>
> (Ofsted 2009: 34)

The use of ICT by the music profession continues to expand the range of music available to all students. For example, music technology encourages more boys to take Music A-level, but it is underused at present, particularly in Key Stage 3 (Ofsted 2009: 6). There are many reasons for this, but perhaps the most obvious one relates to the larger class sizes at Key Stage 3 and the accompanying shortage of technological equipment for a whole class to use. It requires quite a skilful and creative pedagogy to conceive of whole class approaches to the use of music tech-nology for a particular topic given scarce resources. It is much easier when you have smaller classes at Key Stage 4. Other reasons for the comparative lack of usage at Key Stage 3 will be explored below.

These findings are interesting to compare against another piece of recent research conducted on behalf of the Associated Boards of the Royal Schools of

Music (Fautley and Savage 2008). This examined trends in composition and assessment at Key Stages 3 and 4. Two findings are particularly relevant:

- Performance is the major curriculum component at Key Stage 3 and this changes to composition at Key Stage 4;
- Group work approaches to performance and composition dominate the curriculum at Key Stage 3, with more individual engagement with composition at Key Stage 4.

In comparing the findings related to ICT (Ofsted 2009; Savage 2007, 2010) and the broader reflection on types of curricular activities (from Fautley and Savage 2008), it seems certain that the increase in ICT usage in Year 10 onwards, reaching a plateau of around 55 per cent of curriculum time in Year 11 (Savage 2010: 96), can be ascribed to the increasing use of individual activity with composition software such as Sibelius or Cubase. The domination of these pieces of software reinforces the individual, conservative model of music education as discussed above. The larger number of students and the emphasis on group work at Key Stage 3 have meant the ICT usage at this phase is underdeveloped.

4. The missing link

Finally, in this brief overview let us return to the introductory points about a divide between students' experiences inside and outside school —also a feature of the Ofsted study:

> Music technology is changing rapidly and the schools found it difficult to develop their own resources in line with the quality of equipment which students were seeing – and sometimes using themselves – outside school. Consequently, ICT in school could appear dated to them.
>
> (Ofsted 2009: 34–5)

Many teachers, quite reasonably perhaps, embrace ICT in their teaching as just an extension of what they normally do. The adoption and adaptation of pieces of technology becomes just another tool in a long list of potential resources, so when new technologies become available, these models of working are simply transferred to existing frameworks of musical development prescribed within the National Curriculum or GCSE specifications.

This can lead to uncritical responses where, for example, students are placed in front of computers to complete activities that are unmusical, often divorced from a meaningful context, with little sense of purpose and, on occasions, simply a cover for the lack of effective teaching in basic musical skills. Typically these include:

- Unskilful uses of music notation technologies produce scores where considerations of instrumentation have been given cursory attention and instruments play at either impossible ranges or with little thought to specific instrumental techniques (bowing, phrasing, the requirement to breathe, etc.);

- Insensitive and over-enthusiastic approaches to cutting and pasting in music sequencing software lead to compositions that have weak structures, lack of contrast and little, if any, melodic, harmonic or rhythmic variation and development;
- Creative 'borrowings' or 'samplings' of others' work through the opening of access to digital media is carried out with little thought to style, context, reinterpretation or ownership (including intellectual property rights);
- An over-reliance on auto-accompaniments, auto-tuning or other supportive technologies for musical performance provide cover (or an excuse) for the lack of rigorous teaching and training in basic musical skills (such as those required to play together in a group, or sing in tune).

These appropriations of technology into music education are not neutral. They do more harm than good and prevent exchanges of real value.

However, this needs to change. As different technologies are allowed to permeate more deeply, pedagogical approaches need to develop more radically. In other words, differences begin to appear when the extent or the use of technology becomes more extreme. This chapter argues that well-established models related to digital literacy need to be better understood and appropriated within music education. These models will, at least in the short term, co-exist with traditional models of music development. In the longer term, it is hoped that further research will be carried out to explore a fuller degree of integration. It is time to turn our attention to one of these models.

Martin's model of digital literacy

There is an expansive literature associated with the concepts of digital literacy and many models have been described (Bélisle 2006; Gilster 1997; Søby 2003). What follows explores what digital literacy means through a consideration of one such model. Following this, we consider the implications of these ideas for music education with technology.

Martin defines digital literacy as:

> ... the awareness, attitude and ability of individuals to appropriately use digital tools and facilities to identify, access, manage, integrate, evaluate, analyse and synthesize digital resources, construct new knowledge, create media expressions, and communicate with others, in the context of specific life situations, in order to enable constructive social action; and to reflect upon this process.
>
> (Martin 2006: 19)

His more recent research (2009) continues to apply this thinking in the development of three 'levels' of digital literacy:

- digital competence (which Martin believes is a precursor of digital literacy);
- digital usage;
- digital transformation.

1. Digital Competence

This includes:

- skill acquisition with a full range of digital tools;
- finding information;
- preparing and publishing digital resources using software tools;
- various forms of electronic communication and interaction.

Martin acknowledges that many of these elements will build on broader knowledge, skills and understanding obtained in traditional, non-digital (and non-musical) contexts.

2. Digital Usage

For Martin, digital usage embeds skills and concept drawn from digital competence and contextualizes them in real life situations. So, he argues that:

- users draw upon relevant (domain-specific) digital competencies and apply them to specific contexts;
- these competencies are shaped and adapted by the requirements of the situation and the 'digital usages' are, in Martin's phrase, 'uniquely shaped' by the particular expertise of the individuals, their life history and wider experiences.

3. Digital Transformation

This is the ultimate stage of digital literacy where the *digital usages* are developed to facilitate innovation and creativity, stimulating significant change within the personal or professional domain. Martin's research suggests that whilst reflective action is needed at all stages of digital literacy, it becomes essential here. Critical reflection and reflective action is a key requirement for this transformative stage.

Table 11.1 demonstrates what Martin's model of digital literacy might look like in the context of a student's use of a music sequencer:

Table 11.1 Martin's model of digital literacy.

Martin (2009)	Music Sequencer
Competence	Setting up MIDI and audio devices. Learning basic controls and functions for recording, playback, over-dubbing, etc.. Creating basic content. Editing processes such as step, grid, audio or score editors. File outputs and types.
Usage	Contextualisation and linking of sequencer in a broader context, perhaps alongside the use of other digital technologies or traditional instruments. Justification for use of sequencer as opposed to other tools. Advanced use of sequencer for musical purposes. Extending/adapting MIDI sequencer, perhaps through the addition of virtual instruments, to broaden the range of expressive affect. Developing and sharing models of usage with other musicians.
Transformation	Sequencer becomes an intrinsic part of personal performance or compositional practice. Highly creative use of all sequencer functions. Innovative extensions, perhaps even abuses, of sequencer functions that stretch artistic expression.

Developing models for music education with ICT

So far, this chapter has surveyed the current usage of ICT for music education in classrooms across the United Kingdom. It has introduced one model of digital literacy drawn from the research literature. This model will be considered alongside established models of musicianship and musical development that have been well researched elsewhere.

As an example, Table 11.2 shows how Kratus' (1995) developmental model for improvisation could be aligned with Martin's three-staged model for digital literacy.

Exploring sounds and developing simple improvisational processes and products, could all be conceived as requiring a set of ICT skills that are situated broadly within the category of 'digital competence'. The step towards a fluid, structural and stylistic improvisatory approach (levels 4–6 in the Kratus model) would require a more advanced use of ICT, perhaps applying competences to a particular context (a characteristic of digital usage rather than digital competence). Finally, the ability to use musical improvisation to develop a personal style that transcends the stylistic (something that few attain according to Kratus) has similarities to the power of ICT that is shaped, adapted and used by the individual user to transform their approach to an activity and redefine, fundamentally, key aspects of the task and even their identity.

Table 11.2 Combining Martin's and Kratus' models.

Kratus (1995) (improvisation)	Martin (2009) (digital literacy)	Key activities for musical improvisation and technological use
Exploration Process-orientated Product-orientated	Competence	Finding ideas. Exploring ideas. Creating new content. Justifying choices. Skill development. Technical control. Linking ideas and coherence. Structuring ideas. Preparing and publishing final product. Individually meaningful.
Fluid Structural Stylistic	Usage	Application of competences to new contexts. Shaping and development of competences in new contexts. Personalisation of approach. Making connections to broader issues. Socialisation of use and ideas and increasing sense of meaning for others.
Personal	Transformation	Innovative. Significantly creative. Highly critical and reflective. High value for wider context of users.

However, the alignment of these models could be completely unnecessary if one takes the view that the generic processes of learning to improvise are completely independent of any set of tools through which one might access them. In other words, is learning to improvise on a trumpet any different from learning to improvise with your voice, or is that any different from learning to improvise with a virtual instrument like the Seline HD (Amidio 2010)? If your answer is 'no', then the developmental model for musical improvisation presented by Kratus is complete within itself. There is no additional benefit in bringing other developmental models alongside it.

But the tools we choose to use for particular activities, like musical improvisation or performance, do shape those activities in practical, conceptual and philosophical ways. Wertsch's exploration of this point (Wertsch 1998: 27–8) is particularly helpful. He takes an example from the world of pole-vaulting and charts the various rivalries and factions within the sport that emerged at transition points surrounding the adoption of new poles. At one point these even included the possibility of breakaway groups favouring a particular type of pole, and accusations that users of new types of poles were cheating. The history of pole-vaulting itself distinguishes between the various 'eras' of particular poles (On Track and Field, 2009).

It might sound obvious, but the pole is essential to pole-vaulting. It mediates the action between the athlete (the agent) and the goal of hurtling over the barrier at the highest possible height (the context). There is a link between human actions with a pole and the cultural, institutional and historical contexts in which this action occurs. In our context, teachers or students are the 'agents' (to use Wertsch's terminology), the 'cultural tools' are the technologies we are choosing to use, and the context would be, at least in a simple application of his work, the classroom or other learning spaces where students can work informally. Wertsch calls the interplay between agents, tools and contexts 'mediated action'.

Applying this to our discussion, the technologies that we or our students choose to use will allow us to engage with activities in different ways and achieve different outcomes. Learning to improvise in music with the use of a specific piece of music technology is a different but related process to learning to improvise by a more traditional method. To that end, it is a useful exercise to consider different developmental models alongside one another. Whilst they might not match up perfectly, the tensions they facilitate will create an opportunity for thinking differently about how music teaching and learning really works with technology.

ICT and 'cultures of tension'

Peter John takes up this theme in his writing by identifying the tensions that occur when digital technologies are brought alongside an established subject culture like that within music education:

> At the core of this is 'cultures in tension', the idea that the particular discourses that have dominated the educational landscape for more than a century-and-a-half have been thrown into sharp relief by the rise of digital technologies.
>
> (John 2005: 471).

How we respond to this 'cultural tension' is important. It could result in music education retracting and consolidating, with ICT skills becoming situated as part of a wider generic and functional agenda for education rather than being adopted explicitly. This might suit traditionalists who believe that digital technologies threaten or dilute the core values and principles of music education (the 'conservative' approach noted above). Or, it could result in tokenistic pedagogical responses to the adoption of ICT within music education that reinforce traditional approaches (e.g. the uncritical use of music notation software to present a GCSE composition).

John explores this tension through the use of a metaphor (that of a 'trading zone') through which a subject culture (like music) can begin to build bridges with other 'tribes' (like ICT):

> The crucial 'borderlands' between the subject and ICT became transaction spaces or 'trading zones' where exchanges and intense collaborations take place. Each tribe can bring things to the 'trading space' and take things

away; even sacred objects can be offered up and exchanged. This trading process also gives rise to new contact languages which are locally understood and co-ordinated.

(John 2005: 485–6)

However these 'trading zones' offer a space within which cultural tensions can be a positive thing. John's metaphor of a 'trading zone' highlights the transient, evolving and incomplete nature of the relationship between music education and digital technologies. To occupy a 'trading zone' does not mean that we need to abandon our 'sacred home' nor allow the 'profane' to dominate or limit the exchange. Rather, it encourages a process of subtle negotiation that will help develop alternative models and dimensions with music's subject culture over time.

This ongoing process of exchange or interaction between the traditional approaches to music education and broader processes of technological development is something that we can all facilitate. It may lead to an opportunity for a new language or discourse of music education with digital technology to emerge. But this will only happen when the items that are being exchanged are of value. As our analysis of the research at the opening of this chapter has shown, there are plenty of low value exchanges going on between music education and technology in our schools already.

Whilst these implications are important for how we consider the use of an individual piece of technology, they will also have implications for the pieces of technology that we choose to put in our classrooms, and how these are contextualized within our units of work. To what extent are we allowing students opportunities to develop their competencies in choosing which pieces of technology to use in a task (and this would include the 'technologies' of traditional instruments as well as digital technologies), and then asking them to consider and reflect on the consequences of these choices? A lack of critical evaluation about the effects of these choices can have disastrous consequences for our musical products!

So, the extent to which ICT does or does not present a barrier to learning, or is or is not inclusive, is perhaps to the wrong way to think about it. ICT, as a category or series of objects, will not create a barrier any more than, say, a clarinet would create a barrier to learning. As someone with no clarinet skills, giving me a clarinet to perform with would require me to undertake a learning process of some sort before feeling confident to perform a simple piece. How is this different from me giving you a copy of Seline HD and saying perform a piece with this?

The skills that we need to use ICT effectively are well known. They include:

- cognitive skills;
- practical skills;
- communication;
- control;
- reading with meaning;
- writing with meaning;

- functioning effectively in a community;
- applying skills within a social context;
- demonstrating skills;
- enriching and transforming thinking;
- empowering the intellect;
- understanding the relationship between the individual, others and the wider world;
- developing goals and visions;
- conveying thoughts, understanding, interpretation, belief, attitudes and emotions.

But these are also musical skills. The links by now, I hope, are obvious. As teachers, the challenge is finding meaningful and creative contexts within which these skills can be developed systematically.

There are several ways in which teachers can design and implement more structured units of work that integrate digital technologies in musical and creative ways. In order to do this, it will be necessary for teachers to acknowledge a number of key points.

First, recognize that digital music technologies are *different*. They require students to learn a new set of skills in terms of their use and application to particular musical tasks within a unit of work. Time needs to be allowed for this process of development to take place in the unit of work. Students should be given time to experiment and explore a new piece of digital technology as well as master its basic operation. On occasions, teachers will need to dictate outcomes for a particular task; but on others, they can be flexible and allow students to follow their own interests and imaginations within a broader musical context.

Second, recognize that digital music technologies are *broadly similar* to other tools one might want to use. Although this seems contradictory, it really is not! Any given piece of technology has much in common with other pieces of technology that preceded it (we just call those older pieces of technology 'instruments'). So, given their relative historical contexts, is there that much difference between a piano's sustain pedal and a Boss effects pedal? Both affect the sound, both require the use of the foot, both were innovative in their day and had consequences for how composers wrote and performers played.

The consequences of this point for the development of meaningful and creative contexts within which musical skills can develop so that teachers might/should:

- Make links within and between units of work that show students, unambiguously, how music making with digital technology is not so different to music making without.
- Trace the historical, cultural and sociological backgrounds to digital technology in their teaching (they did not just appear; and this can be made a fun exercise too!).
- Try to break down the unhelpful artificial walls that have been built in recent years between music technologists and other musicians. We are all musicians.

Third, meaningful and creative musical contexts for the development of musical skills with technology will be built upon the traditional underpinnings of effective music education, namely an integrated approach to performing, composing and listening. Units of work that place students in front of a computer, isolated, musically and socially, from others, do more harm than good. This is not to say that the individual use of music sequencing software or music notation software does not have a place in a contemporary music education. But if some of the poor practice and ill-conceived approaches that research has identified are to be undone, units of work that rely on such approaches need to be re-contextualized and re-imagined. Teachers need to rediscover the notion of teaching music musically of teaching music technology musically perhaps? As this chapter has argued, the two are not so different.

Developing musical contexts for the effective use of ICT presents significant challenges. But the rewards are also significant when we contextualize digital literacy and the associated range of skills and competencies within the field of music education. We need to take and integrate these alongside those specific musical skills that we know all students require as part of their music education. As teachers, we need to think and act creatively. Perhaps here, more than anywhere, there are benefits in teachers communicating and collaborating with each other. Many of the most creative uses of music technology in teaching take place at the margins of music education. If I can add a personal note here, in my experience this has often been in schools for students with emotional, behavioural and other difficulties; or in community music or other workshop settings; or in schools for students with profound mental or physical difficulties.

For all sorts of reasons, breaking out of the 'silo approach' to music teaching is vital. But perhaps here, in a realm of the music curriculum where many teachers feel uncomfortable and under-skilled, there is a requirement to see and hear what skilful, knowledgeable and creative teachers can do with digital technologies first hand. If finding time to do this is difficult, social media provides a window on the work of many of these practitioners. But we also need to make time to seek out some of these practitioners and prioritize learning about alternative approaches to the use of digital music technology.

Conclusion

New models of musicianship and musical development will develop as we seek to engage young people in a process of music education that facilitates and builds on their emerging fluency with digital tools. These will be far removed from the conservative models of music education with technology that we explored at the opening of this chapter.

Engaging with music through technology is closely related to the broader types of musical engagement that we seek for our students. After all, as we have explored throughout the chapter, digital technologies are not that different from other forms of technology. In this sense, ICT creates no more of a barrier to music learning than anything else might do. ICT, like any technology (including musical instruments), needs to be understood in a particular context. The positive or negative impact it has depends on a whole host of factors, some intrinsic to the tool itself and others spread much more widely throughout that context.

Espeland's questions quoted at the opening of this chapter correctly highlight areas of difference between music education with and without technology. But to focus on these too heavily is to miss the vital connections that all technologies (whether digital or non-digital) have to broader processes of music development and understanding. For sure, there are specific things that digital technology can do that are impossible to do in other ways and these may lead, over time, to the creation of new models of music development. But we are not at that point yet. Rather, as Espeland explores, the relationships between musical activities with digital and non-digital tools is where our attention should be focused.

Perhaps one of the most worrying trends in recent years has been the development of courses and qualifications for 'music technology' that separates a particular type of music student from those identified as traditional 'musicians'. This artificial and divisive approach to music education results in second class musicians (a kind of 'those who can, do; and those who can't, use music technology'). As long as this system remains, teachers will always have the opportunity to opt out and say that music technology is not for them or their students.

As we have seen, the links between music education, musical development and digital literacy are well-founded. The challenge is to provide a unified and integrated model of music education both within and across the Key Stages, making sure that *all* students can use a range of technologies (both digital and non-digital) as they develop their musical skills, knowledge and understanding,

Reflective questions

1 Compare and contrast what your approach might be to a particular sequence of learning with a piece of ICT and to a similar piece of learning without. What differences do you notice? In particular, focus on the ways that you and your students would use ICT in the first approach. What are these replaced by in the second approach? Have you been able to identify any differences in your pedagogy within these two approaches? Which do you feel is more effective? Why?

2 Examine some of the development models for other musical processes such as composing or listening.
   - How do these relate to the models for digital literacy discussed in this chapter?
   - What similarities or differences can you observe?
   - How might they relate to each other?
   - Are there tensions that can be explored creatively?

3 What are the potential new approaches that might be facilitated when music education adopts and embraces digital technologies in a more substantial way?

References

Adams, J. (2010) 'Marcel Proust, Laptop Composer'. Online. Available at www.earbox.com/posts/81> (accessed 15 December 2010).

Amidio (2010) 'Seline HD'. Online. Available at http://amidio.com/seline> (accessed 17 December 2010).

Beetham, H. (2010) 'Beyond Competence: Digital Literacies as Knowledge Practices, and Implications for Learner Development', ESRC Seminar Series: Literacies for the Digital University (LiDU). Also online. Available at http://lidu.open.ac.uk/glasgow-mar-2010.cfmhttp://lidu.open.ac.uk/glasgow-mar-2010.cfm (accessed 25 June 2010).

Bélisle, C. (2006) 'Literacy and the Digital Knowledge Revolution', in Martin, A. and Madigan, D. (eds) *Digital Literacies for Learning*, London: Facet.

Bunz, U., Curry, C. and Voon, W. (2007) 'Perceived Versus Actual Computer-Email-Web Fluency', *Computers in Human Behavior*, 23: 2321–44.

Cain, T. (2004) 'Theory, Technology and the Music Curriculum', *British Journal of Music Education* 21(2): 215–21.

Espeland, M. (2010) 'Dichotomies in Music Education – Real or Unreal?', *Music Education Research* 12(2): 129–39.

Fautley, M. and Savage, J. (2008) *Assessment of Composing at Key Stages 3 and 4 in English Secondary Schools*, unpublished research report for the Associated Board of the Royal Schools of Music, London: ABRSM.

Galison, P. (1997) *Image and Logic: The Material Culture of Micro-Physics*, Chicago: University of Chicago Press.

John, P. (2005) The Sacred and the Profane: Subject Sub-Culture, Pedagogical Practice and Teachers' Perceptions of the Classroom Uses of ICT', *Educational Review* 57:4 (469–88).

Kratus, J. (1995) 'A Developmental Approach for Teaching Music Improvisation', *International Journal of Music Education*, 26: 27–38.

Martin, A. (2009) 'Digital Literacy for the Third Age: Sustaining Identity in an Uncertain World', Barcelona: elearningeuropa. Also online. Available at www.elearningpapers.euwww.elearningpapers.eu (accessed 23 June 2010).

Martin, A. (2006). 'Literacies for the Digital Age', in Martin, A. and Madigan, D. (eds) *Digital Literacies for Learning*, London: Facet.

Ofsted (2009) *Making More of Music*, London, Ofsted. Also online. Available at www.ofsted.gov.uk/Ofsted-home/Publications-and-research/Browse-all-by/Documents-by-type/Thematic-reports/Making-more-of-music-an-evaluation-of-music-in-schools-2005-08 (accessed 1 December 2010).

On Track and Field (2009). Online. Available at www.ontrackandfield.com/main/catalog/2009/polevaulthistory.html> (accessed 29 November 2009).

Orton, R. (1981) *Electronic Music for Schools*, Cambridge: CUP.

Savage, J. (2010) 'A Survey of ICT Usage Across English Secondary Schools', *Music Education Research*, 12(1): 47–62.

Savage, J. (2007) 'Reconstructing Music Education through ICT', *Research in Education*, 78: 65–77.

Savage, J. (2004) 'Working Towards a Theory for Music Technologies in the Classroom: How students Engage with and Organize Sounds with New Technologies', *British Journal of Music Education*, 22(2): 167–80.

Sáinz, M., Castaño, C. and Artal, M. (2008) *Review of the Concept "Digital Literacy" and its Implications on the Study of the Gender Digital Divide*, (Working Paper Series; WP08-001). Online. Available at www.uoc.edu/in3/dt/eng/sainz_castano_artal.pdfhttp://www.uoc.edu/in3/dt/eng/sainz_castano_artal.pdf> (accessed 23 June 2010).

Søby, M. (2003) 'Digital Competence: from ICT Skills to Digital "*Bildung*" ', Oslo: ITU (University of Oslo).

Salomon, G. and Perkins, D.N. (2005) 'Does Technology Make Us Smarter? Intellectual Amplifications with, of, and through Technology', in Preiss, D. D. and Sternberg, R. (eds) *Intelligence and Technology*, Mahwah, NJ: LEA.

Swanwick, K. (1999) *Teaching Music Musically*, London: Routledge.

UNESCO (2006) *Education for All Global Monitoring Report 2006*, Paris: UNESCO.

Wertsch, J. (1998) *Mind as Action*, Oxford: OUP.

Chapter 12

Musical knowledge, critical consciousness and critical thinking

Gary Spruce

People are fulfilled only to the extent that they create their world (which is a human world), and create it with their transforming labor. The fulfillment of humankind as human beings lies, then, in the fulfillment of the world. ... if their work does not belong to them – the person cannot be fulfilled.

(Paulo Freire)

Introduction

The concept of critical thinking is understood in a number of ways. In some definitions it is close to the idea of metacognition – 'thinking about thinking' – whilst in others it describes a process of 'logical thinking' involving the gathering, assimilation and analysis of evidence from which emerges a 'reasoned' conclusion. In his book *Democracy and Music Education* (2005) Paul Woodford suggests that although critical thinking is supposed to 'develop independence of mind' it is almost always equated in curriculum documents 'with the application and development of abstract thinking skills and abilities divorced from social, moral, ethical or political considerations' and that 'Few music teachers realize that this separation of mind and matter is a perversion of what Dewey, one of the fathers of the contemporary critical thinking movement, intended' (Woodford 2005: 95).

In this chapter I will explore critical thinking as part of the framework of critical (social) theory and examine how, as I have written elsewhere, 'properly embedded, critical thinking and understanding enables pupils to make connections between their musical learning in school and their lived reality, and thus empower them as learners'(Spruce 2009: 36). Critical thinking is here conceptualized as a key element in the development of a more socially just society in which all are enabled to fully participate. I will argue however that in order to create the conditions within which critical thinking can flourish, we need to examine the ways in which knowledge is conceptualized and understood and how knowledge, particularly in school, is positioned in relation to the 'knower' or 'learner'. I will suggest that such a reconceptualization will inevitably present challenges to some pedagogical approaches.

I begin the chapter by exploring the philosophical underpinning of some commonly-held conceptions of the nature of knowledge and the relationship of the knower to knowledge; noting through examples from music education the impact these relationships can have on young people's experiences of music in school. Drawing on the ideas of Paulo Freire (1970; 1974) I will then explore how through a process of 'conscientization' leading to critical consciousness, and supported by a critical pedagogy, critical thinking might be nurtured and 'independence of mind' developed within the music classroom. At various points in the chapter I will exemplify the points being made with brief examples or more worked out 'case studies' from music classroom practice.

Conceptions of knowledge and knowledge–learner relationships

Commonly held understandings of knowledge – and ones which inform to a greater or lesser extent many aspects of education in western society – are founded upon two philosophies both of which have their roots in the Enlightenment. The first, sometimes referred to as *transcendental rationalism*, contends that knowledge is objective, 'out there' and transcends time and place. What is true is true at all times and in all places and is unaffected by any aspect of the sensory world. The second, and arguable diametrically opposed philosophy, is that of *empiricism* or *scientific materialism*, which invokes the sensory world in a mechanistic way, holding that what is true is that – and only that – which can be experienced through sensory observation.

The abstract nature of transcendental rationalism, which contends that knowledge is separate from, and unaffected by, any context in which it might be applied, denies the possibility of knowledge and understanding being developed 'in action' i.e. that learning and understanding might occur through the act of *doing*. Scientific materialism/empiricism on the other hand may tell us the way the world is but, as Regelski says, '... no amount of knowledge of the ways things are, can tell us how they ought [to] or could otherwise be' (Regelski 2005: 7).

Although rationalism and empiricism are differing conceptions of the nature of knowledge, they both hold that knowledge exists independently of the knower and is simply awaiting discovery by them and that the knower plays no part in the construction of knowledge. Both of these philosophical positions promote what Woodford refers to as the 'separateness of mind and matter' (Woodford 2005: 95) and are, as Giddens puts it, knowledge which is 'void of self' (Giddens in Schmidt 2005: 5).

Abstract and socially decontextualized knowledge that is 'void of self' reveals itself in music education in a range of ways. These include music theory or instrumental techniques taught and learned separately from any musical application or context and stylistically 'neutral' composing tasks where the stimulus or template does not project or reflect a recognizable musical style or tradition. A consequence of these approaches is that children do not recognize what they are being taught and how they are being taught it as connecting to the lived reality of their everyday lives. As a consequence they experience alienation from musical learning in school.

Wright suggests that the disadvantages that accrue from such alienation are not equally distributed in terms of access and barriers to the acquisition of social capital. Drawing on Bernstein's 'Code Theory' she points out how abstracted and socially decontextualized knowledge particularly disadvantages working class children:

> Bernstein ... argued that working class children were more likely than their middle-class counterparts to use relatively restricted codes which, while not deficient, were primarily context dependent. This derived from the communication systems of families, themselves the products of the divisions of labour. In other words, manual workers acquire different properties of their language orientated to the here and now, compared with the more decontextualized world of the middle-class professionals or employers. Similarly, the middle classes as social and cultural reproducers and repairers rather than producers, require a context-independent, elaborated code. This gives them the vocabulary required to discuss matters beyond those occurring in particular contexts. The fact that schools adopted this elaborated code meant that some working class children tended to be disadvantaged by the dominant of education. The 'fault' however lay with society and its schools, not children or their families.
>
> (Wright 2010: 14)

Transcendental and empiricist conceptions of knowledge are supported and promoted by pedagogical approaches which are characterized by what Freire calls the 'banking concept' of education. Here 'Education ... becomes an act of depositing, in which the students are the depositories and the teacher is the depositor' (Freire 1970: 53). The teacher's role is 'to regulate the way the world "enters into" the students' by organising and controlling 'a process which already occurs spontaneously, to "fill" the students by making deposits of information which he or she considers to constitute true knowledge' (Freire 1970: 57).

The 'banking concept' of education is sustained and supported by, and closely connected to, the commodification, objectification and reification of knowledge that occurs as a natural consequence of knowledge being perceived as something that is independent of the learner/knower. This allows for pedagogies and curriculum content to be appropriated by dominant ideologies resulting in unequal access to, and distribution of, social capital and the perpetuation of inequalities. As Freire writes:

> The banking concept (with its tendency to dichotomize everything) distinguishes two stages in the action of the educator. During the first, he recognizes a recognisable object while he prepares his lessons in his study or his laboratory; during the second, he expounds to his students about that object. The

students are not called upon to know, but to memorize the contents narrated by the teacher. Nor do the students practice any act of cognition, since the object towards which that act should be directed is the property of the teacher rather than the medium evoking the critical reflection of both teacher and students. Hence in the names of the 'preservation of culture and knowledge' we have a system which achieves neither true knowledge nor true culture.

(Freire 1970: 61)

Certain models of Music-Education-as-Aesthetic Education (MEAE) promote the transcendental-rationalist philosophy and 'banking concept' of education in that 'musical works'– which is the usual starting point for MEAE – constitute knowledge that is 'out there' and 'fixed', transcending both time and place. The ideology of music as being 'out there' is promoted particularly in the western classical tradition through the idea that the objectified forms of music – the scores and recordings – are synonymous with 'the music'. Music – or one of its objectified forms – then becomes an object to be taught. Teachers prepare their analyses or descriptions of works of music and 'expound' on these to students in the classroom who are then required to cognitively process and understand (in the sense of memorising and reiterating) the knowledge that has been imparted to them. Students engage with music as an abstract 'object of beauty' which is to be appreciated in a distanced way rather than as something to be actively engaged with and in. However as both Schmidt (2005) and Allsup (2003) point out, MEAE *imposes* on students perceptions and values of beauty that are not necessarily their own and thus such knowledge remains 'void of self'.

Regelski suggests that the study of music as an object – which characterizes MEAE –leads to the teaching of music through 'concepts' which are then treated as 'theoretical abstractions'– they become a form of transcendental rationalism where concepts are perceived as being and meaning the same in every time and place. Regelski contends that '… when concepts are taught or defined their action potential is denied and more often than not it would seem, never get put into musically productive ways' (Regelski 2005: 14).

Take for example the musical concept of triple time. A teacher, adopting a transcendental–rationalist view of knowledge, may believe that a student's understanding of triple time is demonstrated when they can describe triple time as having three beats in a bar and write triple time rhythms on the whiteboard using crotchets, dotted crotchets and quavers. A teacher adopting a scientific–empiricist position might think that students have demonstrated the same understanding if they recognize music with three beats in the bar when they hear it and can clap 3/4 with an emphasis on the first beat. However as Regelski says, none of these examples are 'musically productive ways' (Regelski 2005: 14) of engaging with musical concepts and in the sense in which they are abstracted from any musical context the knowledge gained is 'meaningless'.

Regelski argues that '… in the real musical world concepts are 'open': that is to say that there is not 'one stage at which the concept is addressed once and for all'

(2005: 14). The 'meaning' of triple time in a Strauss waltz is a great deal different from triple time in *Danse Macabre* or the theme to *Last of the Summer Wine* or *One hand, one heart* from *West Side Story* or indeed any other musical context in which it appears. Furthermore that knowledge – that understanding – is not passively received as inert knowledge but knowledge and meaning actively are constructed within the context of personal historicity, musical biographies and musical enculturation. Where 'knowledge' of triple time is most acutely demonstrated is through knowledge that is not 'void of self' but 'full of self'. Students respond to music in 'triple time' in a nuanced and sensitive way recognising the subtleties of difference in its use in different works of music and across different musical styles and traditions. Their performances demonstrate a sophisticated understanding of the nuances of triple time within the different music styles in which they perform and in the personal ownership they take of the concept of triple time in their improvisations and compositions. When these occasions occur, 'knowledge' is no longer independent of them but *part* of their being – of their consciousness. Here, knowledge and the relationship of knowledge to the learner has been reconceptualized to one where it does not exist independently of them but is created by them.

Towards a critical pedagogy of music

Reconceptualizing the relationship between knowledge and the learner/knower such that knowledge is no longer 'void of self' necessitates a radically different approach to pedagogy from that promoted by the 'banking concept' of teaching and learning. It requires a 'critical pedagogy' which supports the process of 'conscientization' whereby one's perception of reality and relationship with the world changes from what Freire refers to as one of 'magical consciousness' (which is fundamentally passive and fatalistic in nature, apprehending the world as 'a given' and immutable) to a state of 'critical consciousness' (Freire 1974: 39). Critical consciousness recognizes the world as a dynamic phenomenon, with inherent contradictions and conflicting ideologies, but within which a person has the power to act and engender change.

Critical pedagogy is characterized by McLaren, and quoted in Abrahams (2005a: 6) as 'a way of thinking about, negotiating and transforming the relationships among classroom teaching, the production of knowledge, the institutional structures of the school, and the social and material relations of the wider community, society and nation state' (McLaren 1998: 45). Here, critical pedagogy, is seen as a means of enabling students to become critically conscious of the power, ideological and relationship matrices that impact on the world. By enabling students to recognize these matrices, critical pedagogy shifts 'the emphasis from teachers to students ... making visible the relationships between them' and affords students opportunities to '... engage in a culture of questioning that demands far more confidence than rote learning and the application of acquired skills' (Giroux 2010: 3).

Allsup (2003), Regelski (2005) and Abrahams (2005a) also offer additional and valuable perspectives on the attributes and characteristics of, and connections between, critical pedagogy, conscientization, critical consciousness and critical thinking. Surveying the work of these three writers yields some common principles which underpin and inform critical pedagogy. In Table 12.1 we identify these and consider how they might emerge from and/or be exemplified through music teaching and learning.

Having established the characteristics and attributes of a critical pedagogy, in the following section we explore how the principles and application of critical pedagogy can help achieve a state of critical consciousness.

Table 12.1 Critical pedagogy and music education

Attributes of a Critical Pedagogy	Manifestations in Music
Teachers are self-reflective, recognize the existence of their own 'consciousness' as being of value but that implicit in this consciousness is their own worldview which is not imposed but used as the basis for a dialectical relationship with students where teachers and students both learn.	Teachers recognize that their own musical biographies and identity will influence their musical 'consciousness' informing their musical values, priorities and tastes which are not necessarily those of their students. They do not impose these musical tastes on their pupils but use them as the basis of a process of musical learning undertaken with their students.
Teaching recognizes students' consciousness of their world and creates contexts and opportunities for this consciousness to be expressed.	Music lessons value and build on the musical experiences and learning students bring into the classroom and provide opportunities not only for students to listen and perform 'their' music but also to discuss its values and purposes.
Teaching connects 'word to world' – or 'music to world'.	Music learning and teaching is not abstracted from real musical contexts. Music teaching is embedded in real musical experiences. Activities that are undertaken would be recognized as musical activities were they to take place outside of school.
No binary opposition is created between 'theory' and 'practice'.	Theoretical understanding is developed through and emerges from immersion in musical practice and is not decontextualized from or allowed to operate as a barrier to direct engagement with music.
Critical pedagogy does not rely on training techniques, methods or primers.	As Giroux says, 'Each class will be influenced by the different experiences that students bring, the resources available, teacher student relationships ...' (Giroux 2010: 5). Training techniques, methods and primers close down the space within which dialectical discourse can occur and where students' consciousness can be expressed.

Critical pedagogy and critical consciousness

Freire argues that true knowledge can only be gained through the development of 'critical consciousness'. Critical consciousness is the state of being that enables critical thinking to occur. In this section, and with the help of some case studies, we explore Freire's concept of critical consciousness and how this might be manifested and developed in the music classroom supported by the principles of critical pedagogy as set out above.

Critical consciousness has resonance with Kant's belief that 'reason is not a passive endowment that discovers logically necessary relations among given ideas (as in rationalism) or among sensory data (as with empiricism)' but rather that 'reason actively constitutes knowledge' (Regelski 2005: 2). Critical consciousness holds that knowledge is not some kind of objective or abstract entity, which is out there and waiting to be discovered or perceived, but rather is actively constructed by the learner. In playing a role in constructing knowledge, rather than simply passively accepting, uncritically 'ideology, doctrine, orthodoxy and mass thinking' (Regelski 2005: 2) the learner can envisage the world not just as something that 'is' (fixed and immutable), but rather as it might be, or should be. The development of critical consciousness therefore represents a challenge to 'authority' and dominant ideologies.

The concept of critical consciousness is predicated on the world as a dynamic phenomenon upon which, and within which, a person consciously acts in the construction of knowledge and understanding. Critical consciousness allows the learner to enter into a dialectical engagement with their world whereby knowledge and understanding are in states of constant change and development, emerging as they do from the 'fruitful collisions of ideas from which a higher truth may be reached by way of synthesis' (Bullock and Trombley 1977; 1999: 222). Critical consciousness recognizes that 'information' is not, and cannot be, perceived in an ideal or pure form but is inevitably mediated by the social and cultural context of the person's consciousness and their personal historicity. As Martin puts it, 'We do not simply register 'objects' but constitute them in ways which can only reflect the particularities of your biographies and our cultures' (Martin 1995: 83).

The development of critical consciousness within music education takes place (at least partly) through a dialectical relationship between teacher and learner where students and teachers are no longer the objects of the educational process but subjects within it. The relationship between the teacher and students changes from one where the teacher teaches a predefined body of knowledge to one where, through a dialectical process, students and teachers together negotiate and construct knowledge, curriculum and pedagogy as a manifestation of the critical consciousness of their worlds.

Allsup, drawing on Marx's definition of 'praxis', provides a starting point for such a process when he suggests that perhaps we should seek to 'uncover the real worlds and real lives of our students ... by simply listening to our students' stories' (Allsup 2003: 9). Box 12.1 takes such an approach as foundation for a dialectical process between teacher and students.

BOX 12.1 THE DIALECTIC PROCESS AS TALK: Musical Biographies

Martha has just taken over as head of music in a non-selective, mixed school in London. Students' attitudes to music in the curriculum are very negative and behaviour in lessons is sometimes poor. Very few students continue with formal music education in school beyond the age of 14 and there is a danger that the school will decide that it is no longer a viable part of the curriculum at this stage.

Martha talks with the students about why they dislike music in school and finds out that they see little 'connect' between the music they experience out of school and what they are asked to do in music lessons. Their opinions and views about what they want to do, learn and experience in music lessons have not been sought. Martha realizes that her own music education as a 'classical' cellist has not provided her with the knowledge and skills she needs to engage with the music that these students value.

She decides to instigate a short 'pilot' project with a Year 9 class on 'Musical Biographies'. Working in pairs as interviewer and interviewee, and then exchanging roles, the students use the available recording technology to create ten-minute 'radio programmes' about their musical lives interspersed with excerpts from the music they value and giving reasons why. Martha also creates a musical biography of her own. They listen to and then discuss each other's biographies and as they do so Martha moves the discussion forward to talk about how their and her musical interests and knowledge results from their lived lives – their enculturation - how it fits into and reflects their lives and how the music projects a particular view of the world - of what's important to them.

Martha now asks them to think about one *recording* they particularly value and try and articulate what it is about it that resonates with them so much. She deliberately does not refer to musical elements or concepts as to do so would be to impose a particular musical worldview on their thinking. Some students talk about the recording in terms of how it makes them 'feel', others refer to the meanings behind the lyrics, others the iconic status in their lives of the recording artist, others the particular skills of the performer(s); only one or two make mention of the formal materials of the music. A whole range of different musical values emerge which are contrary to and different in emphasis from those that Martha presupposed were important in music. Martha finally talks about her favourite piece of music and explains why. As a contrast to the students' focus she deliberately concentrates on the formal properties of the music. They discuss their different perceptions of what they consider to be important in music.

From this process of musical biographies Martha and the students negotiate a way forward for the music curriculum based on a developing understanding of the different music perceptions of the teacher and the students. She realizes that the 'training' approach that she experienced in her music education will not be appropriate here. She understands that the music curriculum and its scheme of work will need to be ever-shifting and fluid and the starting point for negotiation not something that is imposed and fixed.

Freire's conception of the dialectical process between teacher and student is one based upon spoken language. Music however offers the possibility of a much richer discourse between teacher and student based upon and through music. It is in the process of making music – and making music together – that the dialectical possibilities of music are fully realized. Such occasions can take place in any music learning contexts but frequently occur in workshop-type events where Bullock and Trombley's (1977; 1999: 222) 'fruitful collision of ideas' is most easily facilitated.

BOX 12.2: THE DIALECTICAL PROCESS AS MUSIC:
The Improvisation Workshop

Martin is leading an improvisation workshop with a group of Year 10 students (ages 14–15) and their teachers. The students and teachers (and Martin) sit in a circle with their instruments. Martin does not speak but begins with a quiet, syncopated two-bar, Hip-Hop type riff on a bass guitar. After about a minute he signals to one of the group that they should respond to his riff with a single answering riff of their own. He then continues with his riff but begins to place the accents on different notes and beats in unexpected ways. As he does this he glances at the group and smiles. They return the smile thus indicating that they are recognizing what is going on musically and this recognition motivates them to respond by doing similar things with their answering riffs. After about two minutes, and without stopping the flow of the music, Martin gets them to respond to each other's riffs – the ownership moves from him to them – and they begin a process of extending the music and furthering the dialectical process.

Freire proposes that this kind of dialectical relationship can form the foundation for the emergence of 'problem-solving education' where education is seen as the process of posing problems in relation to the world of the learners *and* teachers. He sums up the difference between the banking and problem-solving concepts of education in the following terms: 'The banking method emphasizes permanence and becomes reactionary. The problem-posing education – which accepts neither a "well-behaved" present nor a pre-determined future – roots itself in the dynamic present and becomes revolutionary' (Freire 1970: 65).

BOX 12.3: ENGAGING CRITICAL CONSCIOUSNESS:
Reworking a folk song

A group of GCSE (age 14–16) students work on a composing and performing project based on English Folk Song. The teacher has placed the project in the hands of the students. He has suggested albums and traditional musicians they might listen to and has talked to them briefly about the musical characteristics of English folk music, including a tendency towards modality, the instruments typically used and the social purposes of the songs. However this information and suggestions for listening are presented as starting points which they can choose to use or not.

One of the artists mentioned by the teacher is Maddy Pryor and one student comes across a recording of her singing *My Son John,* a song from the Napoleonic wars which, through the voice of the mother, tells of a soldier who comes home having lost both legs. The words are hard and bitter but touched with black humour:

Refrain:
My Son John was tall and slim
He had a leg for every limb
Now he has no legs at all
For he run a race with a cannon ball

Shortly after beginning work on the song, one of the students finds on YouTube a version of the song sung by Martin Carthy. In his version, Carthy has reworked the lyrics into a contemporary anti-war song specifically protesting against conflicts in Afghanistan and Iraq; the song makes references to cluster bombs and includes lines such as 'Cool Britannia calling for War' but retains the original refrain.

The students recognize how, through the changes to the lyrics and incorporating into the backing band Middle Eastern and South Asian instruments and digitally produced sounds with Middle Eastern resonances, the song achieves a tremendously visceral and emotional power through its acknowledgement of the impact of the conflict on people from all sides. They also recognize that its power lies in the way it maintains its links to its original context of creation over 200 years ago.

A second student then discovers another YouTube link this time of Cathy Berberian performing Berio's *Folk Songs.* The students search the Internet for information about these songs and discover Berio's account of his intentions in composing/arranging them: 'I have given the songs a new rhythmic and harmonic interpretation: in a way, I have recomposed them. The instrumental part has an important function: it is meant to underline and comment on the expressive and cultural roots of each song. Such roots signify not only the ethnic origins of the songs but also the history of the authentic uses that have been made of them' (Berio: 1964).

These two musical worlds come together for the students in a 'fruitful collision' and through these two examples from different musical worlds, they come to understand the way in which folk songs can be reworked to communicate powerful contemporary, social messages without their essential and original meaning being destroyed or lost. Underpinned by this understanding they work together, with support from the teacher when requested, discussing and trying out and testing musical ideas and eventually creating a folk song cycle called *Our Brave Boys* – a title which the songs treat both straightforwardly but in many cases ironically, expressing a strong anti-war sentiment.

They ensure that each song stays true to the spirit of the original, but is given a contemporary feel. They use all the instruments (electronic and acoustic) that they have at their disposal as well as employing digital technology and, in the manner of Berio, employ different instrumental combinations to accompany each song. In addition they rewrite lyrics to address various perspectives of conflict in the world. They perform the song cycle at the next school concert where all present agree that their knowledge does not represent a 'well-behaved presence'.

Conclusion

In the above case studies, and throughout this chapter, I have sought to demonstrate how, through a critical pedagogy which creates musical contexts within which students can develop and express their own critical consciousness, make connections with their own world and become active constructers of knowledge, students' musical knowledge becomes replete with, rather than void of, 'self'.

However the attainment of critical consciousness is not necessarily a 'comfortable' place to be. It carries with it a responsibility that doesn't allow for individual acts to be placed at the door of external factors and authority and thus one becomes – at least to an extent – responsible for one's own destiny: one's own musical destiny. Critical consciousness also brings with it a knowledge of 'self' within one's musical world; of knowing what one knows but with an awareness that the paradoxical nature of being fully human is a knowledge of one's essential 'incompleteness'. Critical thinking and critical consciousness lead people to the knowledge of themselves as essentially 'unfinished, uncompleted beings in and with a likewise unfinished reality' (Giroux 2010: 3). This incompleteness is inherent in the nature of knowledge as being formed from a continuing dialectical relationship with the world where that world is dynamic and ever-changing in relation to the person as a subject within the world. Students (and teachers) come to recognize learning as a fundamentally unending and as a lifelong, ongoing and *liberating* process.

Reflective questions

1   Think back to your own music education. What particular philosophies of knowledge and knowledge–learner relationships do you feel underpinned the way in which you were taught? Do you feel that you were disadvantaged in any way by the conception of knowledge that underpinned the pedagogical approaches of your teachers?

2   Consider your own teaching style. What particular philosophies of knowledge and knowledge–learner relationships do you feel influence the way you teach? Do your pedagogical approaches result from the way in which you were taught or are they consciously chosen?

3   What do you feel are the advantages and disadvantages of a critical pedagogy both generally and in relation to your own teaching? How might you develop your own pupils' critical thinking skills and what impact do you think might it have on them as musicians and their musical development?

References

Abrahams, F. (2005a) 'The Application of a Critical Pedagogy to Music Teaching and Learning', in *Visions of Research in Music Education*. Online. Available HTTP: <http://users.rider.edu/~vrme/v6n1/vision/Abrahams_2005.pdf>

Abrahams, F. (2005b) 'The Application of a Critical Pedagogy to Music Teaching and Learning: A Literature Review', in *UPDATE: Applications of Research in Music Education*, 23(2): 12–22.

Abrahams, F. (2005c) 'Transforming Classroom Music Instruction with Ideas from Critical Pedagogy', in *Music Educators Journal*, 92(1): 62–7.

Allsup, R.E. (2003) 'Transformational Education and Critical Music Pedagogy: Examining the Link Between Culture and Learning', in *Music Education Research* 5(1): 5–13.

Berio, L. (1964) *Folk Songs*, Vienna (Universal Edition).

Bullock, A. and Trombley, S. (eds) (1999) *The New Fontana Dictionary of Modern Thought*, London: Harper Collins.

Freire, P. (1970) *Pedagogy of the Oppressed*, London: Penguin Books.

Freire, P. (1974) *Education for Critical Consciousness*, London: Continuum.

Giroux, H.A. (2010) 'Lessons from Paulo Freire', in *Chronicle of Higher Education*, 57(9): B15–B16.

Martin, P.J. (1995) *Sounds and Society*, Manchester: Manchester University Press.

Regelski, T.A. (2005) 'Critical Theory as a Foundation for Critical Thinking in Music Education', in *Visions of Research in Music Education (Special Edition)* January 2005.

Schmidt, P. (2005) 'Music Education as Transformative Practice: Creating New Frameworks for Learning Music through a Freirian Perspective', in *Visions of Research in Music Education (Special Edition)*, January 2005.

Spruce, G. (2009) 'Teaching and Learning for Critical Thinking and Understanding', in J. Evans and C. Philpott (eds), *A Practical Guide to Teaching Music in the Secondary School*, London: Routledge.

Woodford, P. (2005) *Democracy and Music Education: Liberalism, Ethics and the Politics of Practice*, Indiana: Indiana University Press.

Wright, R. (2010) *Sociology and Music Education*, Farnham: Ashgate.

Chapter 13

Music 14–19: Choices, challenges, and opportunities

Keith Evans

Introduction

The number of young people pursuing music in school in England beyond the age of 14, where it is no longer a compulsory component of the curriculum, remains disappointingly low. Ofsted (2009) reported that only eight per cent of students in 2008 took GCSE music compared to, for example, art and design which had over three times as many candidates. Similarly, almost ten years earlier Harland *et al.* noted that music in school was the most problematic and vulnerable of the three art forms art, music and dance.

> (In GCSE Music) pupil enjoyment, relevance, skill development, creativity and the expressive dimension were often absent.
>
> (Harland *et al.*, 2000: 568)

It has proved difficult to reverse the position where approximately nine out of ten students turn their backs on 'school music' at the earliest opportunity. This is a complex issue and various suggestions have been put forward to explain why the GCSE Music qualification, despite being explicitly conceived as accessible by all abilities, has failed to attract greater numbers of students. These have included its perceived difficulty, its relevance to career aspirations and the level of prescription (Bray 2000; Wright 2002) but, as Lamont and Maton note, these reasons have been 'largely speculative, ad hoc and piecemeal' (2010: 65).

This chapter explores some of the reasons and underlying issues behind the poor uptake of music as a GCSE option including why many students fail to be enthused by the prospect of music as a curriculum subject beyond the age of 14. We argue that the quality of the student experience at Key Stage 3 and teachers' attitudes to inclusion and their own educational backgrounds are crucial. The chapter will also consider whether alternative courses and qualifications have the potential to address young people's disinclination to continue with formal music education once it becomes optional. We explore how the stated aims of the different types of qualification are quite distinct and how these can impact on what the students actually do in their timetabled music sessions.

In conclusion the chapter argues that the fundamental issue concerning the popularity and success of music in education is the extent to which it is taught musically, addresses the aspirations and interests of young people, and is experienced by students as authentic practice. These are the overwhelming factors determining whether or not young people choose to continue with music beyond the age of 14.

Why is music as a curriculum subject unpopular post-14?

At Key Stage 3, in many schools, students find music in the formal curriculum an odd experience that fails to connect with what they see as 'real' music in their lives outside of school (Green 2006). Such disenchantment is therefore unlikely to encourage them to sign up for a course of musical study at Key Stage 4 if they anticipate it will be yet more of the same.

A number of writers turn to sociological theory to explain this disjuncture. Wright (2008) notes a perceived clash of *habitus* between the musical interests and values of the teacher and students. (This term from the French sociologist Bourdieu describes the values and attitudes we hold as individuals that influence the way we behave and react). Therefore, for many students a likely factor as to why they do not wish to pursue music formally in school beyond the age of 14 is that they feel an underlying mismatch between their interest in popular culture and the messages they perceive they are getting from their teacher about the superiority of western art music. This is also expressed in terms of different musical codes between the teacher and many of the students.

> ... by virtue of their predominant western art music background and training, (teachers) tend to use elaborated codes derived from Western European élite culture, whereas students use vernacular musical codes drawn from their musical enculturation received at home and through the media.
>
> (Finney 2007)

The 'élite culture' to which Finney refers is sometimes manifest in the setting of arbitrary hurdles that are imposed by teachers in order to give themselves a small and select group; such as the demand that students play their instrument 'to at least Grade 3 standard'. This is then rationalized through teachers articulating the view that it is the students who fail to match up to the demands of the qualification and overlook their own role in devising an educational experience that might attract and motivate aspiring musicians.

Lamont and Maton (2008; 2010) also draw on Bourdieu and Bernstein, in proposing a legitimation code theory to explain the low uptake for GCSE music. They suggest that the documentation of the UK national curriculum emphasizes either musical knowledge or musical dispositions of knowers whereas music at GCSE represents an élite code where achievement depends on both possessing specialist knowledge and being the 'right kind of knower'. Crucially, they believe that students are aware of this code shift when considering their options for Key Stage 4 and this could partially explain the low uptake for music.

Finally, for much of the twentieth century, music in secondary school has tended to be promoted as 'academic' study. In the time prior to a national curriculum when music's place on the timetable was far from guaranteed it probably served music teachers' purpose to promote music as a high status academic subject; a 'real' subject alongside all other academic subjects. Yet perhaps this is where the root of the alienation that so many students experience towards school music lies. A pseudo-academic curriculum tending to musical analysis, propositional knowledge and with limited opportunity for self-expression is a long way from the practical musical aspirations of most young people and their lived experience of music here and now. Unfortunately, music as an art object distanced from students' experience has been easily perpetuated by teachers who, for the most part, come from a classical music background (Hargreaves *et al.*, 2007) as well as by other teachers simply content to teach the way they were taught themselves.

In summary, authors have identified several reasons why pupils do not choose music post-14. These reasons are most often related to a disjuncture between the 'musics' of pupils and those of teachers, schools and statutory curricula.

Competing aims and philosophies

In an attempt to address the unpopularity of music post-14, there has been a significant and recent expansion in the range of qualifications offered to students wishing to pursue their musical interests in the formal curriculum. Many music departments in schools have positively embraced alternatives to established GCSE and A level qualifications, which now comprise just one route through the variety of 14–19 pathways available to students. This diversity has come about largely through an increase in what can be loosely referred to as vocational qualifications where music is either a discrete focus or a component of a wider course embracing the performing arts or the creative industries. In the case of music these alternatives to more traditional 'academic' qualifications such as GCSE and A-level now account for the majority of examination entries for 14 to 19-year-olds.

While it is debatable whether the academic or vocational labelling of qualifications in music is helpful, there is no doubt that the status of vocational qualifications generally is seen as inferior to that of their academic counterparts by many parties. Throughout secondary education vocational qualifications have an image as the lower-status option and are associated with lower achievers. As the argument goes:

> If 'clever' people are to fulfil their potential ... they need to opt for brainwork rather than handwork, which means the latter becomes the domain of the 'less intelligent'.
>
> (Lucas *et al.*, 2010: 2)

This lack of status can deter some schools or teachers offering these courses to their students despite the fact that they might be more appropriate in meeting their students' needs and aspirations and result in increased take-up for music.

At this point it is worth stopping to consider fundamental aims in offering courses in music beyond a compulsory curriculum, the debates and competing ideologies which impact on decisions about which qualifications are adopted by schools, and what participants hope to achieve from the experience. Have the students signed up for the course because they want to develop as competent musicians and aspire to work in the entertainment industry or do they see studying music merely as a component within a much broader education equipping them for the next stage in their lives? Is it about pursuing a qualification that validates students' interests and achievements or is it more about exposing them to a range of musical styles and traditions to develop aesthetic awareness and appreciation of cultural heritage? The answers to such fundamental questions have a strong bearing on not only the qualifications we offer but, probably more importantly, on how and what we teach. It is worth noting that there are more general competing ideologies of education at stake here too. The traditional liberal–humanist view is that education is about passing on an intellectual and cultural legacy from one generation to another, looking back to 'the best that has been thought and said' in order to equip young people with accumulated wisdom and knowledge to make sense of what is to come. In this view, formal education is concerned with providing students with knowledge that is *not* accessible through direct experience of everyday life:

> Education is not, and should not be, reducible to ideas that are directly relevant to a pupil. It is about imparting the knowledge and insights gained through the experience of others in far-away places and often in different historical circumstances.
>
> (Furedi 2009: 55)

By contrast, others see a more direct and instrumental purpose for education in which young people are supported to grow into responsible citizens with the necessary skills and personal attributes to be self-sufficient and live fulfilling lives. It is not what people know that is important but their ability to adapt and respond to new circumstances. This suggests that students are given opportunities to learn through experience in tasks that are practical and relevant – in fact, characteristics fundamental to vocational learning. This is likely to lead to a project-based approach highlighting skills such as creativity, entrepreneurship, and decision-making.

The stated aims of existing general (i.e. 'academic') and vocational qualifications in music provide an interesting contrast in this regard. The specifications for GCSE Music from all five main examination boards must comply with centrally-determined subject criteria (QCA 2007). These are quite specific and demand that qualifications build on the knowledge, understanding and skills established in the national curriculum. The requirements of range and content are therefore maintained alongside the key concept of integration of practice. Students are expected to understand and appreciate music 'from the past and present, from the western classical tradition and other world cultures' and a balance between range and depth is struck by the demand that specifications set just three to six areas of study. The GCSE qualification is intended to lead to a broad general musical education across a range of styles and traditions with students playing active roles in creating and performing music. The level of engagement with different styles is inevitably going to be fairly superficial and, with limited time to be fully immersed in specific musical cultures, students are hard-pressed to get to grips with the distinctive nature of individual traditions. The solution tends to be a linear curriculum hopping from concept to concept across pieces and styles. Specifications for general qualifications such as GCSE and A-level thus define precisely what is studied and how it is assessed and in many cases this impacts directly on how the course is taught. In spite of the specifications promoting overarching areas of study, in practice most teachers still structure their teaching with discrete lessons covering listening, composing or performing which directly reflect the three areas of assessment. Pragmatically, this is going to be a far cry from, for example, Elliott's idea of 'continuous and active immersion ... meeting significant musical challenges in the context of authentic music cultures' (1995: 246).

In contrast to GCSE, BTEC qualifications are promoted as 'specialist work-related qualifications' that 'give learners the knowledge, understanding and skills that they need to prepare for employment.' (Edexcel 2009: 2) They are qualifications that are proudly claimed to have been developed in the Creative and Cultural Skills sector to give students 'the opportunity to enter employment in the music industry' or to progress to other vocational qualifications in Music and Music Technology. In addition, they aim to give learners 'the opportunity to develop a range of skills and techniques, personal skills and attributes essential for successful performance in working life' (Edexcel 2009: 4). At level two, the exact qualification achieved is dependent on the number of units studied with the Extended Certificate comprising two mandatory units focusing on the music industry and two specialist units, and the Diploma three mandatory units and four specialist units. The range of specialist units is impressive with over a dozen options including performing, rehearsing, improvising, composing, music technology, and world musics. Under the BTEC umbrella it is possible to assemble a highly localized and personalized curriculum and this may have been a further contributory factor in the significant migration from GCSE to vocational alternatives in music during the first decade of this century. Wright (2002) found that students who were asked what they would like a Key Stage 4 music course to include had three common responses: lots of practical work, a choice in the sort of music they study, and plenty of contemporary popular music. Teachers have therefore seen vocational qualifications as a way of responding to this consumer demand and, in particular, to move away from what many regard as potentially alienating content in the GCSE. In fact, there is very little prescription in terms of content set out for BTEC units. Instead, each unit specifies three or four learning outcomes and the skill of the teacher is in devising worthwhile learning sequences and linked assignments in order for the students to evidence how and to what extent they have met the success criteria.

Of course, there are risks that come with such flexibility and freedom and there is no doubt that, for many teachers, this approach requires a totally different mindset. For the teacher who has grown used to the assessment system dictating the learning the idea that it can in fact support and reflect what is taught can be quite challenging. A cynical contributor to a recent online discussion forum picked out a statement from the success criteria in a BTEC performing unit – 'Perform as part of an ensemble, demonstrating an awareness of musical communication' and quipped 'I watched my five-year-old nephew do this at his Sunday school concert with a tambourine!' On the other hand, a more optimistic response would be to capitalize on the qualification's flexibility and plan a course of genuine musical experiences.

Popularity post-14: music making at the heart of the curriculum

It is arguable that whether the course leads to a GCSE or BTEC qualification is irrelevant. Rather, what matters is the way in which music is taught and the opportunities it offers for students to develop knowledge and skills through the core activity of making music. Effective teachers *can* work out ways of helping all students make the most of their musical talents within the GCSE framework. For example, a teacher promoting the view that composing is about the music and not the score enables less conventionally trained musicians to flourish. Similarly, by making performing central to every lesson, the teacher does away with the need for additional instrumental tuition outside of the curriculum as a means of guaranteeing examination success. Such practice is a clear step towards making GCSE music as a post-14 subject inclusive and accessible to all.

However, while many teachers have been able to teach successful, thriving and popular GCSE courses at Key Stage 4, the instinct of others has been to find a solution in the alternative vocational qualifications noted above, that have gained popularity over the past decade. Primarily these have been Edexcel BTEC qualifications at both Level 2 (equivalent to GCSE) and Level 3 (equivalent to A level) but also numerous other qualifications (principally at Level 2) with titles such as Diploma for Music Practitioners (Rock School/Access to Music) or Level 2 Certificate in Music Technology (NCFE).

In particular, the adoption of Edexcel BTEC Level 2 qualifications has proved successful in many schools at increasing the take-up of music at Key Stage 4. Flexibility in terms of the prescribed content enables teachers to create courses tailored to local needs and has the potential to overcome Lamont and Maton's perceived code shift between Key Stage 3 and Key Stage 4. In other words, in schools where take-up for curriculum music is *above* average beyond

Key Stage 4, a determining factor could be that students are *less* aware of the apparent code shift. This is likely to result from more consistent musical experiences either side of the point of transition. Therefore, it is not the choice of qualification that makes the difference but the continuity of practice. The success of music in the 14–19 curriculum at Forest Hill School (see Box 13.1) highlights this point.

BOX 13.1: FOREST HILL SCHOOL – PART ONE

Forest Hill School is an 11–18 boys school in South London with approximately 1400 students. Music is an oversubscribed option at Key Stage 4 and is restricted to 60 students who take Edexcel BTEC level 2 courses in three groups. Music throughout the school is noticeably student-centred. Well-conceived units of work in Years 7–9 based around *Musical Futures* ideas of informal learning and non-formal approaches to teaching (including classroom work shopping and band skills projects) guarantee that, by the time they reach the end of Key Stage 3, boys enjoy making music and are enthused to pursue their interests further. As a student in Year 11 puts it:

> The courses they (the teachers) come up with in Year 8 and 9 really get you into wanting to try it more and find out more in that area.

Building on their work in bands during Year 9, the Key Stage 4 course is taught principally through the medium of jazz and popular music styles. As well as reflecting the interests of the majority, this is consistent with the department's inclusive vision that makes music in Year 10 accessible to all on the basis of what they have done within the curriculum. There is no evidence of any code shift between Key Stage 3 and Key Stage 4 and students see their course merely as a continuation of the music education they started in Year 7. In choosing the option of music in Year 10 boys offer an interesting perspective on the balance between having a passion for music and possessing musical talent:

> When you play together as a group it inspires you more. It still sounds okay even if you are the least talented.

They share a strong belief that their interest in what they are doing facilitates their learning. They have faith that they develop their musical skills in the *process* of doing the course:

> I started getting into it during Year 9. That inspired me to take it further. I *liked* it. It didn't mean that I was *good* at it! The BTEC allowed me to do a musical course while at the same time developing the practical skills.

Students are unable to conceive that anyone who had experienced the same Key Stage curriculum as them would not be able to succeed at BTEC Music.

The practical approach advocated here should not be confused with a focus which prioritizes technical skills. It is concerned with developing students' under-standing of music through *doing* music in contrast to seeking to expose them to great works of art or even a particularly wide range of musical styles. Nevertheless, it can be assumed that increased confidence and versatility in performance arises from the amount of time students spend making music together undertaking 'authentic practice' (see Box 13.2).

BOX 13.2: FOREST HILL SCHOOL - PART TWO

In previous years the music department at Forest Hill School has experimented with other qualifications at level two (including GCSE and NCFE courses) but has gravitated towards BTEC on the grounds that it offers a flexible assessment structure for a course that can capitalize on the students' musical interests. The head of music recognizes that it is the opportunity to perform that enthuses most of his students. Consequently, two of the three groups in each year follow a performance-based combination of optional units (The third group follows a course specialising in music technology).

One of the strengths of the BTEC teaching at Forest Hill is the way that students are involved in authentic practice. The performance-based course is based around the BTEC specialist units *Working as a musical ensemble, Rehearsal techniques for musicians,* and *Developing as a musical performer.* For the students there is no difference between working on performances for school and doing it 'for real'. The two become one through opportunities such as performing before live audiences, sharing work through social media, and recording for an in-house record label. As far as is possible within the context, they operate and are treated as 'real' musicians and this goes some way towards addressing the overtly vocational elements of the qualification (e.g. BTEC Level 2 Unit 1 – Working in the Music Industry).

Most students are aware of progression routes post 16 and most stay on into the school's sixth form where a BTEC level three qualification with a strong emphasis on performing is an option.

There are strong echoes in Box 13.2 of David Elliott's praxial philosophy of music education in which verbal concepts of formal musical knowledge and understanding are secondary to music making in action. The emphasis is on procedural knowledge (non-verbal knowing 'how') rather than propositional knowledge (knowing 'that') where the cognitive activity concerns thinking and knowing 'in action':

> A performer's musical understanding is exhibited not in what the performer says about what he or she does; a performer's musical understanding is exhibited in the quality of what she gets done in and through her actions of performing.
>
> (Elliott 1995: 56)

Developing students' musicianship in this view means organising the teaching into what Elliott calls a 'reflective musical practicum'. In effect, all students learn as musical apprentices. In the real world music making and listening take place within specific contexts and Elliott challenges the one-dimensional, aesthetic view of music in which all styles and traditions tend to be listened to in the same narrow way. He suggests that it is only realistically possible to develop musicianship in the curriculum through activities which are deliberately designed to reflect genuine musical practices, i.e. what he refers to as 'curriculum-as-practicum'. Musicianship is developed through challenging students to solve genuine musical problems in teaching and learning environments as close as possible to real musical practice:

> When small and large performing ensembles are developed ... and students engage in performing, improvising, composing, arranging, conducting, and music-listening projects, then the school music classroom ... becomes a reflective musical practicum: an approximation of real music-practice situations, or musical cultures.
>
> (Elliott 2005: 13)

Without the GCSE specification's areas of study defining in detail what needs to be learned the responsibility transfers to the teacher to devise musical tasks that can provide opportunities for students to display and develop their musical expertise at a variety of levels. Teaching in such a context is arguably far more productive as it is concerned with helping students create meaning out of their experiences and to enable them to construct their own knowledge. The teacher takes on the role of facilitator and, by ensuring that learning activities are set as authentic, real-life problems that need to be solved, gives the learning immediacy and relevance. This is clearly demonstrated in Box 13.3 where the challenge put to the students is no different from that facing the professional music producer.

BOX 13.3: FOREST HILL SCHOOL - PART THREE

In the context of BTEC Unit 7 (*Exploring Computer Systems used by Musicians*) a teacher took advantage of a current remix competition based on OK Go's 'White Knuckles'. For the competition the band had recently made the original multi-track audio available for download and the teacher presented this to Year 10 students as a 24-track audio template in the software *Garageband*. Their task over a series of lessons was to remix this material with the possibility of submitting the results to the online competition.

At the start of the project the teacher modelled some basic functions and possibilities and, while the students worked independently for most of the time, each session included a segment where the teacher introduced new technical and musical possibilities. For the majority of the time the teacher was involved

---

in formative dialogue with individual students. At the midpoint of the project there was a short self-assessment task and there was a more substantial peer assessment process at the end. On both occasions video recording was used to capture students' responses.

It was notable how evidence gathering was embedded into the process - the videos, the teacher's jottings, computer files saved on a regular basis, in addition to the final product.

An unexpected bonus was that the remix competition generated some very high quality submissions from OK Go's fan base and students were motivated by what professionals and expert amateurs were doing on the same task. The task required repeated, extended critical listening but offered an engaging context in which to do it.

As the teacher commented: 'Perhaps the biggest strength of this project was that it didn't just *resemble* a real-world, professional project, but actually *was* one!' The release-quality audio meant that even students with more limited ability were creating something that sounded good and of which they could be proud.

Conclusion

Given the discrepancy between the take-up for examination music courses post-14 and young people's obvious engagement with music in general, it would seem that the responsibility on the teacher to deliver an educational experience that is musical, relevant, and of quality has never been more important. Green's (1999) analysis of musical meaning is of particular relevance here. She suggests that students have a celebratory experience when affirmation by music's inherent meanings (the interrelationship of sonic materials) is accompanied by a positive response to its delineated meanings (the contextual factors). If students are familiar with a particular style through their listening and performing and also appreciate the social context of its production, distribution and consumption, then a course that enables them to develop musically within their preferred style has every chance of attracting committed and motivated musicians. Conversely when they anticipate that an examination course will be dominated by the study of music which has little interest for them and will not allow them to pursue their own musical interests then they are likely not to choose to embark upon it.

The schools where music in the curriculum thrives at Key Stage 4 put music making at the heart of their courses irrespective of whether they lead to so-called 'academic' or vocational qualifications. Whether this 'doing music' takes the form of performing and creating live music or producing music through technological manipulation matters less but, crucially, it is practical learning assessed through measuring what learners can do, rather than what they can remember. This includes how well they adapt their knowledge, skills and understandings to new contexts and means that activities are likely to be framed as problems to be solved rather than facts to be learned. The Case Study in this chapter demonstrates how inspiring teaching has successfully used the structure of a vocationally-related qualification to motivate young musicians, increase numbers continuing music in school beyond Year 9 and certificate their achievements. Whilst noting that a qualification's specification is only a framework of component units, it shows how imaginative teachers can take this as a starting point to plan worthwhile musical encounters.

It requires a good teacher to have the vision and confidence to devise a curriculum of meaningful practical encounters. But it is important that students construct their own knowledge and skills through *doing* rather than having the teacher resort to telling them 'what they need to know' if we are to make music more popular post-14. Indeed, if taught musically and by enlightened teachers, then any specification can be adapted to make meaningful connections with all students and inspire them to take on the subject post-14. In the end the issue of participation in music post-14 has less to do with the branding of the qualification as with the quality of the experience.

Reflective questions

1   Why is music unpopular post-14? In your view what are the relative influences of choice of qualification, school culture and teacher here?
2   How can the tensions between what the specification content and the students' interests be resolved in the music classroom? What are the implications for pedagogy?
3   What are the consequences of excluding music and other arts from the English Baccalaureate?
4   What does a considered and successful course in music 14–19 contribute to a broad and balanced education?

References

Bray, D. (2000), 'An Examination of GCSE Uptake Rates', *British Journal of Music Education,* 17(1), 79–89.

Edexcel (2009) *BTEC Level 2 Firsts Specification in Music,* London: Edexcel.

Elliott, D. (1995), *Music Matters,* Oxford: Oxford University Press.

Elliott, D. (2005) *Praxial Music Education: Reflections and Dialogues,* Oxford: Oxford University Press.

Finney, J. (2007), 'Music Education as Identity Project in a World of Electronic Desires', in J. Finney, and P. Burnard (eds) *Music Education with Digital Technology,* London and New York: Continuum.

Furedi, F. (2009), *Wasted – Why Education Isn't Educating,* London: Continuum.

Green, L. (1999), 'Research in the Sociology of Music Education: Some Introductory Concepts', *Music Education Research,* 1(2): 159–69.

Green, L. (2006), 'Popular Music Education In and For Itself, and for 'Other' Music', *International Journal of Music Education,* 24(2): 101–18.

Hargreaves, D., Purves, R., Welch, G. and Marshall, N. (2007) 'Developing Identities and Attitudes in Musicians and Classroom Music Teachers', *British Journal of Educational Psychology*, 77: 665–82.

Harland, J., Kinder, K., Lord, P. *et al.* (2000) *Arts Education in Secondary Schools: Effects and Effectiveness*, Slough: NFER.

Lamont, A. and Maton, K. (2008) 'Choosing Music: Exploratory Studies Into the Low Uptake of Music GCSE', *British Journal of Music Education*, 25(3): 267–82.

Lamont, A. and Maton, K. (2010) Unpopular Music: Beliefs and Behaviours Towards Music in Education, in R. Wright (ed) *Sociology and Music Education*, Farnham: Ashgate Pub Ltd.

Lucas, B., Claxton, G. and Webster, R. (2010) *Mind the Gap: Research and Reality in Practical and Vocational Education*, London: Edge Foundation.

Ofsted (2009) *Making More of Music – An Evaluation of Music in Schools 2005-08*, (Ref. HMI090085), London: Ofsted.

QCA (2007) *GCSE Subject Criteria for Music*, ref. QCA/07/3463, Crown Copyright.

Wright, R. (2002) 'Music for All? Pupils' Perceptions of the GCSE Music Examination in One South Wales Secondary School', *British Journal of Music Education*, 19(3): 227–41.

Wright, R. (2008) 'Kicking the Habitus: Power, Culture and Pedagogy in the Secondary School Music Curriculum', *Music Education Research*, 10(3): 389–402.

Chapter 14

Partnerships in music education

So — who is the teacher?

Katherine Zeserson

Introduction

Over the last decade, partnership working has become an important driving principle in music education and across the wider cultural learning sector. The publication of Ken Robinson's *All Our Futures* in 1999 catalysed policy and practice debates around creative learning, engaging colleagues across disparate sectors. His vision of an enriched educational system in which professional artists and empowered classroom teachers would work together to help children thrive and grow creatively has inspired teachers, artists, thinkers and planners to test and develop a diverse range of innovative partnership models.

A series of curricular reformations, in the context of a far-reaching national policy debate on creativity in learning, and driven forward via the establishment of Creative Partnership in 2004, has resulted in increased focus upon, and redefinitions of, partnership practice. These new models of partnership have been promoted through, for example, the Music Manifesto in 2005, the evolution of *Wider Opportunities*, the establishment of *Sing Up* in 2007, and the appointment by the then Department for Children, Schools and Families of a Participation Director from 2007 to 2011, one of whose specific goals was to encourage every local authority music service to work in partnership with other local providers. This need for sectoral redefinition has stimulated rigorous and energetic debate between those working in different sectors of music and music education that might hitherto have had very little to do with each other – community musicians, classroom teachers, Music Service staff and managers, professional performing artists - and with it questions of teacher-identity and power relationships.

In this chapter we begin by looking at the context within which partnerships are formed particularly in terms of the changing nature of the 'musical learner' and the potential of partnerships to enrich musical pedagogy. We then move on to considering some of the key issues which need to be addressed in order to ensure that partnerships work effectively. Finally we look at how a 'constellation' model of musical partnership might provide the means for creating effective partnership working which recognizes and values what each and every party brings to the educational process.

Partnerships and the context of musical learning

In considering the context within which music education partnerships are formed we need, perhaps, to consider three factors:

- our understanding of the musical learner;
- the role and identity of the 'music teacher';
- what we are teaching and how it is being learned.

Understanding the learner

To really understand the teacher, we must first understand the learner and particularly what motivates the learner to learn. The motivation to learn may be prompted by various factors and impulses – curiosity, necessity, passion, the desire for approval (see e.g. Kolb 1984; Keller1983). However, what is clear across all theories is that the greater the motivation the more likely learners are to succeed in achieving their goals. So being able to stimulate or connect with student motivation is fundamental to any teacher's efficacy.

The place of music in popular culture combined with the rapid pace of technological development and democratisation have between them radically transformed the wider cultural context for music education. Many children and young people are now coming into music classrooms with an enormous range of musical preferences and references; others perhaps less so depending on their personal circumstances, but none the less the potential is there. This means that our learners may be more knowledgeable, opinionated and personally motivated about their musical learning than previous generations. Harnessing the passions and interests of our learners through being able to work with and from their own musical interests, and taking those as the starting point for deeper and wider exploration, is at the heart of effective music education.

This last decade of debate and development in music education has therefore by necessity included a sharpened focus on consideration of learner individuality and preference. A commitment to negotiated learning goals that take significant account of student voice has become more prominent in some communities of practice within the profession. *Musical Futures*, with its reversal of conventional teacher–student role dynamics in repertoire and stylistic choice-making, is perhaps the best known forum for this approach to classroom practice, but it is widely visible in the work of *Sing Up*, of many *Wider Opportunities* programmes and in the work of countless individual teachers. In addition the relatively recent emergence of the community music movement within music education has played a role in challenging some of the more restrictive orthodoxies of classroom music teaching and its norms through foregrounding inclusive, creative musical learning processes as sites for social and emotional development as well as musical progress and achievement. A high value is placed here on accounting for the feelings, ideas and needs of the individual learner–participant in the context of the group; choices about activities and goals are more likely to be driven by the learner–participants rather than the teacher–leader and there is more likely to be a focus on creative, generative processes rather than instructional or technical ones. Led skilfully, it can be argued that these strategies typically engender high levels of motivation, engagement and satisfaction in learners–participants, as well as musical learning and progression (Moser *et al.* 2005; Price 2008).

Role and identity of the 'music teacher'

In a philosophical investigation of the role of teachers, Shim (2007) writes: 'Teachers not only contribute to the development of individuals and societies but also attain self-realization through teaching. As such, the role of teachers is important as a goal as well as a means.' And he goes on to say: 'Teachers should think things over, look at these things from different perspectives, and come to discover new facts while they are teaching. While teaching, they should realize their own limitations, shortcomings, and flaws, and they should reflect, try to improve themselves, and consequently attain spiritual, moral, and esthetic growth' (Shim 2007: 515 and 516).

As well as understanding students' individual interests and passions, knowing how to identify and meet individual needs in the context of the group is fundamental to ensuring successful differentiation and inclusion. In this plural cultural environment it is increasingly difficult for any individual teacher to be connected to, and confident with, the wide range of genres, styles and sound worlds that young people carry with them and the range and variety of their musical and personal needs. The classroom teacher's confidence and skill in knowing when and how to bring in other teachers–leaders will certainly affect students' opportunity for development and progression.

You could further argue that by approaching the process of teaching in the way described by Shim, the teacher is modelling desirable behaviour to students, and certainly in the case of music teaching, the role of the teacher as the exemplar of learning can be critical to students' capacity to sustain commitment – particularly when learning an instrument. Encouraging a creative and positive attitude to practice through modelling the value of constructive self-criticism and reflection is well-recognized as an effective teaching strategy. We know that realizing our own limitations as teachers and being open with students and colleagues about them is a productive path both to our own professional development and to improving opportunities for our students. However, it can be difficult to sustain this ideal in daily practice despite our best intentions.

Understanding the variety of situational roles the individual 'music teacher' may adopt in the course of a session, a day, a week or a lifetime's work may be helpful in finding shared responses to these questions, and in defusing professional concerns around role identity. In considering music teacher roles from the perspective of partnership working, we can consider the simple grid in Table 14.1.

Table 14.1 Music teachers' situational roles

Situational role adopted	Typical behaviour
Guide	Provides direction, suggests routes of enquiry or action.
Facilitator	Supports interaction and group process; ensures inclusion and progress to goals; encourages personal and collective reflection.
Knowledge provider	Pro-actively introduces information and ideas.
Animateur	Asks questions to provoke personal and collective reflection or action; stimulates debate.
Ally	Advocates on behalf of students; enables realization of ideas.
Trainer	Develops specific technical skills in students.
Beacon	Inspires student motivation and commitment through passion and authenticity.
Role model	Exemplifies and clarifies musical or other behaviours.
Manager	Organises opportunities and resources to support students.

Clearly, any music education practitioner will be more or less comfortable in each of these roles, and at least familiar with them all. The more fluent and fluid we are in moving between these positions in relation to our students' learning, the better we are able to create the best conditions for their progress and enjoyment.

BOX 14.1: THE WATER PROJECT

F, a Year 5 teacher, decided to develop a composition project as part of a term-long Water topic. She was a confident singer with no instrumental playing experience, basic grasp of music notation and a personal passion for blues and jazz. She began the project by teaching her class the songs *Bring me Little Water Sylvie*, *Empty Cup Blues* and *So Much Magnificence* (acting as *Role Model*, *Knowledge Provider* and *Trainer*). Through the half term she acted as *Guide*, *Facilitator* and *Animateur* as small groups of pupils used these songs as templates for their own composition activities, resulting in a set of new *a cappella* songs – a 'Water Cycle'. In the second half of term, she used her effective *Manager* skills to arrange for a small group of A-level students from the neighbouring secondary school, supported by their saxophone teacher, to visit for three sessions to create instrumental backings to be performed by the combined forces of both groups. At the end of term, in response to student enthusiasm (acting as their *Ally*), she arranged for the 'Water Cycle' to be performed in both schools and at the local Arts Centre as part of their Spring Festival. The whole project was so successful, due in part to her inspirational leadership, that a spring composition project is now an annual fixture in the Year 5 learning calendar.

What are we teaching and how is it being learned?

Choosing to introduce a different pedagogic 'voice' or role model is often a key driver for inviting a collaborator into the classroom or setting. Many traditional music styles are taught in a much more directive, master–apprentice style than is common in our classrooms today. It may well be that improvisation or performance sessions led by professional artists may seem to contradict conventions or practices students are learning in other contexts, whilst visiting performers may model technical behaviours at odds with the advice teachers are giving their students. This diversity is an opportunity for students to apply their own critical thinking skills and for the 'home' teacher to contextualize the new experience with reference to familiar norms, and support students to investigate differences between pedagogic approaches as a means of learning more about music; rather than such differences becoming sources of confusion, competition or divisive judgement.

Careful consideration of curriculum content and pedagogical approaches - visible and hidden – combined with equally careful consideration of student interests and needs will underpin decisions about teaching strategies and form the foundations of productive partnerships. Music teaching encompasses a terrific and unique variety of discourses and domains, from the technical to the conceptual and including the imaginative, the kinaesthetic and the social–emotional. Any starting point has the potential to take us anywhere; so what may on the face of it appear a simple matter of information - *this is how to hold the bow* – might lead to a set of bowing exercises designed to improve tone; to a creative improvisation exploring what happens if you hold it another way; to a Dalcroze session on whole body engagement in bowing, or to a discussion about the physics of sound. As teachers we are constantly making choices about how far to confine the learning discourse to a specific goal and how far to allow it to range freely according to students' questions and experiences.

The marvellous variety of opportunities for musical learning generates an equally diverse range of teaching and facilitation approaches. Starting with music-making itself as the core site for musical learning, music teachers–leaders are working in or utilizing solo, small and large group contexts; master–apprentice relationships; collective and peer learning frameworks; instructional approaches; dialogic, investigative strategies and more.

Our experiences as musicians inform and influence our decisions – conscious and unconscious – about what we are teaching and how we teach it, so it follows that individual teachers will animate visible curriculum/session content differently. Teaching from our own experience is uniquely powerful. The authenticity of lived experience radiates an authority which is emotionally engaging and helps to harness and stimulate motivation and equally, when working with unfamiliar material, provide a role model of curiosity and investigative skill. This creates a relationship of equality and shared discovery which is both motivational and inclusive. It is in this regard that partnership delivery is so significant. Knowing how and when to draw on a variety of teachers to support and lead learning enables us to develop richer, more inclusive teaching and learning strategies that can take account of the different ways of learning through which our students will flourish.

BOX 14.2: ELMTREE PRIMARY SCHOOL

Elmtree Primary School is a medium-sized school in a disadvantaged urban area, benefitting from an active and energetic Music Service. There was little instrumental music-making taking place outside of the *Wider Opportunities* violin sessions being delivered in partnership with the Music Service, and few children were taking up the opportunity to progress with instrumental learning. The Music Coordinator convened a series of discussions with the Music Service lead and some local folk musicians, and between them they developed a package of opportunities and experiences designed to introduce a wide range of live music experiences to the whole school in order to stimulate the interest and imagination of students and teachers alike.

The programme included short performances and workshops in whole school assemblies, 'masterclasses' with professional violin players from a variety of genres (folk, classical, jazz) supported by the class teacher, and an extra-curricular ceilidh band combining staff, students and parents. The teaching and learning strategies employed by classroom teachers were complemented by different approaches from visiting musicians that encouraged engagement from children that had not previously expressed an interest in participating in group music-making; in particular the oral teaching approach of the folk musicians caught the imagination of the whole school, leading to the establishment of a culture of short family ceilidhs as part of end-of-term assemblies and celebrations.

A key factor in the success of this partnership initiative was the willingness of the Music Service to help the school identify other local musicians to work with from outside the Service, and also to help the school find extra financial resources to pay the visitors. The importance of this lack of vested interest cannot be overstated.

Developing effective partnerships

Effective partnership working is, therefore, a function of effective relationships, and so thrives on trust, mutual respect and cooperation. However partnership also generates questions, challenges and triggers for change in particular around teachers' roles and identities. Consideration of music education in its broadest sense – incorporating both in and out of classroom contexts – immediately requires us to note that our community of practice is highly plural in skills, backgrounds, professional preparation, objectives, employment status and career structure. This diversity in individual experiences and expectation, coupled with the likely variety of specific goals engendered by learner intentions in different contexts, generates a multiplicity of identity constructs and self-perceptions that impact significantly on both the conceptualization and the implementation of partnerships in music education. The relationship between what we are teaching and who is involved in teaching it is central to effective partnerships in music education. The more attention paid to clarity and alignment of roles before embarking on any level of partnership in delivery, the more successful the outcomes will be.

The development of effective and satisfying partnerships can be said to be underpinned through addressing three key issues.

The first and arguably most critical issue is to recognize that whereas partnership working has the potential to bring tremendous added value to students' lives, and into the lives of those working with children, it also brings into focus questions about power, identity, goals and rewards and can generate anxieties (expressed or unexpressed) about personal competencies in relation to those of a colleague or new professional partner. Competitive defensiveness or concerns around status and hierarchy can then derail and undermine collaborations that might have had great benefit to students in terms of both experiences and outcomes.

It may be the case that the 'home' teacher will be used to working with a particular level of detail in planning and preparation, perhaps even using a specific protocol for capturing lesson plans and so on. Collaborators from different contexts may have quite different approaches to planning, and often if not from a school-based background, may not be accustomed to much documentation of plans. Some musicians may choose not to prepare in a conventional way for their work with students, preferring to operate entirely spontaneously in response to the developing classroom dynamic. Questions of benchmarks, progression and outcomes can also cause difficulty in partnership working, especially in long-term projects and relationships. Just being aware of different approaches can help 'see off' partnership issues before they arise.

The variety of backgrounds and contexts each individual brings with them into the music teaching environment provides a rich opportunity for professional learning. Successful partnerships encompass professional and personal dynamics in equal measure. Partnerships between classroom teachers and visiting musicians are relationships between individuals with shared and agreed goals. Personal role and competency anxieties – *'s/he is a better musician than me'*, *'why don't the students engage with me like that?'*, *'s/he is contradicting me'* – are much more easily resolved when collaborators start from an understanding of each other's practices, gifts and talents in relation to the teaching task at hand, and can see something to learn from each other.

BOX 14.3: A SECONDARY SCHOOL TEACHER AND MUSICIAN PARTNERSHIP

D is a professional musician and educator working as resident musician in a large secondary school, in a three-year programme investigating practical strategies for deploying singing to support learning at Key Stage 3. She works across the curriculum alongside classroom teachers as well as leading after-school and lunchtime singing groups, supporting with school shows and leading a singing group for school staff, as well as a community choir. She is 'embedded' in the staff, spending time in the staff room and participating in whole school training days and staff meetings.

D works in close collaboration with the Head of Music, who is a conservatoire-trained organist and choral conductor. Her own musical background is in music theatre and popular music, and her PGCE is in physics. This difference in perspectives and experience caused some difficulties at the beginning of the relationship, as the Head of Music felt that D's presence in the school implied some criticism of his work to date and had been imposed on him by the Head; whilst D felt awkward and unsure of herself side-by-side with the Head of Music's formal training and music teaching experience, and was uncertain as to why the Head Teacher had established the project without his full buy-in.

However, they both committed to a co-learning process and identified the specific areas of practice they'd each like to develop further as well as agreeing goals for the programme as a whole with the senior leadership of the school. After two years of the partnership, D and the Head of Music had co-written a new Year 7 scheme of work based around ensemble music-making in the classroom, established a system of House Choirs and developed a repertoire base of original songs as well as effectively re-organizing the place of music in the school. They are fully committed to continuing the partnership beyond the original three years as the impact on the whole school community has been so positive, and each of them feels that they learn much from each other's different approaches.

The second issue is the important one of *clarity of purpose*. Why is the partnership being developed? A clear understanding of purpose provides the knowledge that will underpin the choice of collaborators; the content and timeframe of the work; the measures of success and the opportunity for professional development – alongside generating positive outcomes for students. Recognizing and exploring the relationship between context, content and outcomes in the planning process helps to establish goals. Some partnership working relationships will be long term; some entirely transient, but in either case taking time to ensure that everyone has understood and agreed what the purpose of the partnership activity or dialogue is will entirely transform the potential of the relationships. Resolving conflict as partnerships unfold becomes unnecessarily difficult in the absence of these agreements. It is a truism that effective partnership is based on the pursuit of shared goals. Partner norms, expectations and experiences need to be articulated and resolved as far as possible at the beginning of the creative planning journey, and then reviewed throughout as part of the process of continuous reflection.

Having identified clear goals for partnership working, the third issue to be addressed is to explore and negotiate roles. Thinking back to the shifting teacher roles outlined in Table 14.1, it is clear that different skills and qualities will come to the fore as the music teacher and collaborator move in and out of different situational role positions in the 'constellation'. This baton-passing in respect of relationship with student learning processes is where questions of identity and boundaries arise and can become difficult. Understanding yourself in relation to the multiple roles required in effective music teaching, and recognising where you are most and least comfortable will help to create the conditions for productive partnership dialogue. Explicitly balancing skills and qualities in partnership teaching or project leadership allows for a depth of relationship in which trust and mutual respect are more likely to flourish. This in turn creates the conditions for risk-taking and spontaneous creative development in the teaching and learning context.

BOX 14.4: HEDDEN PRIMARY SCHOOL AND GAMELAN

Hedden Primary School is a small school in a metropolitan borough. The school had a good singing culture, with positive commitment from all class teachers and the Head, developed in part with input from a local music organization. The music coordinator wanted to build on this positive platform and develop class teacher confidence further to support instrumental music-making, devising and composing - musical areas in which the school was less strong. The same local music organization had recently acquired a Gamelan, and was in the process of developing a teacher and musician training programme, and was looking for schools with which to pilot and develop this work. They agreed to create a residency project together.

Phase 1 consisted of a week-long residency in which the Gamelan was installed in the school, with every class and every teacher participating in activities. The content of the activities was carefully co-developed between the music coordinator, the class teachers and the visiting musician team (led by a Gamelan specialist who is an experienced ex-secondary school music teacher and including three musicians with little or no experience of working with primary aged children).

All children learned to play a simple melody and added percussion with various instruments, understanding how to play on the off-beat and counting and listening to the melody for their cue to play their individual piece; Class 2 developed some composition work and investigated pulse and rhythm; Classes 3-5 created several small group compositions to tell a story. There were also twilight sessions for teachers and musicians. The whole school then presented the outcomes of their work in a performance to family and friends at the end of the week.

A small group of teachers and musicians led by the music coordinator and the Gamelan specialist reviewed the first week in terms of learning outcomes for children, learning outcomes for class teachers and learning outcomes for the musician team. From this review the next two residency weeks (one in each of the next two terms) were refined, planned and delivered; building on the musical learning and processes and also adding a whole layer about Javanese culture and lifestyle. In between the residency weeks, the music co-ordinator supported class teachers to work with the techniques and experiences gained through working with the visitors. At the end of the year a grand celebration performance involved all staff and pupils.

The programme has been successful in delivering a number of long-term impacts – all class teachers report greater confidence in working with pulse, rhythm, improvisation and composition; children's instrumental music-making skills are growing to match their singing skills; the music organization has developed sound practice and an effective model for its Gamelan programme in primary schools, and the school and the music organization are now planning their next collaboration....

Conclusion

A 'constellation' approach to partnership

The challenge in developing effective partnership lies in balancing viewpoints, capacities and behaviours such that maximum energy is invested in shared endeavour. It's a core part of our human nature to care about our own position in relationships, and to form judgements about our own and others' behaviours. The question then for effective partnership working is how to manage that natural inclination to the benefit of all, ensuring appropriate respect, balance and mutualism. Recognising this shifting matrix of relationships and feelings underpinning musical learning, and considering the nature of partnership working, leads me to propose a *constellation model* of partnerships in music education, based on three core principles – *dynamic tension, shifting viewpoints and mutual reflection*.

Partnership working generates challenges. Tension between different and *shifting viewpoints* (both pedagogical and musical) can be destructive or dynamic. Bringing practitioners into the school environment, whose practice norms are aligned to community contexts or the professional music industry, or even just to a different kind of school, can challenge both the culture of the school community as well as that of the guests. This *dynamic tension* between perspectives can, however, be enormously productive through stimulating debate, the exploration of new ideas and creative invention.

However the multiplicity of pedagogical voices often involved in a young person's music education can provoke the question asked as part of the title of this chapter: 'So – who is the music teacher?' Perhaps the answer is that the music teacher is simply the person from whom a student learns something ... in which case of course there are many music teachers who aren't aware of their role at all. Our students learn from listening to and watching musicians perform, from working things out with their friends, from practising on their own, from talking to all kinds of people. It is of paramount importance that those of us whose role identity is underpinned by the specific training and employment context of 'music teacher' recognize and account for this variety of contributors to our students' learning.

Through developing positive self-esteem in our identity as 'music teachers' (whatever our job title or employment status) we can learn to see the practice of others as an inspiration and a positive provocation, rather than a threat. Then, recognizing that the learners we support have a variety of changing needs which are directly influenced by the process of musical learning itself, we can bring new viewpoints into the teaching and learning environment, or signpost learners to other parts of the musical solar system without ourselves feeling undermined. Engaging in continuous *mutual reflection* with learners and partners then becomes a strategy for building and strengthening the sense of constellation – of being held together around a shared focus, whilst being able to change position and influence according to learner need.

The 'identity' of the 'home' teacher in the classroom - or other context in which students are participating in musical learning - is then as the fixed star around which a 'constellation' of opportunities can orbit. Students whose music teachers encourage and value a variety of investigations, explorations, experiences, questions and experiments will flourish, and will take ownership of music in their lives. Identifying, developing and learning from opportunities for partnerships in music education make this richness possible.

We are professional learners all our working lives, and our reflective practice underpins our efficacy – the more questions we are asking ourselves the more open we are to new ideas, possibilities and opportunities to enrich the lives of our students. Good partnerships blossom into excellent ones when they become sites for deep professional learning and shared reflection between mutually respectful practitioners united in a *constellation* of common purpose. Students learn more than music when they are the beneficiaries of this approach to music education – they learn about the joy and gift of community.

Reflective questions

1 Consider the reason why you might apply the 'constellation' model of partnership working to your own professional context and who your potential partners might be.
2 What benefits would this approach bring to your students and are there any possible negative outcomes?
3 What personal challenges do you think the 'constellation' model of partnership working might present you with?

References

Henley, D. (2011) *Music Education in England – a Review*, London: Department for Education.

Keller, J.M. (1983) 'Motivational Design of Instruction', in C. M. Reigeluth (ed.), *Instructional-Design Theories and Models: An Overview of Their Current Status*, Hillsdale, NJ: Lawrence Erlbaum Associates.

Kolb, David A. (1984) *Experiential Learning: Experience as the Source of Learning and Development*, Englewood Cliffs, N.J.: Prentice-Hall, Inc.

Moser, P. and McKay, G. (eds) (2005) *Community Music – A Handbook*, Lyme Regis: Russell House Publishing.

Price, D. (2007) *From Vision to Practice - Musical Futures*, London: Paul Hamlyn Foundation.

Robinson, K. (1999) *All Our Futures*, London: National Advisory Committee on Creative and Cultural Education.

Shim, S.H. (2007) 'A Philosophical Investigation of the Role of Teachers: A Synthesis of Plato, Confucius, Buber, and Freire', in *Teaching and Teacher Education* 24: 515–35.

Music Education Code of Practice at www.soundsense.org/metadot/index.pl?iid=25842&isa=Category

Part IV

Professional Development

Chapter 15

Teachers and pupils as researchers

Methods for researching school music

Tim Cain and Pamela Burnard

Introduction

This chapter is about teachers and pupils researching musical teaching and learning. Our goal is to offer a thoughtful treatment of the role of school-based research in the teaching and learning of music and to synthesize relevant literature. Teacher research is not new but the challenge for teaching to become more 'evidence-based' (e.g. Hargreaves 1996) has given new impetus for teachers to be researchers (Stenhouse 1975). Assuming that teacher research is primarily undertaken so as to improve the quality of teaching, this chapter explores the affordances and constraints of teachers undertaking research with their pupils, and pupils as researchers. It explains why some traditional approaches to research are inappropriate for teachers, researching in their own classrooms, and it describes two, commonly used and helpful approaches: case study and action research. It explores ways of involving pupils in research – consulting pupils, involving them in decision-making and generating their own research. Throughout, it draws on studies by teachers and their students, with varying degrees of support from university researchers. We hope that it will act as a starting point for music teachers wishing to undertake and encourage research in their own schools.

Teachers as researchers

Researchers research; teachers teach. In this traditional view, researchers do the intellectual activities, while teachers get on with practical matters, putting educational research into practice. However, the last 40 years have seen an increasing interest in teachers as the generators, as well as users, of research. In the UK, the 'teachers as researchers' movement is generally thought to have began with the work of Lawrence Stenhouse and John Elliott, who worked with teachers to research and improve their educational practice, especially in the Schools Council Humanities Project (Rudduck & Hopkins 1985). Stenhouse argued that improvements in the curriculum would only be effective if teachers developed and tested them in the classroom.

Since that time there has been a steady increase in the quantity of educational action research by teachers. In a recent survey of over 4,000 teachers in England,

33 per cent agreed (or strongly agreed) with the statement, 'In the last 12 months, I have undertaken my own research and enquiry to improve my practice' whilst 60 per cent agreed or strongly agreed with the statement, 'I would like more opportunities to do my own research to improve my teaching' (Poet, Rudd & Kelly 2010). The same survey found that the chief reason for engaging with research was teachers' intrinsic motivation to maintain and improve their practice. So it seems likely that, when teachers undertake research, they research aspects of their own practice. Researching their own practice has a number of advantages because as a teacher they understand their own situation in much more depth and detail than an external researcher. They might also be free of the pressure to publish felt by university researchers. However, it also has major constraints, which can best be explored by considering the role of the teacher and teacher as researcher in the classroom.

The teacher in the classroom

'Teaching', says Elliott (2007) is 'an intentional activity directed towards bringing about learning outcomes for pupils' (p. 558). A teacher's purpose, inasmuch as she is teaching, is to motivate, inspire, direct or otherwise encourage learners to develop how they think, and what they do. Such development is usually incremental and specific to disciplines such as music, and teachers also teach matters around socially acceptable behaviour. This purpose places teachers in a leadership role within their classrooms, with a mandate to influence their students. They are both 'in authority' and 'an authority' (Hammersley 1993). Accountable to various stakeholders for their teaching (e.g. school managers, parents, local and national governments) teachers nevertheless exercise professional judgments about how local and national policies are interpreted and operationalized in their classrooms. Teaching is therefore suffused with values – the teacher's, informed by (or perhaps sometimes, in resistance to) others in the immediate and wider social milieu.

There might have been a time when teaching was largely a matter of imparting information but not now:

> A shift has taken place from a technical, rationalistic view of teaching as mastery of subject knowledge and discrete pedagogical skills to one which recognizes that teaching is a relatively unpredictable and cognitively complex activity, characterized by decision-making, negotiation for meaning and reflection in action.
>
> (Crasborn *et al.*, 2008: 501).

The influence is not unidirectional (from teacher to students); rather, the teacher listens attentively and observes perceptively, altering her teaching, in the interests of achieving better mutual understanding. Teachers sometimes stand back to observe their students, to give them independence, to allow them to learn from each other or to learn from making (safe) mistakes, but such 'standing back' (a pedagogical concept discussed extensively in a school-based study by Grainger, Burnard and Craft 2006) is always constrained, to a greater or lesser extent, by the teacher's responsibility to influence. Teachers' roles are co-constructed, in a dialectic of mutual influence with their students.

In a classroom, a web of meanings surrounds the teacher's attempts to influence. How students answer a teacher's question is not only affected by their understanding of that question. It is also affected by their understanding of the teacher's intentions (e.g. to check understanding, prompt or embarrass); by their understandings of how the teacher might respond to their answers (e.g. with praise, encouragement or sarcasm) and by how they expect their peers to understand their answer (e.g. as seeking approval, flaunting knowledge or flouting authority). Such understandings are heavily influenced by personal histories and previous experiences and, because school students change enormously during compulsory schooling, their understandings change. 'That the present is different from the past is one of the safest of generalizations ... what we carefully observed yesterday will certainly be different tomorrow' (Winter 1989: 49). One implication of this is that, in continuously adapting to changing relationships and social environments, students are constantly learning. Teachers cannot cause learning, in the sense of bringing learning into being but they can influence its focus, speed and direction. Additionally, although we like to compartmentalize phenomena, thinking of classrooms, lessons, school subjects and so on as discrete entities, the boundaries between them are constructed, not given (Whitehead and Rayner 2009). We divide students into 'classes' to be taught 'subjects' in 'lessons', and these divisions give us an appearance of clarity and control. But the divisions are artificial and, to some extent, arbitrary constructions – what happens in one lesson, at one time, influences what happens in other lessons, at other times.

Implications for teachers' research

Because the classroom is complex, it makes little sense for teachers to research their classrooms in traditional, scientific ways as, for instance, when medical researchers research the effects of a particular drug. Teaching is not like giving 'treatments' to 'research subjects' so any attempt to research it as if it were, is likely to result in poor-quality research, particularly when samples are small and unrepresentative, as is usual, in individual schools.

However, traditional, scientific approaches to research, such as large-scale surveys and randomized, controlled tests, are not the only ones possible. During the past 40 years or so there has been an increasing quantity of research in what is called the 'interpretive paradigm'. Arguing that people (the object of study) interpret their worlds in individual ways, and that there is no objective standpoint from which we might view others, 'interpretive' researchers study lived experiences; subjective understandings that are uncovered more by interviews than questionnaires, and by observations in 'real life' settings rather than controlled environments. Whereas the traditional, scientific research approach assumes that the commonalities among people are most worth researching, the interpretive approach assumes that what is worth researching is the detail, the uniqueness of particular people, institutions or events within the contexts that partly define them. The interpretative view resonates with another important idea in education – the idea that knowledge is constructed by individual minds, in social interactions.

Case study

A case study is 'the study of the particularity and complexity of a single case, coming to understand its activity within important circumstances' (Stake 1995: xi). The aim of case study is to investigate something important in detail. The researcher focuses on a particular person, group or system (the 'case') and makes a sustained attempt to understand it, in all its complexity. The research report provides 'thick description' (Geertz 1973) so that a knowledgeable reader can use the report to better understand similar people, groups or systems. Gage (1989) located the disciplinary roots of this approach in anthropology. It requires the researcher to be closer to what is being researched than traditional scientific research methods, and its research methods include interviews and observations in natural settings.

One example of a teacher's case study is Finney (1987) – a study of a group of 15-year-old boys as they became rock musicians. Finney's study was helped by the fact that, although he was the boys' teacher, he was not acting as their teacher in the situation under study. At the start of the research he acted in a caretaker role because the group used his teaching room to rehearse in; towards the end he became their recording engineer and he told the boys about his research, negotiating terms in which he interpreted events as he saw them but shared, with them, his research findings. Finney (1987) can be used to inspire teachers' case studies: it is possible for teachers to focus on individuals or groups and by judicious use of interview and observation, create thick descriptions that provide insights that help to develop understandings of similar individuals or groups. However, teachers' case studies of their own students should always consider their own influence because the teacher's authority and influence makes it difficult to step back and research the 'case' without simultaneously influencing it in some way. (For a teacher to ask a student, 'how do you respond to my teaching?' is to ask, 'how do you respond to my question, 'how do you respond to my teaching?' in a context where I am expected to influence your thinking?'). Thus teachers' case studies are not so much studies of students or classes as such; they are inevitably studies of students or classes as both influenced by, and interpreted by the teacher; to some extent they are studies of relationships. (For other examples of case study teacher research, see Burnard's (1995) case study of her Year 12 class and de Vries' (2003) case study of a 10-year-old girl's musical preferences within the context of piano lessons).

Action research

The most common approach used by teachers to research their own practice, is action research. Action research is undertaken by practitioners into their own practice, in order to improve it. It starts with questions like, 'how can I improve what I am doing?' (Whitehead 1989). In addressing such questions, action researchers investigate their own practice, plan improvements, implement the improvements, evaluate the intended and unintended consequences and reflect on these, in order to plan further improvements. At each stage, the researchers collect data, so that their evaluations are grounded in evidence. This sequence is often described in a diagram such as Fig. 15.1.

The general process is very similar to that of rehearsing music (Cain 2010) and more generally, reflective practice (Dewey 1933; Schön 1983). However, whilst reflective practice is usually conceptualized as continual, private, experiential and largely unarticulated, action research is generally thought of as a specific project and is more occasional, public and collaborative (Tripp 2003). Action research goes further than reflective practice also because it involves the specific collection and interpretation of data, is published to an audience beyond the research participants and, like all research, makes a contribution to theory. Different writers emphasize different aspects of action research. For some, its main purpose is to generate practical changes (Elliott 1991). Others emphasize collaboration, and the way in which an action research project can bring people together to change an aspect of their working practice (Kemmis & DiChiro 1987). For others, a major benefit of action research is self-knowledge and a greater understanding of how teachers' values are realized or denied in their practice (Whitehead & McNiff 2006). Others emphasize that action research generates knowledge of different types, including skilful actions, propositional knowledge, presentational knowledge and acquaintance knowledge (Heron & Reason 1997).

Doing action research

Finding a focus for an action research topic requires some thought. Because action research is time-consuming, it is important that teachers choose a focus that is worth giving time, as well as intellectual and physical energy. Useful

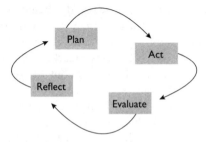

Figure 15.1 An Action Research Spiral.

starting points include questions like, 'How can I improve what I am doing?' (Whitehead 1989) and 'What will happen if ...' (Cochran-Smith & Lytle 1993). The latter question is particularly creative because it opens up possible thoughts – 'What will happen if I use my lessons as a whole-class jam session?'; 'What will happen if I let the students choose how they want to learn?'. It is helpful for teachers to consider why the chosen focus is important. Contrary to the scientific approach to research, action research holds that the teacher's subjective views and feelings are an important part of the research; they count as data, to be analyzed. Once a suitable focus has been found, the action research begins with a 'reconnaissance' in which teachers observe details of a problematic situation and try to understand it as fully as possible, reflecting on what is problematic and asking others to collaborate in research. Books and articles can help develop an understanding of the situation, as a precursor to planning improvements.

Planning and implementing interventions

The planning stage involves imagining a better situation; in one type of action research, it is called 'dream' (Reed 2007). It involves imagining what an ideal situation would look like, and deciding what actions might move the present situation closer to this ideal. In this stage, teacher–researchers consider what evidence would convince them and others that the situation had indeed moved closer to the ideal. At the 'action' stage, teacher–researchers put their plans into action and collect data to show the extent to which they are meeting their ideals, bearing in mind that it is possible for there to be unintended consequences, not all of them good. The more common forms of data tend to include the researcher's reflective diary, their observations, students' work, questionnaires and interviews with students or others. Teachers often involve a colleague, as a 'critical friend', to cast a critical eye over the data. Because action research typically generates huge quantities of data, it is important that teachers focus only on whatever is most useful, 'reading' and 're-reading' the data to find evidence of improvement and for unintended consequences.

Reflecting

Because the researcher is central to the situation under study, classroom action research should include an element of self-study, including consideration of the researchers' aims and values – what they were attempting through the research, and how these intentions were rooted in their theories, beliefs and values. To avoid using students as 'research subjects', teacher–researchers should involve their students, including them in decisions about the research aims, planning, processes and ownership. (Action research is also strengthened through collaboration with colleagues although music teachers sometimes have few colleagues to call on). Ethical issues, which include teacher–student relationships, are particularly important in teachers' research because of the teacher's leading and influencing role – it is all too easy for teachers to claim to have instigated successful changes without reference to the voices of their students, who might think otherwise. It is also necessary to consider relevant contextual aspects – broadly, the historical, political and social contexts which significantly influence the situation under study. And, like all research, teacher research contributes to the building of theory through the generation of knowledge, in a broad sense. In reflecting on the research, teacher–researchers can consider how the knowledge they have gained contributes to knowledge more generally – linking with, and building on, knowledge that is reported elsewhere. This involves a shift from statements like, 'we have made this successful change' to, 'through making this change we have learned matters which extend what we and others already knew'.

Reflection should therefore focus on all these areas: the teacher, the students, the contexts and the theoretical knowledge, as it develops through the research. A good starting point is to ask questions such as:

- What did the students do?
- What did they learn?
- How worthwhile was it?
- What did I do?
- What did I learn?
- What will I do next?

Thoughtfully answering these questions after each lesson in a series can lead to new insights, about self, students, contexts and theoretical knowledge, and a renewal and re-invigoration of teaching (Cain 2008).

Case descriptions of teachers' action research

Musical exploration using ICT

Christopher Ward's (2009) project involved 189 of his school students, aged 11 to 16. The study aimed to enable the students to '… enjoy creating original and distinctive musical pieces using the potential and advantages of ICT'. 'Original and distinctive' meant 'within a 3-dimensional soundscape … where tonal, notational and other boundaries are dissolved' (p. 157). Ward consciously created an informal class atmosphere in which his students created analogue multi-tracked recordings, used MIDI and audio sounds to underscore a movie clip and manipulated imported and created samples (including dishwasher and motorcycle sounds). The students also experienced a workshop with Trevor Wishart, a notable electro-acoustic composer.

Data was collected during lessons, as part of his regular practice. This was mainly qualitative: questionnaires with open questions, students' evaluations of their own and others' work, video interviews with students and a colleague (critical friend), students' work and 'informal monitoring' (participant observation). Ward also kept 'lesson logs' to record his own perceptions after every lesson.

Ward described the work that his students did, and illustrated their responses to it, with quotes from some of the students. He explained the changes in his practice, and in his relationships with his students. He also explored how music technology can contribute to the development of creativity, relating his work to Loveless (2002; see Ward 2009 for further details).

Behaviour management in the classroom

At the time of the research, Jo Mattock was a trainee teacher, undertaking an action research assignment. She started by video recording herself teaching, and she used the recordings to analyze three lessons on her first placement. The video allowed her to observe herself closely:

> There are moments when I am hunched over, sometimes with my arms folded, which creates a very negative, insecure impression ... there are occasions when I fidget and fiddle for example with a pen lid ...

At the beginning of her lessons she sometimes felt that she was inconsistent, responding to some pupils' poor behaviour by telling them off and to similar behaviour in other pupils by sending them out of the room. She found that she became emotionally involved in situations, sometimes becoming defensive and occasionally confrontational.

She explored the literature, practical advice which was firmly supported with theoretical underpinnings, often from psychology. From Rogers (1998) she understood the functions of behaviour management in terms of socializing individuals, providing for their moral development, their personal maturation and in providing emotional security. From Cowley (2003) she learned the importance of setting clear expectations, appearing authoritative, applying sanctions in a fair and graduated way, of reacting from the head rather than becoming emotionally involved, and avoiding confrontation. By applying her reading to her interpretation of classroom events she began to understand the need some pupils have for attention and said, 'It was important for me to make sure that I did not reinforce negative behaviour through giving students attention when they misbehave'. At the same time, she recognized a need to help the students to develop positive self-images.

Following this reconnaissance, she drew up an action plan which included the following points:

- decide on personal expectations for a class
- develop a personal plan for responding to misbehaviour
- stay calm, positive, polite and non-confrontational
- use non-verbal signals (body language, facial expressions), wait for silence.

Because most of the poor behaviour happened at the start of her lessons she developed starter activities to focus the class. For instance, because a particular class arrived from PE lessons, in twos and threes, she wrote down a simple activity on the board that they could do at their own pace, and was better able to engage students individually.

Jo analyzed her improvements by studying transcripts of lessons before and after the plan. These were partly a matter of making expectations clear, partly to do with self-presentation and partly to do with language. In an early lesson she was assertive but confrontational but she developed a more non-confrontational approach and monitored the development of this. In conclusion Jo wrote:

> This assignment has allowed me to address the issues that gave me the greatest concern and demonstrate how I have systematically improved in these areas ... it has given me a good foundation to build upon in the future.
>
> (see Cain *et al.*, 2007 for further details.)

Pupils as researchers

Researchers research; teachers teach; students learn. Recent years have seen a challenge to this traditional view and a wealth of support for the idea of consulting pupils about their own experiences and processes of learning. We know that pupils themselves have a huge potential contribution to make as active players in music education. We also know that pupils can and should participate, not only as co-researchers in the co-construction of their own particular learning environments, but, as research partners in examining questions of music learning and any other topics pertinent to what happens in and around schools.

The significance of learning from pupil perspectives or pupil consultation (or 'pupil voice' as coined in some literature) on education and learning in particular is most striking when pupils are seen as 'key informants' (Rudduck & McIntyre 2007: 193) in making explicit what child-meaningful engagement is. Consulting pupils means talking with pupils about things that matter in school music. It may involve the ongoing process of having regular conversations about teaching and learning music, seeking advice from pupils about curricula issues, music initiatives, forthcoming concerts, programming, assessments or units of work; inviting comment on ways of solving problems that are affecting the teacher's right to teach music and the pupil's right to learn music; inviting evaluative comments on recent developments in schools or classroom policy and practice. For some teachers, this might seem a time-consuming and daunting prospect. What pupils say can be discouraging, it can be hard to listen to and it can be negative, and it can require teachers to reflect on their assumptions about 'tried and true' approaches. And yet, as music teachers seriously committed to pupil engagement in highly effective music learning, we need to know what works and what doesn't work for them.

The pioneering work of Jean Rudduck (1999) on the concept of 'student voice' highlights the importance of pupil perspectives: their having things to say about their learning and having opinions that matter about in-school and beyond-school music cultures. Rudduck points out that consulting pupils – 'through looking at teaching, learning and schooling through the eyes of the student' (p. 51) – can lead to a transformation of teacher–pupil relationships and to pupils having a new sense of themselves as members of a community of learners. After demonstrating that pupils tend to do better when they are more involved as active participants in their own learning, she focused on various ways in which teachers and students can create 'a communal venturing forth'. While music teachers might worry that consulting pupils could unleash a fury of criticism directed at them and their teaching, this is not usually the case. Many music teachers might be surprised by the fact that what most pupils ask for aligns remarkably well with a substantial body of music education research and theory. For example, pupils can generate their own research questions and designs to explore preferred ways of learning, hindrances to learning, what counts as learning, what is enjoyable about learning. Topics can move from classroom to school practices.

There are various ways of approaching pupils as participants in the teacher's research. Rudduck and McIntyre (2007) identified different stages of pupil voice research, each with their own characteristics and potential and strategies for accessing pupils' perspectives and ways of implementing such strategies.

The standard repertoire for eliciting pupils' attitudes to learning used to be based on interviews[1] or a 'quick survey in the last few seconds of the lesson with no discussion of the outcomes with pupils and no obvious follow-through' (p.195). In the 1990s, a second stage evolved which recognized the potential for exploring 'pupils-as-consultants'. The recognition of children as a social group whose views should be valued in fruitful communication heralded further studies involving collective mind-mapping exercises in class and discussions about classroom practice. In the next phase, researchers explored the potential of *pupil consultation* in particular contexts given 'differences between classrooms, both within and across schools' (p.194). This involved more *shared participative enquiry* either where pupils were acting in a co-researcher role with teachers or where pupils were generators of their own research questions and enquiry. Either way, the outcome of the research saw pupils involved in decisions at individual and class levels and where suggestions (i.e. findings from the research) might, or might not, be acted on. However, accounts where pupils' ideas have been adopted at a 'whole-school' level, including:

(i)   where there has been 'a serious and authentic commitment to listen and learn' (p. 196);
(ii) where pupils ideas were adopted from classroom practice to school practice; and
(iii) where change occurred to improve all aspects of school life,

– remain scarce.

Often teacher-researchers incorporate a dual- or multi-focused research design, using between-method methodological triangulation to increase the validity of research findings, and adopting two or more methods both *to obtain pupil's views* on music learning and *to engage pupils as co-researchers* (rather than simply 'participants') in the teacher's research. The third form of pupil consultation is to set up pupils as generators of their own research questions, research design, research facilitation and write ups.

Pupils as generators of their own research

Unsurprisingly, pupils adopt the role of researcher and generate their own research questions easily and enjoy conducting their own research projects. Groups can work on their projects in their own free time, and pay careful attention to the analysis and consideration of findings. Pupils take great pride in the knowledge that people from within and outside the school are interested in what they have to say about their experiences. The number of educational researchers and practitioner–researchers interested in pupil perspectives, pupil voice research and pupil consultation in music education is increasing (see Finney and Harrison 2010[2] and Cook-Sather 2010 for edited books which showcases teachers and pupils as researchers working along a continuum from co-researchers in the teacher's research to pupils as generators of their own research).

Facilitating pupil-generated research

We now have persuasive evidence that encouraging young people to enquire and research schools and classrooms themselves is at the heart of good teaching. We also know that when teachers encourage their pupils to engage in enquiry systematically, and with a concern for evidence, that pupils become adept learners in direct correlation to the degree to which they take increasing responsibility for their own learning. The quality of learning deepens as they develop as autonomous, self-directed, and hopefully, lifelong musical learners. Valuing what pupils say and responding to what they say (as researchers) emphasizes respect for pupils and empowers them as learners (Kellett 2005).

Before embarking on their own research projects informed consent must be obtained from both pupils and parents. It is also important that the pupils should fully understand the constraints and opportunities of being a researcher, including the power dynamics and ethical and resource constraints.[3] These elements, together with an awareness of the importance of reflexivity and basic research skills training, follow as a seven-phase plan for teaching pupils to be researchers and can be implemented in a cycle of three hours over four weeks (see FLARE 2009 the classroom resource for training pupils to become researchers; Frost, 2006 the school-based study from which the classroom resource originated). Training pupils in the basic skills of research includes:

1   *Introducing research*: exploring pupils' perceptions of research.
2   *Becoming a researcher*: introducing pupils to the work and responsibilities of young researchers including being ethical, skeptical and systematic, and providing the basis for thinking about what research is and what young researchers do.
3   *Understanding what research is*: allowing pupils to reflect on their ideas about the purposes of research and the role of data.
4   *Deciding what to find out or change*: supporting pupils in deciding a research focus.
5   *Collecting data*: introducing pupils to a range of ways to collect data and evaluating these methods for their strengths, weaknesses and ethical challenges.
6   *Analyzing data*: introducing pupils to using codes, memo-ing and counting for the analysis of data.
7   *Designing an ethical research project*: supporting pupils in designing an ethical research project.[4]

Once their research training is complete, pupils can be given up to six weeks in which to plan and complete their own research project. One hour's dedicated class time can be provided each week, together with voluntary opportunities to work during the lunch hour one day a week. In defining their research foci children can select an aspect of their lessons for investigation with their peers.

Supporting young researchers

One very effective form of data collection which pupils can easily use as researchers of their own topics is *talk-based consultation* such as conversations, discussions and interviews. While each approach differs in the degree of formality it offers, all three approaches can build into a habit of constructive dialogue about learning and help establish and sustain an open relationship between pupils and teachers in and across schools. Two examples follow:

(i)   Using focus group interviews in conjunction with video-stimulated reviews of class music lessons can offer pupils interviewing other pupils a powerful tool for focusing on learning. Using a hand-held or wall-mounted video camera, pupils can engage in mutually oriented issues to stimulate discussion between pupils following a music session. Pupils can conduct a follow-up video-stimulated review in which pupils (and teachers) can recall and reflect on key moments, or episodes, of learning. Pupils can share their thoughts on important moments which have influenced the direction of their learning and how learning is experienced differently by different students. The identification, charting and account of critical incidents in learning are important in helping the pupil voice to be heard and become a significant part of the organizational and learning culture of the classroom (see Burnard 2004; Woods 1993. From these reviews both pupils and their teachers learn that there are multiple perspectives and multiple vantage points; they come to recognize that who is allowed to speak, to whom, what they are allowed to say, and what language is permitted, is significant when trying to establish a meaningful dialogue).

(ii) Using talk-and-draw techniques can offer strategies for pupils interviewing other pupils about their experiences of musical learning across different modules or within and beyond school settings. Possible prompts that the pupil–researcher might use are these: 'Thinking back over your experience of … what does it mean for you?'; 'Can you show me by drawing how you might represent what … means to you?'; 'Talk to me about what you have drawn'. Students' responses can be rich in information if you provide something concrete for them to talk about. Find an image or picture that you think is relevant to the topic you wish to explore with them and ask them to explain what is going on. Images of classroom activities can be useful for pupils interviewing other pupils on their views about tasks, classroom activities, musical tastes, on using computers or any number of different issues concerning music learning specifically and learning generally. Drawing 'Rivers of Musical Experience' can also be useful. Pupils give each other written (or oral) instructions to reflect on the critical incidents or musical events which impact on their musical lives, both positively and negatively, and to mark them on the bends of a diagram of a winding river. The instructions can emphasize that writing about, discussion and consultation about engagement in music and the learning process, whether formal or informal, in school or out of school, can provide a valuable testimony to the possibility of alternatives (see Burnard 2004; Burnard & Hennessy 2009; Burnard & Bjork 2010).

Case descriptions of pupils as researchers and co-researchers

The following case descriptions from teacher–researchers in England, illustrate how pupils' can be co-researchers in the teacher's research (see Case Studies 1 and 2) and where pupils are generators of their own research questions and pupils researching their own assessment of learning (see Case Study 3).

Case study 1

Secondary school music classroom: pupils as co-researchers

Fiona works as a secondary music teacher in a Norfolk school. She is researching her own classroom practice by consulting students on what makes a good lesson and a good teacher. She is committed to the notion that school improvement requires listening to students to see learning from their perspective. Whilst her school is not directly involved in any agendas linked to student voice research, student views on learning are recognized by senior management as being important for developing understanding about learning. Fiona collaborates and consults closely with her students and, in the classroom context, regularly creates opportunities for listening to students' views on learning. She is very interested to know whether/when students are deeply dissatisfied and disgruntled, and encourages students to give voice to their views about learning. In the process of consultation and evaluation, she encourages both students and teachers to share their views about teaching and learning in music. This leads to changes in her teaching practice. Fiona video tapes all her lessons and, together with her students, regularly observes and reflects on learning. Both the teacher and the students focus on the ways each define and construe learning while participating in classroom practices, as a community working together to improve and enhance learning. The engagement with learning is made more visible through the use of video taping as a tool for reflecting, seeing and noticing, showing and articulating musical learning and students' musical voices. Fiona is presently looking at designing a 'Students-as-Researcher' programme to suit the needs of her music classes. What is important here is that while Fiona, the individual teacher, is committed to see and work with her students differently, she still feels that she functions on a 'cultural island' set apart from and having no interaction with mainstream values and practices in the school. This matters a lot to Fiona who is wanting to realize the potential of her initiatives outside her own classroom and also reach out beyond her department (see Burnard, 2004).

Case study 2

Primary school music curriculum planning and creative learning: pupils as co-researchers

James is an AST music teacher and deputy head at an inner London primary school. He is very keen to engage pupils creatively with music that is relevant to their musical lives. He is very interested in hearing about how pupils explain their understanding of creativity and creative learning in their musical lives. James's interest in pupils' voices and introducing pupils to the work and responsibilities of young researchers is so that their participation in research could play an active role in the school's planning and implementation of music education. James started thinking about the conversations, discussions and interviews he'd had and reflected on with his pupils. He wanted to understand more about his pupils' creativity and about the kinds of creative learning fundamental to pupils in and out of the school learning environment. James consulted closely and worked intensively with one year group, resulting in the development of resources to help each child collect data. Different tasks within the research were set. For example, while some were carrying out the research, others were preparing the outline of their research report and presentation. With support from staff, parents and senior management, James set about co-researching with his class to develop a new curriculum. James incorporated several ideas that emerged during this consultation process and integrated them across the curriculum in terms of musical repertoire, ways of working, invited guests from the community and experts on new technology and creativity (see Biddulph 2010).

Case study 3

Secondary school music assessment: pupils as researchers

Carole works at a Cambridgeshire state-funded high school. Her pupils are researching their own self- and peer-assessment practices as a way of developing more effective practices. Encouraging pupils to be creative (more often through self-expression) is considered an important part of the school's ethos. Most activities in class music lessons focus on group work. The students' progress in music is assessed every six to eight weeks through pre-planned structured assessment tasks. Each unit of work ends with a formal assessment where the students are asked to *self-* and *peer-assess* their work prior to engaging with the teacher's views which are generally offered towards the final stages of preparation. Assessment criteria are developed by the pupils following pupil research to ascertain a shared understanding of what constitutes levels of work and to help set targets for the next unit. There is genuine ongoing participation and engagement with learners about their learning. Pupils are encouraged to be creative in both musical process and outcome, using their imagination in making connections to given themes. In this exemplar, roles are blurred and overlap. Pupils mentor and learn from each other. The teacher empowers pupils to be involved in making recommendations and evaluating the creative dimension of their own work. In the light of pupils' views, teachers discuss and rethink aspects of assessment practice. This provides a strategy for improving assessment practices that works across the school (Leong, Burnard, Jeannert, Leung, & Waugh 2011).

Implications for researching with pupils

Three exemplifying ways in which pupils can be actively involved in shaping their education come to mind: (1) being open to hearing people's experiences (2) finding a metaphor to look at the questions from a different angle, and (3) knowing that experience is complex and that finding creative ways to access experiences is a challenge and a thrill. We come to know that no one can see the whole and no one picture is complete. The teacher–researcher's journey as with the pupil–researcher's is to further understanding into their own and their peer's education, to depict the outcomes of meaning-making, and to bring together different views to inform future teaching and learning.

Three basic assumptions should underlie the teacher–researchers' dispositions towards the pupils they are studying. First, pupils are smart. They know how to get along in the world they inhabit. They know what works and what does not work. The only way to get as smart as they are about their world is to learn from them. Second, pupils make sense. What may appear from the outside to be dysfunctional activity, from the inside, makes sense. The only way to understand how pupils' actions make sense is to listen and observe very carefully. Third, see the pupils as co-researchers, providing valuable insights into their own personal experiences, their correlations and meanings.

Finding out, as Geertz (1973) put it, 'What the devil people think they are up to', requires paying careful attention to them and respecting their abilities. This is what is so important about becoming a teacher–researcher and a pupil–researcher and learning how to bridge the gap between the pupil, the subject, and how schools are required to operate their learning agendas. By bringing the voices of pupils to the surface and by recognizing the role of imaginative inquiry, it is possible for teachers as researchers, as with pupils as researchers, to create and co-construct knowledge that is not only new, but also has the capacity to transform school music.

Reflective questions

On 'teachers as researchers':

1   To what extent do you think teachers can set aside their responsibility to influence, in order to research their students?
2   What sort of findings can be generated by teachers' case studies? How can such findings help to develop the practice of teaching?
3   What sort of knowledge was generated by Ward's and Mattock's action research?

On 'consulting pupils about teaching and learning and pupils-as-researcher':

4   Do you think it possible for teachers to learn from pupil consultation (i.e. pupils generating their own research)? What are the biggest challenges? For pupils, is it the challenge about showing in their talk that they are seeking to improve the content and the performance of the music in schools? Explore the challenges for pupils and teachers.
5   How can music teachers and their students go about developing consultation as a whole-school strategy? Discuss this in the light of your experience.
6   What can pupils generating their own research on musical learning tell us about the social conditions of learning in the music classroom?
7   Make a persuasive case for the relationship between pupil consultation, engagement and learning in music.

Notes

1 Interestingly, in the early phases of student voice research, observation data was not used as a consultation approach in schools but just as a research tool for investigation classroom phenomena. Student voice was once largely about students as data (see 'Sustaining Pupils' Commitment to Learning: The Challenge of Year 8', Rudduck, Wilson and Flutter 1998); then it became connected to practice through teacher research and school improvement strategies (see Students' voices: what can they tell us as partners in change' by Rudduck, Wallace and Day 2000).

2 For a complete list of National Association of Music Educators (NAME) publications visit www.name.org.uk.

3 It is essential that participants fully understand what the research entails, what it is for, and their role within it; to disguise one's intentions (as a researcher) compromises both the researcher and the participants (Erikson 1967). Children are encouraged to ask questions and can withdraw from the research at any point if they feel uncomfortable. Other considerations include an assurance of the confidentiality of any expressed opinions and the use of pseudonyms to ensure anonymity in order to safeguard the participants rights and increase their confidence (Hitchcock & Hughes 1995).

4 For more details see Frost 2006; see FLARE 2009.

References

Arnot, A., McIntyre, D., Pedder, D. and Reay, D. (2004) *Consultation in the Classroom,* Cambridge: Pearson Publishing.

Biddulph, J. (2010) 'Exploring Creative Learning in School and Out of School Contexts: A Phenomenological Case Study', unpublished Master of Education thesis, University of Cambridge.

Burnard, P. (1995) 'Task Design and Experience in Composition', *Research Studies in Music Education,* 5(2): 32–46.

Burnard, P. (2004) 'Pupil – Teacher Conceptions and the Challenge of Learning: Lessons from a Year 8 Music Classroom', *Improving Schools,* 7(1): 23–34.

Burnard, P. and Bjork, C. (2010) 'Using Student Voice Research to Understand and Improve Musical Learning', in J. Finney and C. Harrison (eds) *Whose Music Education Is It? The Role of the Student Voice,* Solihull, West Midlands: National Association of Music Educators (NAME).

Burnard, P. and Hennessy, S. (eds) (2006/2010) *Reflective Practices in Arts Education,* Dordrecht: Springer.

Cain, T. (2008) 'The Characteristics of Action Research in Music Education', *British Journal of Music Education,* 25(3): 283–313.

Cain, T. (2010) 'Music Teachers' Action Research and the Development of Big K knowledge', *International Journal of Music Education,* 28(2): 1–17.

Cain, T. (forthcoming) 'Too Hard, Too Soft or Just About Right: Theoretical Underpinnings of Music Teachers' Action Research', *British Journal of Music Education.*

Cain, T., Holmes, M., Larrett, A. and Mattock, J. (2007) 'Literature-Informed, One-Turn Action Research: Three Cases and a Commentary', *British Educational Research Journal,* 33(1): 91–106.

Cochran-Smith, M. and Lytle, S. (1993) *Inside-Outside: Teacher Research and Knowledge,* New York: Teachers College Press.

Cook-Sather, A. (2010) *Learning from the Student's Perspective: A Sourcebook for Effective Teaching*, Boulder, Colorado, USA: Paradigm Publishers.

Cowley, S. (2003) *Getting the Buggers to Behave*, London: Continuum.

Crasborn, F., Hennissen, P., Brouwer, N., Korthagen, F. and Bergen, T. (2008) 'Promoting Versatility in Mentor Teachers' Use of Supervisory Skills', *Teaching and Teacher Education*, 24: 499–514.

Creswell, J. (1998) *Qualitative Inquiry and Research Design: Choosing Among Five Traditions*, Thousand Oaks, CA: Sage.

deVries, P. (2003) 'A Case Study of a 10-year-old's Musical Preferences Within the Context of Studio Piano Lessons', *Music Education International*, 2: 51–67.

Dewey, J. (1933) *How We Think: A Restatement of the Relation of Reflective Thinking to the Educative Process*, Boston: D.C. Heath.

Eliott, J. (1991) *Action Research for Educational Change*, Buckingham: Open University Press.

Elliott, J. (2007) 'Making Evidence-Based Practice Educational', in M. Hammersley (ed.) *Educational Research and Evidence-Based Practice*, London: Sage/Open University.

Finney, J. (1987) 'An Investigation into the Learning Process of a Group of Rock Musicians', Unpublished Master's thesis, University of Reading, UK.

Finney, J. and Harrison, C. (2010) (eds) *Whose Music Education Is It? The Role of the Student Voice*, Solihull, West Midlands: National Association of Music Educators (NAME).

FLARE (Forum for Learning and Research Enquiry) (2009) *Active Enquiring Minds: Supporting Young Researchers*, Chelmsford: Essex County Council.

Frost, R. (2006) 'Students as Researchers: an Investigation in One Primary School', unpublished Master of Philosophy Thesis, University of Cambridge, UK.

Gage, N.L. (1989) 'The Paradigm Wars and Their Aftermath: A 'Historical' Sketch of Research on Teaching Since 1989', *Educational Researcher*, 18(7): 4–10.

Geertz, C. (1973) 'Thick Description: Toward an Interpretative Theory of Culture', in C. Geertz (ed.) *The Interpretation of Cultures*, New York: Basic Books.

Grainger, T., Burnard, P. and Craft, A. (2006) 'Pedagogy and Possibility Thinking in the Early Years', *Thinking Skills and Creativity*, 1(2): 26–38.

Hammersley, M. (1993) 'On the Teacher as Researcher', *Educational Action Research*. 1(3): 425–45.

Hargreaves, D.H. (1996) *Teaching as a Research-Based Profession: Possibilities and Prospects*, London: Teacher Training Agency.

Heron, J. and Reason, P. (1997) 'A Participatory Inquiry Paradigm', *Qualitative Inquiry*, 3(3): 274–94.

Hitchcock, G. and Hughes, D. (1995) *Research and the Teacher: A Qualitative Introduction to School-Based Research*, 2nd edn, London: Routledge.

Kellett, M. (2005) *How to Develop Children as Researchers: A Step-by-Step Guide to Teaching the Research Process*, London: Paul Chapman Publishing.

Kemmis, S. and Di Chiro, G. (1987) 'Emerging and Evolving Issues of Action Research Praxis: An Australian Perspective', *Peabody Journal of Education*, 64(3): 101–30.

Leong, S., Burnard, P., Jeannert, N., Leung, B. and Waugh, C. (forthcoming, 2011) 'Assessing Creativity in Music: International Perspectives and Practices', in G. McPherson and G. Welch (eds) *The Oxford Handbook of Music Education*. New York: Oxford University Press.

Poet, H., Rudd, P. and Kelly, J. (2010) *Survey of Teachers 2010: Support to Improve Teaching Practice*. Online. Available HTTP: <www.gtce.org.uk/documents/publicationpdfs/teach_survey10.pdf> (accessed 6 April 2011).

Reed, J. (2007) *Appreciative Inquiry: Research for Change*, London: Sage.

Rodgers, B. (1998) *You Know the Fair Rule*, London: Financial Times/Prentice Hall.

Rudduck, J. (1999) 'Teacher Practice and the Student Voice', in M. Lang., J. Olson., H. Hansen and W. Bunder (eds) *Changing Schools/Changing Practices: Perspectives on Educational Reform and Teacher Professionalism*, Louvain, Belgium: Garant Publishers.

Rudduck, J. and Flutter, J. (2000) 'Pupil Participation and Pupil Perspective: Carving a New Order of Experience', *Cambridge Journal of Education*, 30(1): 75–89.

Rudduck, J. and McIntyre, D. (2007) *Improving Learning Through Consulting Pupils*. London: Routledge.

Rudduck, J., Wilson, E. and Flutter, J. (1998) *Sustaining Pupils' Commitment to Learning: The Challenge of Year 8*, Cambridge: Homerton Publications.

Rudduck, J., Wallace, G. and Day, J. (2000) Students' Voices: What Can they Tell Us as Partners in Change? In K. Stott and V. Trafford (eds) *Boys and Girls in the Primary Classroom*, Buckingham: Open University Press.

Schön, D. (1983) *The Reflective Practitioner: How Professionals Think in Action*, New York, NY: Basic Books.

Stenhouse, L. (1975) *An Introduction to Curriculum Research and Development*. London: Heinemann.

Thomson, P. and Gunter, H. (2006) 'From "Consulting Pupils" to "Pupils as Researchers": A Situated Case Narrative'. *British Educational Research Journal*, 32(6): 839–56.

Tripp, D. (2003) *Action inquiry*. Online. Available HTTP: <www2.fhs.usyd.edu.au/arow/arer/017.htm> (accessed 24 June 2011).

Ward, C.J. (2009) 'Musical Exploration using ICT in the Middle and Secondary School Classroom', *International Journal of Music Education*, 27(2): 154–68.

Whitehead, J. (1989) 'Creating a Living Educational Theory from Questions of the Kind, "How Do I Improve My Practice?"', *Cambridge Journal of Education* 19(1): 137–53.

Whitehead, J. and McNiff, J. (2006) *Action Research Living Theory*, London: Sage.

Whitehead, J. and Rayner, A. (2009) *From Dialectics to Inclusionality: A Naturally Inclusive Approach to Educational Accountability*. Online. Available <www.jackwhitehead.com/jack/arjwdialtoIncl061109.pdf> (accessed November 2011).

Winter, R. (1989) *Learning from Experience: Principles and Practice in Action Research*, London: Falmer.

Chapter 16

Professional development and music education

Vanessa Young

Introduction

Some might say we've never had it so good! The past decade has perhaps been one of the richest in terms of developments and initiatives in music education. *The Music Manifesto* launched in 2005 marked a new injection of enthusiasm for and commitment to music education. In November 2007 a £332 million funding package for music education was announced. For primary schools, this spawned the National Singing Programme, *'Sing Up'* which aimed to put singing at the heart of every primary school curriculum, and the *'Wider Opportunities'* programme to give all Key Stage 2 pupils the chance to play an instrument. At Key Stage 3, arising out of the work of Lucy Green (2002), *'Musical Futures'* was developed, offering a radical new approach to music teaching for both pupils and teachers at Key Stage 3. In addition the *'In Harmony'* programme inspired by Venezuela's *El Sistema* (http://en.wikipedia.org/wiki/El_Sistema), provided free instrumental tuition and orchestral involvement to children in some of the country's most deprived areas. Music technology too has become much more significant, and teachers now have a whole panoply of ICT resources to support children's musical learning. Most recently, the curriculum has been subject to the *Henley Review* (2011), a government commissioned review which has resulted in a National Plan for Music (DFE: 2011). In tandem with these initiatives we have seen a renewed interest in music outside the school context with television programmes such as 'Britain's Got Talent', 'Pop Idol', and 'Glee'. Indeed the whole area of informal learning in music (i.e. outside the traditional structures of school and the formal curriculum) has recently gained recognition for the lessons this kind of engagement has for the classroom (Folkestad 2006), and there is a new democratic sense that yes, music truly is for everyone!

Whilst of course welcoming such developments and in no way underestimating their importance, new approaches make new demands on those at the frontline – the teachers. In order for any initiative to be implemented, teachers must engage with it; understand it; interpret it and then develop the necessary skills to put it into practice. Without teachers who are willing and able to do this, nothing at all can happen. Effective professional development for teachers of music in school must therefore be the cornerstone of any improvement in children's musical learning.

So how well are music teachers supported in developing their learning? According to Ofsted (2009), not as well as they should. This might appear strange given the apparently conducive climate described above. Initiatives such as *Wider Opportunities* for example should have provided excellent professional development for primary music teachers and instrumental teachers. The problem is that these opportunities are not often maximized with the class teacher and specialist instrumental teacher working collaboratively. There is often insufficient dialogue between them, and involvement has been too short to have any lasting impact (2009:3). It is also the case that teachers often lack both understanding about musical progress and the professional development opportunities to discuss it with each other. Indeed, many music teachers are professionally isolated. Helpful continuing professional development (CPD) and challenge is rare; and even more worryingly perhaps, developments in music education have gone unnoticed or been disregarded (Ofsted 2009: 5–6).

How can this be the case? It is especially puzzling and frustrating given the raft of support initiatives that have been put in place for music teachers over recent years. These include: the Key Stage 2 Music CPD programme, run by Trinity Guildhall and The Open University, available free to all instrumental teachers to support the *Wider Opportunities* initiative; access to the *Sing Up* materials, and regional practical CPD workshops. Professional websites such as *Teaching Music* (www.teachingmusic.org.uk) were set up to support school music teachers, and the National Association of Music Educators has been trying to reach out to classroom music teachers with useful and relevant publications. Perhaps then we need to look further than mere availability and accessibility and think about other factors.

What then constitutes effective professional development (PD)? Research into teachers' perceptions of CPD (Hustler *et al.*, 2003) found that most teachers still thought of it in terms of traditional approaches or methods such as courses, conferences and INSET days – i.e. as experiences and events. This implies that it is something done *to* teachers, with teachers mere passive recipients. Effective PD must be about more than this. If it is ever to have impact on the classroom, it must involve teachers in pro-actively learning how to learn and transforming their knowledge into practice that in turn enhances the musical learning of their pupils. The processes involved in all this are necessarily complex, concerning not just the cognitive understanding of teachers but also their emotional commitment and resilience and their willingness to engage both individually and collectively.

The 'who?'

So who are these teachers and how do they see themselves? Professional identity has been described as the 'enduring constellation of attributes, beliefs, values, motives and experiences in terms of which people define themselves in a professional role' (Ibarra cited by Patrick and McPhee in McMahon *et al.*, 2010). This is a rich and complex mix of factors. We need to know and understand teachers as individuals within a profession if we are to have any idea of how their development can be maximized. Pre-service or early career teachers for example may well have a different perception of themselves from those experienced teachers nearing retirement who may have a more stable sense of their own identity. Whatever stage in their career they are at however, aspects of identity such as confidence can fluctuate; any teacher can have moments of great self-doubt. The introduction of new music technologies for example could be highly challenging for those who might be described as 'digital immigrants' (as opposed to 'digital natives') Prensky (2001). For staff who are older and more experienced but not brought up with technology this kind of challenge can cause real anxiety, or at worst lead to a state of 'denial', where the new initiative is simply not acknowledged or accommodated and therefore has no chance of being assimilated into the teacher's practice.

Regardless of experience, the increase in state control and introduction of a centralized and prescriptive curriculum appears to have weakened the professional confidence of teachers and lowered morale. Teachers are required to 'deliver' frequently-changing new curricula and are held ever more accountable not only for the performances of their pupils, but ultimately – with the publishing of results and league tables – for the success of their schools. Treating teachers as 'naughty children' (Hargreaves 1994) who need to come into line and keep up to the mark is unlikely to help teachers to flourish and embrace new ideas.

Indeed, as Hargreaves points out, this kind of rhetoric of professionalism simply seduces teachers into consorting with their own exploitation. Furthermore, the prescriptive nature of the changes in education means there has been little room for dissent.

The 'what?'

Clearly all professional development involves some kind of change – but from what and to what? It is perhaps not always recognized that dearly held values and beliefs, not to mention consciously adopted educational ideologies, play a crucial role in the process. If we accept that learning involves change, not just of practice but also of understanding and belief, then we can see just what a tall order learning through professional development is. Firstly, it could be the case that teachers are asked to change their practices to something which 'goes against the grain', contradicting what might be long held convictions about how children learn or how teachers should teach. This was certainly the case soon after the National Curriculum was introduced when a number of experienced teachers reluctantly left the profession, feeling that the changes they were being asked to make were simply too compromising. Secondly, if there is a gap between beliefs and suggested practices, change will only occur if that gap is recognized. Ofsted noted that the Key Stage 3 Strategy for Music was often ignored by those who (wrongly in their view), felt it covered ground with which they were already familiar (Ofsted 2009: 6)

Prescription of curriculum together with the emphasis on accountability has impacted on professional development for teachers of music, particularly in primary schools. When the school is identifying priorities for development, those areas that are subjected to national testing are always liable to take precedence, leaving little time for other areas. As one primary teacher commented in research carried out for the DfES: 'Not much of music, loads of NLS (National Literacy Strategy)' (Hustler *et al.*, 2003: 67).

More insidious is the problem at the initial teacher education stage. Student teachers on teaching practice can find themselves infected and demoralized by the practice and attitudes of teachers in schools where the foundation subjects have lost their status and position in the curriculum. Primary student teachers often have inadequate input in music on their courses. They often report that they have been told not to plan for music in their school placement as it is 'covered by a specialist', or 'done *en masse*', or 'not on the curriculum that term', or even not done at all. Furthermore, they are often given little or no opportunity either to observe the teaching of music (good or otherwise) or teach it themselves.

The 'where?'

The context within which PD takes place is also significant. Avalos (2010) in her review of the last ten years of teacher PD in a range of 21 countries, remarks on the extent to which we have moved away from the traditional in-service training model towards a 'situated' model; that is to say professional development that takes place in the workplace. Indeed, the nature of PD, it could be argued is continuous and embedded in teachers' everyday lives. 'Teacher learning occurs every time a lesson is taught, an assessment is administered, a curriculum is reviewed, or a professional journal or magazine is read …' (Guskey (2000) cited in Darleen Opfer *et al.*, 2010). Borko makes the point that to understand teacher learning, we must study it within these multiple contexts, taking into account both the individual teacher-learners and the social systems in which they operate (Borko (2004) cited in Opfer *et al.* (2010)).

School cultures, structures and organizations however can either facilitate or constrict workplace learning, particularly PD that involves whole-school enquiry. In James and McCormick's study, those teachers who found it most difficult to develop were those who felt constrained by a 'policy culture that encouraged rushed curriculum coverage, teaching to the test and a tick-box culture' (2009: 982). Avalos (2010) found too that in the quest for higher examination scores, teachers tend to be provided with 'outside experts' to teach them how to produce results in the short periods of time demanded by their education systems. The success of a 'situated model' relies on input from and engagement in the wider context where, through collaboration and challenge, existing ideas can be reviewed, current practice analysed and interpreted; new ways of working considered and trialled. Imants (2002) proposes that schools may need restructuring if they are to become contexts for teacher learning. Subject departments for example can have positive effects on PD provided they operate as communities that seek to have influence on the whole school environment. This is a problem for small secondary music departments where the lone music teacher is isolated. It can also be challenging in a primary school where there may not be the interest, commitment, expertise or resources for collaborative PD in music.

The 'when?'

Alexander (2010) is critical of the approach to teachers' development introduced by the government as part of the workforce reforms. This was conceived as simply progression through five career points and their related 'standards': from newly qualified (Q) to 'advanced skills' (A) with the same basic repertoire at every stage. This is problematic given that teachers have very different needs at different stages in their careers.

At the initial training stage, student teachers need to operate within a limited repertoire to start with, feeling more secure with firm parameters and guidance based on what good teaching entails with some sense of conformity to that which is given and advised. Some kind of set of standards indicating the required competencies may be quite appropriate at this stage and the importance of a good role model in music is evident. It is a different story with experienced teachers. 'Expert' teachers not only act differently from novices, but also think in fundamentally different ways; and the problem is that these advanced modes of thinking are largely tacit, making them difficult to identify and 'measure'. Just as novices need a 'bounded' repertoire, so experienced teachers need to be freed from rules and prescription and given the autonomy to act creatively and instinctively.

These 'standards', designed to 'raise standards', could have the effect of actually depressing them, constraining experienced and talented teachers from problematizing teaching in an innovative and autonomous way. Being expected to remain subservient to government 'rules' throughout their career could explain why many teachers find much 'policy-informed' CPD to be insufficiently challenging (Alexander 2010). The qualitatively different needs of teachers at these career and experiential stages is not often discussed, but differentiating approaches to teachers' learning in this way would seem to be a key criteria for effective PD in music – which we ignore at our peril.

The 'how much?'

So how much PD do music teachers need for their learning to be effective? The issue of time and professional development is a tricky one. The current Government extols some practices in other nations and regions and cites Singapore as an example in the White paper:

> We provide our teachers with 100 hours of professional development each year... If you do not have inspired teachers, how can you have inspired students?
> (Singapore Education Official, quoted in Barber and Mourshed,
> White Paper 2010)

Clearly 100 hours of time is substantial compared with what most music teachers in this country experience, and should, just on that basis alone, be expected to make a significant difference to the nature of any learning. As Hargreaves points out 'To increase the amount of innovation and reduce the time for its implementation is like increasing the speed of an aeroplane when you are rapidly losing height with your nose pointing towards the ground' (2003: 1). But is it just a matter of quantity? To continue the aeronautical metaphor, do more 'professional development hours' (like 'flying hours') make a better teacher (or pilot) merely through practice and experience, or is there more to it than that? There is a big difference between getting better at teaching music through simply 'doing more of it', and initiating a whole new approach such as *Musical Futures* into your ongoing practice.

The 'how?'

A new initiative in teacher education in the UK (see DfE 2010) is the creation of a national network of Teaching Schools. These schools have a leading responsibility for providing both initial teacher training in their area and professional development, moving teacher development away from the influence of local authority advisors and university tutors, and from others outside the school. 'Other schools will choose whether or not to take advantage of these programmes, so Teaching Schools will primarily be accountable to their peers' (DfE 2010). Whilst this may seem sensible on the face of it, there is danger in this kind of provision.

A strategy that is school-based and subject to market forces in this way could lead teachers further into a 'tips for teachers' kind of culture; with teachers evaluating the effectiveness of PD on how immediately useful or enjoyable it was, rather than how ultimately thought-provoking and profound its impact. The approach becomes purely pragmatic with its emphasis on skills and competencies. This discourages the kind of reflective and critical thinking that is a pre-condition for transformative professional development. In 1993 with specific reference to music, Swanwick and Paynter remarked that: 'we face a continual onslaught by those who seem to regard teacher education as ...picking up a few tips from a mentor 'on the job' (Swanwick and Paynter 1993: 6). This is particularly problematic for primary generalist trainees in music. Lack of knowledge on the part of mentors (and peers) leads to inadequate guidance and a paucity of role models.

The 'so what?'

Finally, how do we know when effective professional development or teacher learning in music has happened? It is easy to under-estimate the complexity of the stages and pathways involved in what is essentially a transformative process, and consequently notoriously difficult to evaluate in terms of impact. Who is to say, for example, that the improvement in *this* child's musical understanding is directly attributable to *that* teacher's improvement in their musical subject knowledge;

their better understanding of effective music pedagogy; their newly-found insights into how musical learning children should be assessed? If no immediate improvement in (measurable) learning is detected, does that mean that no learning has taken place on the part of the teacher? Does it indeed mean that no learning has taken place on the part of the pupil?! The notion of cause and effect here is problematic. The 'change' that has occurred could simply be in terms of a teacher's new understanding, perhaps even as a result of having assumptions challenged. Such learning may need a 'gestation' period, particularly if the process has been a painful one (as it can be when dearly held practices have to be abandoned).

It might be more relevant and certainly more realistic to acknowledge at any one point, where the 'change' is located – in the teacher herself or in the pupils she teaches and therefore at when and how impact could or should be demonstrated. Actually seeing the impact in the classroom in terms of pupil learning could take some time. This is problematic in a system where the performances of schools, teachers and pupils have been so inextricably bound up together. A teacher's career development is now heavily dependent on measurable performance against measured pupil outcomes which relate to predetermined criteria and targets.

Discussion

In any teacher development that is contextualized and situated, we need to take account of:

- *Intellectual Capital,* the knowledge that is created, shared or exchanged;
- *Social Capital,* the relationships, networks and cultures that exist within the school; and
- *Organizational Capital* which includes the leadership, the school's ability to managing change and the development of communities of practice (Hargreaves 2003: 3).

If we are saying that the most effective professional development is that which leads to 'transformation' then we need to be clear not just what that means but how it can be achieved. Such transformation won't just happen by itself or through top-down imposition. *Organizational Capital* is important here. It has to be engineered by imaginative and courageous school leaders who are prepared to take risks. Innovative schools are those that are proactive and seize the agenda, avoiding simple compliance.

In terms of *Intellectual Capital,* we need a particular perspective on the music curriculum and knowledge. If we are not to become a profession of mere technicians, delivering a centrally prescribed curriculum we need to maintain a critical perspective. Such an approach demands open and receptive (rather than defensive) schools and teacher training institutions as well as confident teachers and students who have time to reflect and question, in other words a culture which welcomes enquiry. This commitment to enquiry in turn implies provisionality and therefore uncertainty. If we support the notion that 'ownership of the curriculum is a prerequisite to understanding' (Kushner 1994: 42) then the curriculum needs to be regarded as a hypothesis to be tested, rather than as a syllabus to be followed; pedagogical approaches need to be continually 'trialled' rather than prescribed; learning outcomes need to become valued for their unpredictability as much as for their predictability and we need to once more acknowledge that what we teach is not necessarily what pupils learn (Stenhouse 1975)

> There are those who choose the swampy lowlands... they speak of experience, trial and error, intuition and muddling through. Other professionals opt for the high ground. Hungry for technical rigour, devoted to an image of solid technical competence, or fearful of entering a world in which they feel they do not know what they are doing, they choose to confine themselves to a narrowly technical practice ... .
>
> (Schon in Day 1993: 91)

We need to choose the 'swampy lowlands' as opposed to the 'high ground' if we want teachers of music to really engage in learning that will develop their practice.

What would good teacher education in music look like? First it is worth looking at how not to do it!

BOX 16.1: CASE STUDY 1 – HOW NOT TO DO IT

As a music coordinator in a primary school in the 1980s, I had all the zeal (and naiveté) of a 'hero innovator' having just completed a post-graduate diploma in Music Education. With ambitious ideas for whole school development in music I was determined to initiate a radical structural change (moving away from the model I had inherited) i.e. the generalist teachers teaching their own classes for music. This ambition was ideologically driven. I felt that music was 'for all', and that the current arrangement reinforced the notion that music was only for the few who could 'do it'!

The head teacher gave me his blessing although he said he could only allocate one staff meeting slot to initiate the change. I called all teachers to an extended staff meeting and workshop (the head teacher was too busy to attend). My intention was to outline the rationale for the change to the teachers, introduce ideas to motivate them and get them started through a practical workshop, and then plan for action. I was dismayed to find that the teachers were quite unconvinced as to why this initiative could possibly be a change for the better ... To finish the story, the initiative was eventually imposed by the head teacher and the necessary structural changes took place.

Unsurprisingly, there was considerable resistance from some of the teachers which resulted in music lessons often being side-lined in favour of other activities in the classroom, and the quality of the music curriculum as experienced by the children at that stage was of variable quality.

This salutary experience bears some analysis. Schools are complex systems and, for change to occur, some key prerequisites need to be in place (Knoster 2000). These include vision, skills, incentives, resources and an action plan. This can be represented in Figure 16.1.

There needs to be a *vision* in terms of what effective music education in the school should look like as well as what constitutes effective professional development processes. This *vision* involves not just a sense of purpose to take ideas forward, but also knowledge and understanding i.e. Intellectual Capital (Hargreaves 2003). Ofsted (2009) reported that head teachers readily admitted that they did not have the depth of understanding required to improve their music provision. This was certainly the case with the head teacher in Box 16.1. Although he supported the change in principle and wanted to be supportive of the 'change agent', he did not have an in-depth understanding of what it was I trying to achieve. The teachers were simply not convinced by what was being promoted. Any attempts to share *vision* with the teachers then fell on stony ground.

Because the teachers were confused about what they had to do, and why they had to do it, they lacked *incentive*. This resulted in a lack of momentum: a resentment of the new arrangements; avoidance; a reluctance to 'have a go' and also resistance to guidance and support offered. This is the problem when an initiative is seen to be imposed, and not based on a convincing rationale. Where was the evidence that things were not working as well as they were? ('If it ain't broke …?'). Philosophy and ideology were hardly a sufficient foil for the pragmatism that ruled.

Vision	+ Skills	+ Incentive	+ Resources	+ Action plan	=	Change
	+ Skills	+ Incentive	+ Resources	+ Action plan	=	Confusion
Vision		+ Incentive	+ Resources	+ Action plan	=	Anxiety
Vision	+ Skills		+ Resources	+ Action plan	=	Resistance
Vision	+ Skills	+ Incentive		+ Action plan	=	Frustration
Vision	+ Skills	+ Incentive	+ Resources		=	Treadmill

Figure 16.1 Essential factors in the management of change (Knoster, T., Villa, R. and Thousand, J. (2000))

It is not just a question however of having a clear *vision*; teachers need to have the *skills* to improve their music teaching or that of others. This includes not just musical skills and knowledge, but also the professional and pedagogical *skills* that are integral to all subject teaching. We know that there is a good deal of anxiety within the teaching of music in primary schools for example, due to lack (perceived or otherwise) of *skills*. Furthermore, if the music specialist is to support and promote the development of non-specialist primary teachers, they also need the professional *skills* associated with that kind of enterprise. The planned workshop was designed not only to start to develop new *skills*, but also to convince the teachers that they already had many of the necessary *skills* needed to teach music to their classes. What it actually revealed was a great deal of anxiety; and because of the lack of shared *vision* and *incentive*, the teachers' willingness to practice and develop these *skills* was limited.

No initiative can be implemented without the necessary *resources*. These include staffing, time and accommodation as well as equipment and materials. Although the case study school was well catered for in terms of musical *resources*, expecting the teachers to teach music in their classrooms was particularly problematic as the school was open plan. In terms of staff 'having a go', fear of exposing their inadequate *skills* in this public environment acted as a further inhibiter. The staff meeting time allocated was clearly inadequate to effect such a radical proposal in the first place and there was also little follow-up time allocated to allow the necessary support of teachers in their classrooms. This led to a good deal of frustration. Ofsted (2009) commented that teachers who called themselves 'non-specialists' were able to provide good music teaching when they were supported effectively. However, the subject leader needs time to do the job effectively. This includes working alongside the teachers in the classroom as well as monitoring the music curriculum for quality.

To ensure implementation all effective development needs an *action plan* which does more than just monitor. The *action plan* should cater for long-term development and include points over the year(s) when work is shared; successes celebrated and issues reflected upon and problematized. From these 'events', new ways of working are identified and taken forward. The initiative in Case Study 1 lacked the planned coherence that was needed to really 'embed' it into the life of the school. Imants (2002) claims that there are two essential mechanisms for the promotion of school-based learning: 'collaboration' (in terms of developing communities of practice) and the use of 'feedback'. An *action* plan taking account of these could have included: an audit of staff experience and needs; staff workshops; demonstration lessons; peer coaching; assemblies to share work; concerts that included work-in-progress, perhaps with children articulating the processes they had gone through to complete their compositions; periodic review and development meetings. This is in addition to simply allowing the teachers to investigate any focus of enquiry in their classrooms. As well as formally planned activity such as this, we also need to acknowledge the role of informal learning in relation to PD. Teachers do learn a great deal experientially and serendipitously.

The problem with such learning is that it often leads to 'unconscious competence' and is therefore not formally reflected or acted upon; articulated or shared. The building of a culture of curiosity and enquiry within the organization could allow for such experiences to act as a springboard for further systematic investigation.

Wise teachers readily learn from their students. Much attention has been given recently to the role of the student voice (Finney and Harrison 2010; Rudduck and McIntyre 2007). Finding out more about what the children feel about their classroom music during the development in the Case Study School, could have provided a fascinating evidence base for the work and perhaps added significantly to the badly needed incentive. The views of pupils could have given rise to the focus for enquiry in the first place or at least helped to shape the nature of the investigation. They could also have contributed to finding solutions and changing practice.

BOX 16.2: CASE STUDY 2 – ONE WAY OF DOING IT

JS learned to develop her practice through talking to and consulting her pupils. In one specific example, she cites a *Musical Futures* (MF) project in which her pupils were involved. One of the key aims of the project was to 'personalize' their learning. In spite of the 'bottom up', informal nature of the whole MF approach she noticed that the process did not seem to be engaging all pupils. Devising a system which involved students in ranking six different approaches, she gained significant insights. In spite of the apparently open-ended nature of the approach, the students felt that they were not given enough choice in the way they worked. Whilst they respected the importance of the teacher's role and knowledge, they complained that 'they [teachers] can ruin the work or change it … they can take over the song and give ideas that aren't practical for the group'. As a consequence, she made significant changes leaving more of the decision-making to the pupils. This led not only to a high level of commitment, but also to enhanced relationships between her and the students. Perhaps most significantly, it also led Jenny to question the whole notion of 'personalized learning', enhancing her understanding of 'shallow' and 'deep' personalization (Leadbeater 2006). She realized that in some schools, the idea of personalizing the learning had become little more than tracking individual student progress …. (in Finney and Harrison 2010).

This excellent example of teacher development is all too rare. The harsh reality is that teachers are often better at teaching traditional content than they are at learning for themselves or from others (Hargreaves 2003: 3).

The notion of 'Teacher as Researcher' here may have some mileage, particularly if we think of research as 'systematic enquiry made public' (Stenhouse 1981). This would allow practitioners to explore new ideas, question and challenge existing ones and develop their practice based on real evidence from the classroom, not to mention discussing findings with colleagues both in and beyond the school. The problem here is that many teachers view 'research' as remote and inaccessible - the business of academics rather than busy teachers. At the same time, many teachers who regularly reflect upon and change their practice are not conscious that this could potentially be research. It is a relatively short step from intuitive judgement and action based on informed reflective practice to more systematic investigation. Handscomb and MacBeath (2003) propose the term 'Teacher as Enquirer', as a way of reconceptualizing the role. This suggests one who, in the spirit of good teaching, is keen to reflect upon and critique his or her own practice, trying out new ideas and systematically evaluating the impact of any subsequent change in practice.

All this of course requires teacher (re)empowerment coupled with a great deal of trust (Social Capital) challenging notions in the current culture of 'top-down' bureaucratic mistrust. In terms of Organizational Capital, schools in turn would need to move from what might currently be seen as an 'audit' model (developed as a result of the rigorous school inspection regime) to one which embraces this kind of open-ended enquiry the research-engaged school. A model where it is 'in the interest of its pupils to be critical of received wisdom and sceptical of easy answers' (Handscomb and MacBeath 2003). In such schools, the notion of teachers first and foremost as learners would be embedded in the culture.

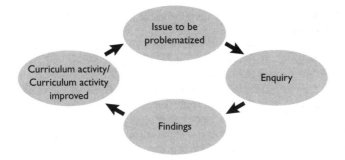

Figure 16.2 Teacher as enquirer process.

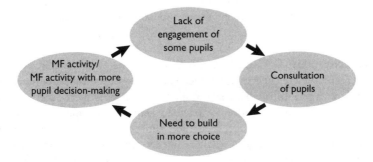

Figure 16.3 Example of teacher as enquirer process from Case Study 2.

The importance of the external perspective should not be underestimated. If schools are not going to 'mull around in their own ignorance' or develop a kind of 'group think', knowledge needs to be broadened and extended. With an external engagement of any depth, teachers are encouraged to 'step outside' their day-to-day situation; to listen to different viewpoints, and alternative strategies. Their existing understanding is deepened, stretched or even challenged by learning about the work of others, including experts in the field. This new knowledge generates new hypotheses which are then 'tested' and further insights are gained, allowing a more informed, critical analysis of the work of others. In other words, there is a dialectic between theory and practice which promotes objectivity and which at its best leads to profound change within the teacher herself, and therefore also within her classroom.

Those communities of practice referred to earlier need to extend beyond the individual school to other teachers and other schools. This is particularly so where individuals are not school-based or part of a school community. Such as many instrumental teachers. In these instances other ways need to be sought to bring teachers together to investigate and share their practice such as in Box 16.3.

BOX 16.3: CASE STUDY – ANOTHER WAY OF DOING IT

The ABRSM Certificate in Teaching for instrumental teachers has built into its course design the requirements for all teachers to 'peer review'. Each teacher video-records a sequence of lessons focusing on a particular area of development of their choice e.g.: improvisation; sight reading; interpretation. The video recordings are brought to the session for discussion and critiqued by both mentor and peers. The issues that arise, together with relevant reading, then feed into the students' assignments. This requires the teachers to write a critique of their own teaching and indicate the impact on their practice. The quality of discussion and thinking that this process engenders is impressive, not just in terms of analyzing practice but also in the role it plays in exposing teachers to new ideas which often challenge their existing understanding of teaching and learning. A major benefit of these sessions is the opportunity for teachers to observe other modes and styles of teaching. One session which included both string and guitar teachers – each from very different instrumental traditions, generated an indepth discussion on whether or not different styles and genres should be taught (learned).

The teachers in this (Box 16.3) are in effect involving themselves in small-scale action research where their own practice is being systematically examined, with some external input, through a series of small-scale investigations, and as a consequence there is a firm foundation for practice to be adapted and improved.

Many teachers do of course reflect upon and experiment with their practice, but for larger-scale innovation, teachers need to investigate together and then share the knowledge that arises. Teachers can respond better to innovations driven by peers than from 'superiors' or 'experts'. Observation, trial and error, talk, narrative, (because much knowledge is tacit), coaching, mentoring ... These should be regular features of school life and professional development. This does not mean however that all teacher development in music should take place simply within the school context. If a measure of criticality is high up on the agenda, then this implies an injection of ideas and provocative questions. We do, however need to think carefully about where this 'external' input comes from. As Day (1993) points out, schools often lack the culture, teachers often lack the energy or the knowledge, consultants are often ruled by the profit margin, and LAs are often forced to peddle the latest government initiative. Even higher education is sometimes subject to commercial and accountability pressures. With carefully chosen partners however, there are rich pickings to be had.

Conclusion

What we might conclude from this is the holistic, complex and interdependent nature of educational experience for pupil and teacher. For too long, perhaps we have separated out the processes of teaching, pupil learning, curriculum development and teacher development in our scramble to make the world of education a tidier place. If we want to develop deep learning approaches at all levels in education we need to do something more risky, providing student teachers with 'pedagogical space to develop their own ideas, to inject something of themselves into their learning and to make and to substantiate ... their own truth claims in and on the world' (Hallam and Barnett in Mortimore 1999: 148). What holds good for student teachers holds good for teacher development in all its guises – in fact holds good for all learners.

In meta-cognitive terms, we need to recognize when and where learning takes place. Learning is not something that happens 'out there' when something is done to us. If we trace back and identify those moments when a real shift in our understanding has taken place, we realize that these 'eureka' moments happen often when we least expect them, but then move us qualitatively onwards in terms of our understanding. It is impossible to prescribe these moments, plan for them or even predict them. In that case, we could argue, the best that we can do is to provide the optimum conditions for these moments to take place. If, however, we take the view of teachers as researchers or systematic enquirers as a way of thinking, we can do better than that.

Ultimately, wherever the provision for teacher development in music is located, we need to transform our understanding of it from a 'training' model to a 'learning' model. Whatever the curriculum for music looks like, one could argue that the main value of any curriculum is the extent to which it is not implemented, but investigated. Many teachers, understandably, cry out for stability. On the contrary, I would argue that the curriculum should never stop changing; it should never be finished; we should never be satisfied. Change and development is perceived as threatening precisely because it is imposed by others and therefore implies a loss of control. We must therefore reclaim the initiative, re-interpreting the curriculum every time we engage with it.

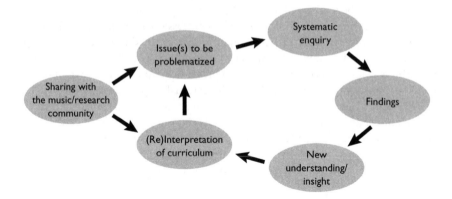

Figure 16.4 Teaching as reinterpretation of the curriculum.

With this scenario (represented by Fig. 16.4) we see 'Teachers as Enquirers', exploring their own practice, sometimes alone, sometimes in collaboration with colleagues, sometimes with external partners, sometimes with pupils, provide a potentially powerful force within the profession. Teachers' serious questions about teaching music merit serious enquiry, the findings of which deserve to be taken seriously, not just by the profession, but also by the government and the community. This of course means not simply implementing the latest government agenda, but trusting the profession to have integrity and to do what is right by their pupils.

Reflective questions

1 What has been the most significant learning for you in teaching music? Think carefully about the context. Was this an informal or formal learning situation?
2 What would help you become a better teacher of music? Analyse the relevant factors involved in your answer to this question. What are the implications for your own professional development?
3 To what extent would you describe yourself as conforming to the 'teacher as enquirer' model?
4 What do you/your school do which meets the Knoster (1991) '*Management of Change*' criteria. How could you take more account of these?

References

Alexander, R. (2010) *Children, Their World, Their Education: Final Report and Recommendations of the Cambridge Primary Review*, London and New York: Routledge.
Avalos, B. *Teacher Professional development in Teaching and Teacher education over ten years* (Editorial). Available online: http://dx.doi.org/10.1016/j.tate.2010.08.007

Darleen Opfer, V., Peddar, D.G. and Lavicza, Z. (2010) 'The Role of Teachers' Orientation to Learning in Professional Development and Change: A National Study of Teachers in England' *Teachers and Teacher Education*, 1–11.

Day, C. (1993) 'Reflection: a Necessary But Not Sufficient Condition for Professional Development' *British Education Research Journal*, 19(1): 83–93.

DCSF (2009) *Making More of Music: Improving the Quality of Music Teaching in Secondary Schools*, Ofsted.

DfE (2010) *The Importance of Teaching: The Schools White Paper*, DFE.

DfE (2011) *Music Education in England: A Review by Darren Henley for the Department for Education and the Department for Culture, Media and Sport.*

DfE (2011) The Importance of Music – A National Plan for Music Education. DFE–00086–2011.

Finney, J. and Harrison, C. (2010) *Whose Music Education Is It?*, *NAME Handbook 2010*. London: National Association of Music Educators.

Folkestad, G. (2006) 'Formal and Informal Learning Situations or Practices vs. Formal and Informal Ways of Learning' *British Journal of Music Education*, 23(2): 135–45.

Green, L. (2002) *How Popular Musicians Learn: A Way Ahead for Music Education*, Ashgate Popular and Folk Music Series.

Handscomb, G. and MacBeath, J. (2003) *The Research-Engaged School*, Colchester: Essex County Council, FLARE.

Hargreaves, A. (1994) *Changing Teachers, Changing Times: Teacher's Work and Culture in the Postmodern Age*, London: Cassell.

Hargreaves, D. (2003) 'From Improvement to Transformation', keynote lecture presented at International congress for School Effectiveness and Improvement, Schooling the Knowledge Society, Sydney Australia, January 2003.

Hustler, D., McNamara, O., Jarvis, J., Londra, M. and Campbell, A. (2003) *Teachers' Perceptions of CPD*, DfES Research Report RR429.

Imants, J. (2002) 'Restructuring Schools as a Context for Teacher Learning' *International Journal of Educational Research*, 37: 715–32.

James, M. and McCormick, R. (2009) 'Teachers Learning How to Learn', *Teaching and Teacher Education*, 25: 973–82.

Knoster, T., Villa, R. and Thousand, J. (2000). 'A Framework for Thinking About Systems Change', in R. Villa and J. Thousand (eds) *Restructuring for Caring and Effective Education: Piecing the Puzzle Together*, Baltimore: Paul H. Brookes Publishing Co.

Kushner, S. (1994) 'Against Better Judgment: How a Centrally Prescribed Music Curriculum Works Against Teacher Development', *International Journal of Music Education*, 23: 34–45.

McMahon, M., Forde, C. and Martin, M. (2010) *Contemporary Issues in Learning and Teaching*, London: Sage.

Mortimore, P. (ed.) (1999) *Understanding Pedagogy*, London: PCP.

Prensky, M. (2001) 'Digital Natives, Digital Immigrants', from *On the Horizon*, NCB University Press, 9(5), October 2001.

Rudduck, J. and McIntyre, D. (2007) 'Improving Learning Through Consulting Pupils', *ESRC Teaching and Learning Programme*, London: Routledge.

Stenhouse, L. (1975) *An Introduction to Curriculum Research and Development*, London: Heinemann.

Swanwick, S. and Paynter, J. (1993) 'Teacher Education and Music Education: an Editorial View', *British Journal of Music Education* 10(1): 3–8.

Websites

www.name.org.uk (accessed 29 August 2011)
www.phf.org.uk/page.asp?id=770 (accessed 7 January 2011)
www.teachingmusic.org.uk/ (accessed 7 January 2011).

Index

Please note that page references to non-textual content such as Boxes, Figures and Tables will be in *italics*, while the letter 'n' will follow references to Notes.

Abrahams, F., 189, 190
ABRSM Certificate in Teaching, *254*
abstraction, 120, 121
accommodation, 68, 74
accountability, 109, 111, 112, 224, 244
action research, 227–9; behaviour management, 230–1; case descriptions, 229–31; case study, 226; interventions, planning and implementing, 228; and reflection/reflective practice, 227, 228–9; *see also* research; teacher-generated research
activity theory, 38
Adams, John, 55, 170
Adorno, T., 57
aesthetic experiences/education, 4, 11, 15, 92; aesthetic education movement in music, 86, 87; grounded aesthetics, 41
affective cognition, 74
Afro-Caribbean youth culture, 41
A-levels, 172, 201
Alexander, R., 246
alienation, musical, 120, 199
All Our Futures (Robinson), 209
Allsup, R. E., 188, 190, 191
American music educators, 85, 86, 89
American society, 87
anticipation, 38, *39*
Apple, M. W., 24
appreciation, through subjective musical experiences, 10–12
Arnot, M., 29
art, accessibility to masses, 87
Art As Experience (Westbrook), 87

artefacts, musical, 119, 120, 123, 124, 131
assessment, vs. evaluation, 111
assessment for learning (AfL), 155, 159–62
assessment for self-directed learning (SDL): description of SDL, 154–5; framework, 162–5; in music education, 153–67
assessment of learning (AoL), 155–9, 162; application of strategies to SDL, *160–1*
assimilation, 68, 74
Aston, Peter, 35
audience-listening, development, 72, 75
authority, 224
autonomous art, 55
autonomy, musical, 119, 121
auto-pilot, 78–9
Avalos, B., 245

Ball, Stephen J., 110
Bamberger, J., 66, 74, 77, 78
banking approach to education, 16, 187–8, 189, 193
Barnes, Jonathan, 4, 137–52
Barrett, M. S., 67, 73
Basis for Music Education, A (Swanwick), 12
behaviour management, 230–1
Benedict, Cathy, 4, 102–17
Bentley, Arnold, 35, 65
Berberian, Cathy, *194*
Berger, Peter, 20
Berio, L., *194*

Bernstein, Basil, 5, 198; background/
   career, 25; Code Theory, 187; policy
   and pedagogic device, 3, 20, 26–30;
   sociology, contribution to, 25–6;
   on trainability, 21
Black youth, New York Bronx, 41
Blitz, London, 144, *145*
Bohlman, P. V., 122
'bolt-on accessories,' 153, 154
Borko, H., 245
Bourdieu, Pierre, 5, 124, 198
Bowe, Richard, 110
Britten, Benjamin, *145*
Brown, Donald, 137
Brown, S., 53
Bruner, Jerome, 91–2
BTEC qualifications, 201–2, *204, 205*
Buber, Martin, 36
Bullock, A., 193
Bunting, Robert, 68–9
Burnard, Pamela, 5, 38, 73, 223–41

Cage, John, 35
Cain, Tim, 5, 157, 223–41
Cameron, David, 98, 102, 105, 110
capitalism, 86, 87, 94, 95, 96, 107, 108;
   consumer, 42, 43, 45
Carnegie Hall, 131
Challenge Monitoring Indicators, 38, *39*
Challenge Seeking Indicators, 37–8, *39*
Challis, M., 112
Cheung-Yung, Jane, 78
child-centred creativity, 34
chords, 65, 66
Christianity, 18n
Clarke, Kenneth, 24
'CLASP' (model of musical experience),
   12
classical music, 53–4; hegemony of,
   156; ideology, 158
*Classical Music and Postmodern
   Knowledge* (Kramer), 119
Clegg, Nick, 102, 105
Clift, S., 50
Code Theory, 187
Cold War politics, 4, 86, 88, 89, 93, 97;
   and multiculturalism, 95–6
collaboration, 130, 137, 215, 227; *see
   also* partnerships in music education
Colwell, R. J., 94
commodification, 122
commoditization, 120

communities of practice, 254
Concerto for Turntables and Orchestra
   (Prokofiev), 130
conscientization, 186, 189
'constellation' approach to partnerships,
   5, 216, 218–19
consultation, talk-based, 234
consumer capitalism, 42, 43, 45
consumption vs. production, 40–1
contextual musicianship, as musical
   understanding, 13–14
continuing professional development
   (CPD), 243, 246
control of knowledge, 23, 24, 25, 30
Cooksey, J., 105
Copland, Aaron, 88, 89
Core State Standards Initiative, US, 108
Cowley, S., 230
Crain, W., 64
Crasborn, F., 224
Creative Age, The (Pope), 45
Creative and Cultural Skills sector,
   BTEC qualifications, 201
creative genius, 3, 34, 37
creative music, 34–6
Creative Partnerships scheme, UK, 144,
   209
creativity, 3, 33–47; consumption vs.
   production, 40–1; creative pedagogy
   in music education, 43; definitions, 3,
   45; discovery of self as creative being,
   138; domain, flow of, 36–40;
   facilitating, 36; little 'c' and big 'C,'
   37–40, 42–3, 137; material sonic
   culture, 41–2; music making and
   school life, *44*; as necessary symbolic
   work, 40–2; pupil-generated research,
   236–7; as a social good, 33
Creech, A., *52*
criteria sharing, 159, *160*
critical consciousness, 189, 195; and
   critical pedagogy, 191–5; engaging,
   193–4
critical cultural workers, music teachers
   as, 14–16
critical incidents, in learning, 234
critical musicality, 15
critical pedagogy: and critical
   consciousness, 189, 191–5; of music,
   189–90; for music education, 59–62,
   190
critical thinking, 185–96

cross-curricular approaches to education, history, 138
cross-curricular approaches to musical teaching and learning, 4, 139–48; double focus cross-curricular teaching, 148, *149*; hierarchical, 139–41; importance, 150; interdisciplinary, 143–6; multidisciplinary, 141–3, 144; opportunistic, 146–7; playful and rigorous, 139
Csikszentmihalyi, M., 37, 38
cultural construction of subjectivity, 126
cultural consumption, 40–1
cultural prophecies, philosophies of music education as, 9, 10
cultural universals, 65
'cultures of tension,' and ICT, 178–81
curriculum-as-practicum, 205
curriculum planning, primary school music, 236–7

dangers of music, 55
Darleen Opfer, V., 245
Davies, Brian, 23
Davies, C., 67, 72
Day, C., 255
de Vries, P., 226
Death of Klinghoffer, The (Adams), 55
Debord, Guy, 108
decontextualization, 27, 119, 120, 121, 186
Deliège, I., 66
delineated meaning of music, 53
democracy, 92; democratic mission of schools, 96; democratic realists, 88; paradox of, 113–14; participatory, 86, 87, 88
Democracy and Music Education (Woodford), 185
democratic realists, 88
development: accommodation, 68, 74; assimilation, 68, 74; cultural universals, 65; hierarchy, notion of, 65; horizontal dimensions, *78*; individual, 76–7; musical, 64–81; quantitative and qualitative, 64; stages concept, 64, 73; Swanwick/Tillman developmental spiral, 67–72; theories, 64–7; vertical dimensions, *78*
developmental research: reliability issues, 74–5; un-notated compositions,

cluster analysis, 68, 74; validity questions, 72–4
developmental spiral (Swanwick/ Tillman), 3, 67–72; layers, 68–71; un-notated compositions, cluster analysis, 68
Dewey, John, 9, 13, 17, 142; and social justice, 85, 86, 87, 90–4, 96, 98
dialectical process, *192, 193*
digital competence, 175, 176
'digital immigrants,' 244
digital literacy model (Martin), 174–5, *176*
digital technologies, 118, 130, 180
digital transformation, 175
digital usage, 175
diversity (musical) and educational inclusion, myth of, 121–4
domain creativity, flow of, 36–40; gatekeepers, 37, 42
double focus cross-curricular teaching, 148, *149*

Eagleton, T., 42
Edexcel BTEC qualifications, Level 2, 202
Education Act 1988, 22
educational environments, designing, 16
educational music, absence of strong epistemological discourse for, 52
Educational Policies Commission, NEA, 90
Eglinton, K., 41
Eklund-Koza, J., 94
elite culture, 198
elites, corporate, 88, 89
Elliott, David, 3, 13–14, 124, 128, 201, 204, 205
Elliott, John, 223, 224
Elmtree Primary School, *214*
emotion, music as expression of, 57, 58
Emotion and Meaning in Music (Meyer), 91
empiricism, 186, 187, 188
enjoyment of music performance, 11
Enlightenment, 186
Eno, Brian, 130
equality, 86
Erikson, Erik, 64
Espeland, M., 170, 182
ethics, 228–9
ethno-musicological research, 13

evaluation, vs. assessment, 111
Evans, Keith, 5, 187–207
expansion, 38, *39*
expression, 67, 68; expressiveness, personal, 70
extension, 38, *39*

Fautley, M., 153, 161
feedback, 159, *160*
female composers, 50, 56
female singers, 56, 60
film music, 144
Finney, John, 3, 33–47, 198, 226
Fitz, J., 22, 26, 30
'flipping,' 164, 165
flow: Csikszentmihalyi's dimensions of, 38; of domain creativity, 36–40; Indicators, 37–8, *39*; little 'c' and big 'C,' 37–40, 42–3, 137
Fly Me to the Moon, 43
folk music, 157, *193–4*
Folk Songs (Berio), *194*
Folkestad, G., 4, 163, 164
Forest Hill school, South London, *203, 204, 205–6*
form, 67, 68, 69, 70–1, 74, 119
formal learning, 163, 164
formalism, 68
formative assessment (assessment for learning), 155, 159–62
França, Cecilia Cavalieri, 72, 75
Freire, Paulo, 185, 186, 187–8, 193
Froebel, Friedrich, 138
Froehlich, Hildegard, 21
functional tonality, 57
fusions of horizons, 59

Gadamer, H. G., 59
Gage, N. L., 226
Gamelan acquisition, Heddon Primary School, *217–18*
Gammon, V., 23
Gane, P., 109
Gardner, H., 37, 73, 142
GCSE (General Certificate of Secondary Education): music as option, 187, 200, 201, 202; and music technology, 172, 178
Geertz, C., 238
gender stereotypes, and music, 55–6
genius, creative, 3, 34, 37
German analytic tradition, 92

gesture, 38, *39*, 67
Giddens, Anthony, 22, 186
Giroux, Henry, 15
Glass, Philip, 43
global postmodern, 41
glocal culture, 44
Goble, J. S., 132
Goehr, Lydia, 119
Goodall, Howard, *51–2*
Gramsci, Antonio, 23, 24, 30
graphic representations, 67, 72
Great Depression, 87, 94, 97, 98
Green, Lucy, 15, 21, 60, 76, 118, 121; on meaning of music, 53, 55–6, 206; on SDL, 153, 154, 156, 159; *see also Musical Futures* project
grounded aesthetics, 41
Guskey, T. R., 245

habitus, 198
Haikus, musical, 145–6
Hall, S., 41
Hallam, S., *52*
'Hammered Out' (Turnage), 42–3
Hancox, G., 50
Handscomb, G., 253
Hargreaves, D. J., 65, 67, 73, 79, 244, 247
Harland, J., 187
Heads, shoulders, knees and toes (song), 141
headteachers, 105
Hedden Primary School and Gamelan, *217–18*
hegemony, 23, 24, 30; of classical music, 156
helix, developmental, 68, 73
Henley, Darren, 114
Henley Review, Secretary of State's guidelines, *51*
hermeneutic windows, 126
Hertfordshire Pathfinder Project, 154
Hess, J., 119
hierarchy: and development, 65; hierarchical cross-curricular teaching and learning, 139–41
high culture, 43, 123
High Fidelity practices, 128–9, 130, 131
high status western art music/music knowledge, 120, 121, *123, 125*, 130; High Fidelity practices, 129

historians, American music education, 97
homophobia, 50
horizontal progression, in music, 77, *78*
House, Robert W., 89, 92
Huckabee, Mike, 95
human universals, 137
Huntington, Samuel, 114

ICT *see* information and communications technology (ICT)
ideology, 121; classical music, 158; definitions, 132n; and music, 56, 120
Imants, J., 245, 251
improvisation: Kratus' developmental model for, 176; workshop, *193*
In Harmony programme, 242
inaccessibility, musical, 88
incentive, 250, 251
individual development, 76–7
individual musical experiences, 10–12
informal learning, 79, 163, 164
information and communications technology (ICT), 4, 170; and 'cultures of tension,' 178–81; developing music education models with, 176–8; limited student experience at Key Stage 3, 172–3; MIDI sequencing, 171; musical exploration using, 229–31; prioritizing use of in music education for older students, 171–2; recent research into usage in classroom, 171–4; score-writing, 171; useful skills, 179–80; *see also* digital technologies; music technology
inherent meaning of music, 53
instructional discourse (ID), 28
Intellectual Capital, 248–9, 250
interdisciplinary cross-curricular teaching and learning, 143–6
interpretation, 59–60
interpretive paradigm, 225
iPads, 169

James, M., 245
Jameson, Frederick, 42, 43
jazz, 92, 130–1
John, Peter, 178–9
Jorgensen, Estelle, 16, 33
justifications for music in curriculum, 48–63; civilizing, 49; completion of

expression, meaning and understanding, 49–50; critical pedagogy for music education, 59–62; current context, 50–3; emotional, 49; instrumental, 49; liberal, 49; music as 'hard' discipline, 49; rational, 49; soft and hard, 3, 48–50, 51, 52–3, 57, 58, 59, 61; symbolic, 49; therapeutic, 49; wider meaning of music, 53–9

Kant, Immanuel, 191
Keller, M., 132n
Kellogg, John Harvey, 50
Key Stage 2 Music CPD programme, 243
Key Stage 3: and future GCSE options, 187; limited student experience with ICT at, 172–3; unpopularity of music as curriculum subject, 198; *see also* *National Strategy Key Stage 3 Music Programme* (*NSKSMP*), England
Key Stage 4, 198, 201, 202, 203, 206
knowledge: aesthetic mode of knowing, 11; control of, 23, 24, 25, 30; decontextualized/recontextualized, 27, 119; empiricism, 186, 187, 188; high status *see* high status western art music/music knowledge; and knowledge-learner relationships, 186–9; and musical alienation, 120; personal, 9; thinkable/unthinkable distinction, 27; transcendental rationalism, 186, 187, 188; as 'void of self,' 186, 188, 189
Kohlberg, Lawrence, 64
Kontakte (Stockhausen), 130
Kramer, L., 119, 126, 129
Kratus, J., 176, *177*
Kushner, S., 105

Lamont, A., 187, 198–9, 202
Langer, Suzanne, 66
language: linguistic development, 66; music as, 3, 58–9
Latino youth, New York Bronx, 41
Lawson, D., 103, 105
layers, developmental, 68–72; cumulative, 71–2; idiomatic, 71; manipulative, 70; personal expressiveness, 70; sensory, 70; speculative, 70–1; symbolic, 71;

systematic, 71; vernacular, 70, 78; *see also* development; Swanwick/Tillman developmental spiral
legitimation, 121–2, 124
Leonhard, Charles, 89, 92
Lincoln Centre, New York, 130–1
linear development, 105, 156, 157; linear progression, in music, 77
linear time, 57
Lucas, B., 199
Lyon, J., 104, 106

MacBeath, J., 253
Mahlmann, John, 108, 109
manifestos, 104, 105–8
manipulative power of music, 55
Marsh, K., 72
Martin, A., 174–5, *176*
Martin, P. J., 57, 191
Marx, Karl, 87, 191
'mash up,' 42
'mask of neutrality,' 29
material sonic culture, creativity, 41–2
materials, 68, 70
Maton, K., 187, 198–9, 202
Matthews, Francesca, 4, 118–34
Mattock, Jo, 230, 231
McCarthy, Joseph, 88
McCormick, R., 245
McIntyre, D., 232
McLaren, Peter, 189
McMahon, M., 243
McMurray, F., 96
MEAE (Music-Education-as-Aesthetic Education), 188
meaning of music, 53–7, 206; inherent and delineated, 53
meanings and values (musical), understanding, 12–13, 14
Mellers, W., 34, 36
melodic vs. rhythmic development, 66, 72
Meyer, Leonard, 91
military–industrial complex, US, 86, 89, 90, 93
misogyny, 50, 60
modelling, *161*
modernism, 42, 43
Moog, H., 67
multiculturalism, 95–6
multidisciplinary cross-curricular teaching and learning, 141–3, 144

music: as dangerous, 55; as domain of creativity, 37; educational, absence of strong epistemological discourse for, 52; as exclusive, 54–5; as gendered, 55–6; 'good,' 119, 120, 156; and ideology, 56, 120; as language, 3, 58–9; making up, 113; as manipulative, 55; as multi-layered, 67, 68; vs. 'musics,' 156–7; primary purpose, prior eighteenth century, 132n; as propaganda, 56–7; social structures, reflecting, 57; 'specialness' notions, 51; as 'superior' or 'inferior' subject, 141; and technology, 169–84; western art *see* western art music; wider meaning of, 53–7
Music A-level, 172
Music Education Council, 52
Music Educators National Conference (MENC), 90, 94, 108, 115n; Centennial Conference, 95
Music Manifesto (2005), 209
music teacher educators, 85, 86, 89, 92; Music Educators National Conference (MENC), 90, 94, 95, 108, 115n
music teachers: as critical cultural workers, 14–16; role and identity, 211–12, 243–4; *see also* teachers
music technology, 169–84; digital literacy model (Martin), 174–5, *176*; inherent conservatism in musical pedagogies with technology, 4, 171; limited student experience with ICT at Key Stage 3, 172–3; and Ofsted, 171, 172, 173; prioritizing use of ICT in music education for older students, 171–2; recent research into ICT usage in classroom, 171–4; students' experiences inside and outside school, 173–4; *see also* information and communications technology (ICT)
Music Working Group, National Curriculum, 23, 24
musical artefacts, 119, 120, 123, 124, 131
musical biographies, *192*
'musical delinquency,' 92
musical development, 64–81; audience-listening, 72, 75; criteria, 65; evaluating students' work, 77; implications for curriculum, 76–7;

informal opportunities, 79; melodic vs. rhythmic, 66, 72; pioneering studies, 67; progression, 77; theories, 64–7; *see also* development
musical entrepreneurship, 110
Musical Futures project, 60, 77, 127, 153, 154, 155, 166, 210, 247; development, 242; National Curriculum, and, 157, 158, 161; *National Strategy Key Stage 3 Music Programme* (*NSKSMP*), and, *160, 161, 162*
musical identity concept, 79
musical meanings and values, understanding, 12–13, 14
musical structure words, 142
musical understanding, 12
Music-Education-as-Aesthetic Education (MEAE), 188
musicians: contextual musicianship, as musical understanding, 13–14; professional and amateur, 12
'musics,' notion of, 156–7
music-sharing sites, 130
My Son John (song), *194*

National Association of Music Educators (NAME), 26, 239n
National Curriculum, 27, 102–17, 244; calls to reform education, 103–5; creation, 22, 103, 104, 149; as fixed and defined, 104; locality in music curriculum design and development, 104–5, 108–11; manifestos, 104, 105–8; model banks, 115; and *Musical Futures* project, 157, 158, 161; national data bank, suggestions for, 111; portfolios of program structures, 111, 112, 115; possible futures/practices, 111–13; Review of Music Education document, September 2010 Press Notice, 107; teaching as reinterpretation of, *256*; unpopularity of music as curriculum subject, 198–9; vertical curricular design, 110, 111; *see also* National Curriculum for Music, English; Ofsted
National Curriculum for Music, English, 4, 22, 23, *52*, 75, 105, 118, 169
National Curriculum Handbook for Secondary Teachers in England, 107

National Curriculum Key Stages 1 and 2: Handbook for Primary Teachers, 107
National Curriculum Music Working Group, 23, 24
National Defense Education Act 1958, US, 89
National Education Association (NEA), 90, 92
National Plan for Music, 242
National Standards movement, US, 108, 111
National Strategy Key Stage 3 Music Programme (*NSKSMP*), England, 23, 28–9, 153; and *Musical Futures* project, *160, 161, 162*
Nattiez, J. J., 58
Nazi regimes, 55, 56
NEA (National Education Association), 90, 92
neoconservatives, 88
neoliberals, 88, 97
New Deal program, 94
New York Bronx, youth of, 41
Northern Ireland, cross-curricular approaches, 138
notations, 67
Numminen, A., 11

Obama, Barack, 108
objectification, 121
Office of Education, US, 89, 93
official recontextualizing field (ORF)/ official field of change, 26, 27, 29
Ofsted, 243; and music technology, 171, 172, 173; and National Curriculum, 106, 115n1; and post-14 musical education, 187
O'Hear, Anthony, 24
On Knowing: Essays for the Left Hand (Bruner), 91
opportunistic cross-curricular teaching and learning, 146–7
ORF (official recontextualizing field), 26, 27, 29
Organizational Capital, 248, 253
originality, musical, 143–4; *see also* creativity
'othering,' musical, 122, 123

paradox of democracy, 113–14
participative enquiry, shared, 232

participatory democracy, 86, 87, 88
participatory practices, 127–8
partnerships in music education,
    209–20; 'constellation' approach to,
    5, 216, 218–19; and context of
    musical learning, 210–14; Creative
    Partnerships scheme, UK, 144;
    curriculum content, 213–14; dynamic
    tension, 218; effective, developing,
    214–18; Elmtree Primary School,
    214; Hedden Primary School and
    Gamelan, 217–18; mutual reflection,
    219; role and identity of 'music
    teacher,' 211–12; secondary school
    teacher and musician partnership,
    215–16; shifting viewpoints, 218;
    situational roles, 212; understanding
    the learner, 210–11; Water Project,
    212; see also collaboration
Pascall, David, 23, 24
Paynter, John, 3, 35–6, 113, 247
pedagogic device (Bernstein), 26–30
pedagogic discourse (Bernstein), 28
pedagogic recontextualizing field (PRF),
    26, 27, 29
peer assessment, 159, 161, 237, 254
pentatonicism, 57
Perkins, D. N., 170
personal knowledge, 9
Pestalozzi, Johann Heinrich, 138
philosophies of music education, 2–3,
    9–18; contextual musicianship as
    musical understanding, 13–14;
    reflection, 16; subjective musical
    experiences, appreciation through,
    10–12; understanding musical
    meanings and values, 12–13, 14
Philosophy of Music Education, A
    (Reimer), 10
Philpott, Chris, 1–6, 48–63, 120,
    153–67, 154–5
Piaget, Jean, 64, 67–8, 73, 162
Pierce, C. S., 58
pitch, 11, 65
Plato, 55, 142
Plowden Report (1967), 138
Plummeridge, C., 51, 105
Polanyi, M., 9
pole-vaulting, 177–8
policy and practice in music education,
    20–32; actors in policy arena, identity
    of, 26–8; Bernstein's policy and

pedagogic device, 3, 20, 26–30;
    National Curriculum see National
    Curriculum; outcomes, 26; persons
    benefiting from policy and persons
    omitted, 29–30; from policy to
    practice, 22–5; resources, 26, 28–9;
    sociology/sociological perspective,
    20–2, 25
political agendas, separating of conscious
    and unconscious, 15
Pope, R., 45
popular culture, 43, 210
popular music, 41, 92
portfolios of program structures, 111,
    112, 115
post-14 musical education, 158,
    187–207; competing aims/
    philosophies, 199–202; Forest Hill
    school, South London, 203, 204,
    205–6; music making at heart of
    curriculum, 202–6; unpopularity of
    music as curriculum subject, 198–9
Postgraduate Certificate in Education
    (PGCE), 1
postmodernism, 42, 43, 44–5
praxial approach to music curriculum,
    14, 118–34, 204; High Fidelity
    practices, 128–9, 130, 131; high
    status western art music, 120, 121,
    123; knowledge and musical
    alienation, 120; music curriculum as
    praxis, 124–31; musical diversity and
    educational inclusion, myth of,
    121–4; participatory practices, 127–8;
    presentational practices, 125–7;
    Studio Art practices, 129–31
praxis, 124–31, 191
prejudice, 54–5, 59
Prensky, M., 244
presentational practices, 125–7
PRF (pedagogic recontextualizing field),
    26, 27, 29
primary context (Bernstein), 27
primary schools: examples, 143, 214,
    217–18; hierarchical cross-curricular
    teaching and learning, 141; music
    curriculum planning/creative
    learning, 236–7
Process of Knowledge, The (Bruner), 91
professional development (PD), 179–80;
    action plan, 251; case studies, 249,
    252, 254; context, 245–6; degree

required, 246–7; evaluation of, 247–8; identity of teachers, 243–4; Intellectual Capital, 248–9, 250; and music education, 242–58; Organizational Capital, 248, 253; skills, 251; Social Capital, 248, 253; standards, limitations, 246; Teaching Schools, 247; types of change, 244–5; vision, 250, 251

Prokofiev, Gabriel, 130

propaganda, music as, 56–7

Pryor, Maddy, *194*

pupil consultation, 232

pupil-generated research, 231–3; case descriptions, 235–8; facilitating, 233–5; implications for researching with pupils, 237–8; primary school music curriculum planning/creative learning, 236–7; pupils as co-researchers, 235–7; pupils as generators of own research, 233; secondary school music assessment, 237; secondary school music classroom, 235–6; supporting, 234–5

pupils: aged 14 and over *see* post-14 musical education; Assessment for learning (AfL), 159–62; as consultants, 232; as researchers *see* pupil-generated research

quantitative progression, in music, 77

questioning, 159, *160–1*

Rancière, J., 113, 115

randomized controlled trials, 225

reason, instrumentalist notion of, 90

Reay, D., 29

re-contextualization, 16, 26–8, 29

referentialism, 68

Reflecting Others project, 112

reflection/reflective practice, 227, 228–9; mutual reflection, 219; reflective musical practicum, 205

Regelski, T. A., 188–9, 190

regulative discourse (RD), 28

reification, 120

Reimer, Bennett, 3, 10–11, 13, 14, 60–1, 89

repertoires, 16

research: action research *see* action research; interpretive paradigm, 225; musical exploration using ICT,

229–31; pupils as researchers, 231–3; reductionist organization of, 66; research methods, school music, 223–41; scientific, 225–6; secondary forms of representation, 67, 72; teachers as researchers, 223–6

resources/resource distribution, 26, 28–9, 251

Review of Music Education, 107

Review of Music Education document, September 2010 Press Notice, 107

rhythm, 65, 66, 72

Rickover, Admiral Hyman, 89, 91

Riley, Terry, 43

Rittel, H., 102–3

Robinson, Ken, 148, 209

Rogers, B., 230

Rogers, Carl, 33

Rogers, R., 122

Roosevelt, Franklin D., 94

Rousseau, Jean-Jacques, 138, 142

Rowe, D., 107

Royal Schools of Music, Associated Boards, 172–3

Rudduck, Jean, 231–2

Salomon, G., 170

Samba Band, 38, *39*

Samba Batucada, 128

Sash, The (Irish ballad), 54

satisfaction, 36

Savage, Jonathan, 4–5, 112, 169–84

scaffolding, *161*

Schippers, H., 14

Schmidt, Patrick, 4, 102–17, 188

school life, and music making, *44*

Schools Council Humanities Project, 223

Schools White Paper, The, 107

scientific materialism, 186

scientific research, 225–6

Scotland, cross-curricular approaches, 138

Scruton, Roger, 24

Seashore, Carl E., 65

Second World War, 87; Blitz, London, *145*

secondary schools: case example, *203*; cross-curricular approaches to musical teaching and learning, 141; music assessment, 237; music classroom, 235–6; promotion of music as

'academic,' 199; secondary school teacher and musician partnership, *215–16*; *see also* GCSE (General Certificate of Secondary Education)
secondary systems, 67, 72
Seeger, Peter, 88, 89
self-assessment, 159, *161*, 237
self-assignment, 37, *39*
self-correction, 38, *39*
self-directed learning (SDL): application of AfL strategies to, *160–1*; description, 154–5; *see also* assessment for self-directed learning (SDL)
Seline HD (iPad instrument), 169, 177, 179
sequential participation, 127
Serafine, Mary Louise, 66
serialism, 92
serious music, 92
sexism, 60
Shepherd, John, 57, 60
Shim, S. H., 211
signs, 58
'silo approach' to music teaching, 181
Silva, M. C. C. F., 72
simultaneity, 66
simultaneous participation, 127
Sing Up scheme (National Singing Programme), 77, 209, 242
Singapore, 246
singing, 50, *51*, 56
skills, 132, 251
Sloboda, J., 66
Small, Christopher, 21
Social Capital, 120, 248, 253
Social Context Indicators, 38, *39*
social justice and music education, 85–101
social structures, music reflecting, 57
social values, 13, 20
Socialist Realism, 57
sociology/sociological perspective, 20–2; and Bernstein, 25–6
sonic culture, material, 41–2
Sound and Silence (Paynter and Aston), 35
sound materials, 66, 72, 73–4
specialized discourse (Bernstein), 27
spiral, developmental *see* developmental spiral (Swanwick/Tillman)
Spruce, Gary, 1–6, 4, 5, 118–34, 185–96

stages concept, development, 64, 73
standardized testing, 95, 96
Stenhouse, Lawrence, 223
Stockhausen, Karlheinz, 130
student voice, 231–2
Studio Art practices, 129–31
subjective musical experiences, appreciation through, 10–12
succession, 66
summative assessment (assessment of learning), 155–9
suprasocial phenomenon, 54
surveys, 225
Swanwick, Keith, 3, 13, 14, 64–81, 105, 158, 162, 247; *Basis for Music Education, A,* 12; objectives for music teaching, 67; on tribal dimensions to music meaning, 59–60
Swanwick/Tillman developmental spiral, 3, 67–72, 73; expression, 70; form, 70–1; materials, 70; reliability issues, 74–5; validity questions, 72–4; value, 71–2; *see also* development; developmental research; layers, developmental
symbolic value, 69
symbolic work, creativity as, 40–2

Tagg, P., 54
talk-and-draw techniques, 235
talk-based consultation, 234
Tarfuri, J., 67
target setting, 159, *161*
Taruskin, Richard, 55
teacher-generated research, 223–6, 238, 252–3; behaviour management, 230–1; case descriptions, 229–31; case study, 226; implications, 225–6; planning and implementing interventions, 228; reflection, 228–9; teacher in classroom, 224–5; *see also* pupil-generated research
teacher-proof curriculum, 16
teachers: in classroom, 224–5; critical cultural workers, music teachers as, 14–16; purpose, 224; as researchers, 223–6; role and identity, 211–12, 243–4; *see also* music teacher educators; music teachers
Teaching Schools, 247
technical mastery, 71
technique, 68

technology, music *see* music technology
'theme park' metaphor, 157
Theorell, T., 53
'thick description,' 226
thinkable/unthinkable knowledge, 27
Third International Conference of
    Education, Heidelberg (1925), 36,
    44
Tillman, June, 67, 68; *see also*
    Swanwick/Tillman developmental
    spiral
tones/tonality, 57, 66
Towards a Theory of Creativity (Rogers),
    33
trainability, 21
transcendental rationalism, 186, 187,
    188
Treitler, Leo, 119
tribalism, 50, 55, 59–60
triple time, musical concept, 188–9
Trombley, S., 193
Turino, T., 124, 125, 127, 129, 130,
    131, 132–3n
Turnage, Mark Anthony, 42–3

UN Convention on the Rights of the
    Child, 147
United Kingdom, 96, 104; 'limited
    engagement' process of early 1990s,
    109; National Curriculum in *see*
    National Curriculum
United States: in 1940s and 1950s,
    93–4; American music educators, 4,
    85, 86, 89, 92; American society/way
    of life, 87, 88; Cold War politics, 86,
    88, 89, 93, 95–6, 97; military–
    industrial complex, 86, 89, 90, 93;
    and National Curriculum, 108;
    National Defense Education Act
    1958, 89; National Standards
    movement, 108, 111; Office of
    Education, 89, 93; politics during
    Great Depression/Second World
    War, 87, 94
utopian music, 55

validity questions, 72–4
value, 67, 68, 69–70, 71
values: musical, 12–13, 14; of
    researcher, 228; social, 13, 20; in
    teaching, 224

verbal descriptions, 67, 72
vernacular, 70, 78
vertical curricular design, 110, 111
vertical progression, in music, 77, *78*
vision, 9, 250, 251
Visual Material Culture, 41
vocational qualifications, 5, 199, 206
Voices Foundation, *52*
Vygotsky, L. S., 76

Ward, Christopher, 229
Water Project, *212*
Webber, M., 102–3
webs of meaning, 59
Welch, G., 105
Wertsch, J., 177
Westbrook, R. B., 87
Westerlund, Heidi, 2–3, 9–18, 60
western art music: dominance of, 122–3,
    158; high status, 120, 121, *123, 125*,
    129, 130; presentational practices,
    126; skills and understandings related
    to, 132
western classical music, 53–4
What develops in musical development?
    (Bamberger), 66
wholeness, 36
Wider Opportunities program, 209, 210,
    242, 243
William III, King, 54
Willis, P., 41
Wishart, Trevor, 229
women composers, 50, 56
women singers, 56, 60
Woodford, Paul, 4, 60, 85–101, 185
Woods Hole Conference (1959), 91
Wright, Ruth, 3, 20–32, 187, 198, 201

Yale Seminar on Music Education
    (1963), 91, 92, 93, 94
Young, Michael, 120
Young, Vanessa, 5, 242–58
Younker, Betty Anne, 38
Youth Music, 77

Zacharias, Jerrold, 91
Zeserson, Katherine, 5, 209–20
Zimmerman, M., 65, 67
Zinn, Howard, 87
zones of proximal development, 76